Social Justice

This book explores the political and philosophical underpinnings of exclusion and social injustice in India. It examines social movements, anti-caste uprisings, reformers like Ambedkar and Narayana Guru and writers like Foucault and Serres to establish a link between the political and social milieu of the idea of nationhood. Going beyond the legal framework of justice, the essays in the volume reassemble the social from popular perception and the margins, and challenge Rawlsian and Eurocentric paradigms which have dominated discourse on social injustice. The volume also draws on instances of history as well as contemporary issues, as well as locating them in the context of social and post-colonial theory.

An intellectually stimulating yet subaltern engagement with the idea of justice, the volume will be of great interest to scholars and researchers of social theory, law, modern South Asian history and social exclusion and discrimination studies.

K. V. Cybil is Associate Professor, Department of Humanistic Studies, Indian Institute of Technology (BHU), Varanasi, India. He has published articles with *Economic and Political Weekly* and the *NMML* New Delhi on Indian practices of social exclusion and injustices. Before joining IIT BHU, he also taught at Ambedkar University Delhi, University of Calicut (Christ College), University of Delhi, India and Mahatma Gandhi University, Kerala, India.

Social Justice

Interdisciplinary Inquiries from India

Edited by K. V. Cybil

Routledge
Taylor & Francis Group
LONDON AND NEW YORK

First published 2019 by Routledge

2 Park Square, Milton Park, Abingdon, Oxon, OX14 4RN
605 Third Avenue, New York, NY 10017

Routledge is an imprint of the Taylor & Francis Group, an informa business

First issued in paperback 2020

British Library Cataloguing-in-Publication Data
A catalogue record for this book is available from the British Library

Library of Congress Cataloging-in-Publication Data
A catalog record for this book has been requested

ISBN: 978-1-138-50504-9 (hbk)
ISBN: 978-0-367-73074-1 (pbk)

Typeset in Sabon
by Apex CoVantage, LLC

This book is dedicated to JNU Campus for more than a million reasons in the wake of its individual and collective struggles against the powers that be that instilled in me a desire for a better sense of social justice.

Contents

Contributors

Soumyabrata Choudhury is Associate Professor at the School of Arts and Aesthetics at Jawaharlal Nehru University, India. He has authored *Theatre, Number, Event: Three Studies on the Relationship of Sovereignty, Power and Truth* and articles on ancient Greek liturgy, the staging of Ibsen, psychoanalysis, Nietzsche, Schiller and Hegel. He has directed theatre productions based on the works of Dostoevsky, Shakespeare, Premchand, Mudraraksha, Artaud, Buchner, Kafka and Prakash, and has acted in a number of productions. His current research involves a detailed reading of B. R. Ambedkar's works in the light of their political and philosophical implications.

K. V. Cybil is Associate Professor, Department of Humanistic Studies, Indian Institute of Technology (BHU), Varanasi, India. He has published articles with *Economic and Political Weekly* and the *NMML* New Delhi on Indian practices of social exclusion and injustices. Before joining IIT BHU, he also taught at Ambedkar University Delhi, University of Calicut (Christ College), University of Delhi, India and Mahatma Gandhi University, Kerala, India. He has an abiding interest in Anthropology and Political Science. He is interested in the systems for the development of writing, music, films etc. in contemporary India. He has published articles on marginal literature and political movements against the backdrop of an emergent threat to democracy in India from various corners. He has been associated with the Social Science Research Council, New York (2005), Indian Council of Social Science Research, New Delhi (2012) and the Nehru Memorial Museum and Library, New Delhi (2013) as part of research fellowships. He is the author of *From Ritual to Republic: Death* *as a Democratic Discourse* (2012). He has published several research articles related to Indian politics in *Economic and Political Weekly*, *Indian Journal of Political Science*, *Indian Journal of Social Work*, etc. His doctoral research was completed at Jawaharlal Nehru University, India, in 2002, and he was associated as a Research Associate with the Department of Sociology in the University of Delhi, India, from 2007–12.

Michael Dusche works as a freelance researcher in the field of legal and political anthropology and political theory. In 1999, he obtained his PhD in Philosophy from the University of Frankfurt, Germany. After joining the Centre for German Studies at Jawaharlal Nehru University as a lecturer, he has held various research and teaching positions in Germany and India, including at the University of Erfurt 2005–9, Jawaharlal Nehru Institute for Advanced Studies 2009–10, Centre for the Study of Developing Societies, Delhi 2013–14 and Manipal Centre for Philosophy and Humanities 2014–16. Currently, he lives in Ruhland, Germany.

Neshat Quaiser taught in the Department of Sociology, Jamia Millia Islamia, New Delhi, India. His research interests include social theory, historical sociology of medicine (with reference to encounter and exchange between unani/indigenous and Western systems of medical practices) and the public sphere during colonial/post-colonial India, Muslims and Islam in the Indian subcontinent, Partition studies, social history of the Urdu language and literature, colonialism, post-colonial law and legal theory, and media and cultural studies.

Sundar Sarukkai is currently Professor of Philosophy at the National Institute of Advanced Studies, Bengaluru, India. He is the author of the following books: *Translating the World: Science and Language*, *Philosophy of Symmetry*, *Indian Philosophy and Philosophy of Science*, *What Is Science?* and *The Cracked Mirror: An Indian Debate on Experience and Theory* (co-authored with Gopal Guru).

Vidhu Verma is currently Professor at the Centre for Political Studies, School of Social Sciences, Jawaharlal Nehru University, New Delhi, India. She was educated at the universities of Delhi, JNU and Oxford. She has also been Chairperson of the Centre for Political Studies (CPS), the Gender Sensitization Committee against

Sexual Harassment (GSCASH) and the Centre for the Study of Discrimination and Exclusion (CSDE). Her areas of research include comparative political theory, feminist political theory, state and civil society, affirmative action policies and social justice in India. She has recently edited and contributed to a volume on *Unequal Worlds* and articles in several journals. She has been a visiting fellow, Maison Des Science de L'Homme, in 1994 and in 2006. She was Senior Fellow, Indian Council of Social Science Research, 2008–10. She has been involved with many projects as Director, Political Institutions (Collaborative), UPOE, JNU, 2005–7; Member, Minorities in India, UPOE, JNU, 2014–17; and currently Principal Investigator of a sponsored project on 'Changing Conceptions of Legal Justice in India', ICSSR, 2014–15.

Acknowledgements

I would like to begin with the contributors of the chapters to this volume. We collaborated successfully for a seminar titled 'Social Justice as a Question of the Empirical Sciences' held 11–12 December 2014, at the Nehru Memorial Museum and Library (NMML), New Delhi. I was a junior fellow at the NMML in 2013, and the plans for the seminar were conceived during this term. A concept note was circulated, and I received positive responses from several scholars, from which a select few participated with their papers in the seminar. After the successful completion of the seminar, I was inspired by colleagues and friends to bring out the seminar papers in the form of a book.

I was working as an assistant professor in Christ College, Irinjalakuda in Kerala, and I had very few resources to think of a publication proportionate to the enthusiasm with which the seminar was received in Delhi. Nonetheless, I contacted the paper presenters and kept in touch ever since, and the book here is a result of the dedication of these authors to the very seminar in which they all willingly participated. It has been in that way completion of a long journey for me in which I have been applauded most heartily by these colleagues of mine. I take this opportunity to express my sincere gratitude towards them.

I would also like to thank out of the bottom of my heart the two reviewers who gave a very insightful reading to my proposal, gave me the most crucial comments and recommended the book for publication at Routledge.

I owe bottomless gratitude to Gopal Guru, who presented a paper in the seminar but could not write a chapter for the book as he was completely caught up with commitments of a different kind. In the years 2015–16, when I was compiling the chapters for this volume, I understand he must have given more public speeches than ever because of increasing atrocities against Dalits. His presence has been felt throughout the compiling of this volume, and when it goes to press without his article, I can only imagine how much its readers would have gained if it had been otherwise. But that does not subtract from my own gratitude to him for having patiently entertained my requests for the article despite his situation. I have responded to two of his articles (both so integrally tied up with the theme of this book) in *Economic and Political Weekly*, and have had a very fruitful association with him that way since 2009. I wish and hope his proposed chapter for this book is completed before long and falls into the right hands for publication.

Jinu Abraham with the Mental Health Action Trust, Kozhikkode and Faizan Ahmed, independent researcher based in New Delhi, both produced brilliant papers for the seminar, and I owe my gratitude to them for having kept the discussion alive long after the seminar in personal conversations and emails. I also wish them good luck with their papers in taking them to a due destination as their talents demand. Meanwhile, I cannot exclude the names of Mahesh Rangarajan, the then-director of the NMML, and his colleagues Indira Vancheswer and Nisar Kizhakkayil for their valuable contribution in organising the seminar. Regarding the seminar and its concept note, valuable inputs were given to me by George Varghese. G Aloysius and Abey Koshy both contributed in different ways in elaborating the theme for the seminar.

After the seminar, in compiling the papers into a book, the path was a most difficult one, and I would not have lasted through it but for the persistence of my contributors in this book. I also thank Madhav Tankha for his support here, in bringing out the papers in a book form. I consider it my privilege to be collaborating with each and every one of them and will do so in the future, too.

All errors and omissions are only mine.

Introduction

K.V. Cybil

Imagining the Third World, a post-colonial society, and engaging with the study of Social Sciences, makes it next to impossible to evade a question of social justice with respect to the field of one's engagement. It is a concept that works its way slowly through the process of research to create a zone of discomfort before the researcher has to finally make his or her own conclusions. Though popularised by John Rawls as a concept, it has a longer history than its patron(s) may have thought of. This book is certainly not an attempt to come to grips with the contemporary or state-of-the-art theory of Social Justice, although two of its chapters[1] speak volumes in this respect. It is rather an attempt to break the veneer of Eurocentric theory that covers this concept in order to break into the actuality of justice (or injustice) hidden by this concept.

Social justice, global justice

Gayatri Chakravorty Spivak's *A Critique of Postcolonial Reason* (especially its chapter on History) has made this (injustice) abundantly clear, where the work of John Rawls is situated squarely within its antecedents of liberalism and with respect to multiculturalism that creates a tabula rasa for the Eurocentric theory to reduce post-colonial culture as the lives of the migrant from the Third World represented it – as it is experienced in the First World. Citing Derrida, she contends that a 'hieroglyphist prejudice' arising from Europe's encounter with Chinese language in its early modernity has compelled it to admire what it cannot understand (notwithstanding the current knowledge of Chinese as a script). This initial European hallucination has set for itself an ethnocentric pattern and a post-colonial reason, which according to Spivak 'operates the culturalist excuse for Development, for example, encountered in John Rawls' Political Liberalism' (Spivak 1999: 281).

Not surprisingly, therefore, Rawls withdrew from the difference principle (related to social or distributive justice) when he formulates the law of the peoples in contrast to his earlier take on global justice as subject to the law of nations (Rathore 2017). Rawls makes a distinction between the law of nations (at an earlier stage of his theory) and the law of peoples (at a more recent stage in his theory), and because of his withdrawal from the difference principle in the latter, allows 'socio-economic injustices at the global level that would not be tolerated within a single nation' (Rathore 2017: 104).

The sanctioned ignorance in/with which the post-colonial subject is imagined in the Social Sciences (Spivak 1999: 164) gives us more reasons to doubt the Rawlsian axiomatic of veiled ignorance. Stanley Cavell (1996) has tried to make Rawls more accommodative within the post-colonial framework by highlighting his concept of conversations of justice as a moot point. Commenting on Veena Das, who tries to argue that it is possible for Social Sciences to engage with a category like pain (contextualised here against the Partition of India and the incidents of violence following it) through a philosophical investigation into the location of pain, Cavell states that Rawlsian conversations of justice may conceptually apprehend the reconciliation processes of mourning onset by accidental death of kin, especially by women in families in India. Still, his commentary would stop short of assessing how justice will converse with the Aghoris who consume flesh of the corpse to liberate entrapped souls from accidents, as cited by Veena Das (1996: 91). The limits of knowledge being sanctioned as ignorance is a repeated hurdle that comes up when Rawlsian framework is employed in premises remote from those of Eurocentric theory.

By some internal design or default, John Rawls' theory of justice as fairness has been made to appear like a partial remedy for post-colonial societies, with grave forms of injustice considered sanctioned by ignorance as well as given to sanctioned ignorance. The one important and crucial reason behind this is its failure to account for the forms of injustice that are ascribed to birth/descent (Rathore 2017: 158). His theory of 'the veil of ignorance' though persuades the argument for justice, as fairness leads its seeker into the wilderness in terms of understanding what are the limits of 'ignorance' in a post-colonial society? A theory of liberal politics and representative government that is backed by the Rawlsian conception of justice would add to these woes because in a society like India, representative government is considered by its rigid casteist organisation to be ignorant of its limits. While remaining elected legislators of a representative assembly in the country, a majority of the representatives take it for granted because of their caste background to be safely 'ignorant' of the people or the problems faced by them in their respective constituencies. Mediations or solutions to problems faced by people are given a chance to representation only through channels controlled by norms of social exclusion. In short, this biography of the representative government in India has transformed the limits of government to that of a social corpus becoming visible as the signs of an embalmed caste system in its mode of representation. This is one reason why Rawls may be only infrequently invoked with relation to the concept of Social Justice in India, though he is a recent innovator of this concept. One reason that this is admitted to be so by Amartya Sen, who has been a great supporter of Liberalism, is 'the contemporary – and largely Western – pursuit of political philosophy in general and of the demands of justice in particular has been, I would argue, limited and to some extent parochial'(quoted in Rathore 2017: 107). Rathore, meanwhile, though praising Sen's critique of the Rawlsian framework's parochialism, rallies for a theory that will account for caste-based discrimination in India. To refocus attention from global to social justice, he calls for a 'turn now to a certain aspect of the Dalit problem; specifically, a peculiarly perplexing one wherein the notion of global justice gets ironically reflected in an antagonistic position toward the more direct and local goal of (social) justice' (ibid: 110).

Marx, Derrida, Spivak

By and large, with most problems on Social Justice in India, we do find reference to Karl Marx, a thinker who is not considered a champion of liberal politics or representative government. Reiterating the need for an Indian theory for the study of politics which also foregrounds the lived experience of the people of the country, Rathore defends his notion of the people (a large majority of which is poor and Dalit):'Is this some crypto-Marxism that sees the universality of the proletariat now reflected in Dalits? Well, the briefest of brief answers is probably very simply *yes*' (ibid: 26–7).

Anupama Rao (2013) considers the question of social justice as a confluence of the thoughts of Karl Marx and Ambedkar as it was lived out in the interim or the in-between years of the World Wars in Mumbai when Ambedkar spearheaded a Dalit renaissance in India. The most important channel for this was provided in Mumbai by the workers' movement, especially of the textile mills, which was led by the Communists. Radical intervention by Ambedkar was required to retain the rights of Dalits as workers when the trade unions concerned showed no direct interest in them. He kept writing in the journals about the Dalits and led a movement in the streets for the depressed classes. The dialectics of body as value for the worker and body as dispossession for the Dalit posed for Ambedkar the crucial challenge of Social Justice as a problematic in the 1930s and 1940s workers' movement of Mumbai. The distinction he maintained between depressed classes and Dalits – the former as a governmental term and the latter as a political and literary term – indicate the subtlety with which he raised a platform for consciousness to fight the caste system (Brahminical Hinduism) while engaging Marxism.

A friendly dispute with Marx and the Marxist problematic of social justice is dealt with by Spivak (1999: 261) in respect to the politics of woman in post-colonialism as a subject of history. She argues that the Marxist framework of economics left out a discussion of the family (natural exchange) or politics of reproduction to be conducted through anthropological debates that wind up eventually with the incorporation or assimilation of differences under the hegemonic power relations of colonial knowledge (ibid: 261–2). Her radical proposition that the silence of the subaltern (woman in post-colonial society in this context) is an artificial silence accomplished through the twin projects of imperialism and patriarchy also engages with Marxism in confronting the question of intellectuals and power in a post-colonial society.

Spivak advances the Derridean concept of justice to reiterate the presence of Marxism in resisting the reduction of justice to a global phenomenon (ibid: 423–31). Justice as the experience of the impossible is a negation with sublation that Spivak proposed instead. In that way, ethics and gift (as given time) also are experiences of the impossible. Law, Politics and Time that owe themselves to these experiences derive their structure from Justice, Ethics and Gift, which by themselves remain without structure. Yet she summarises the process of deconstruction not merely as reaching the point of complicity in reading a text with its trope – as detropification, but as the registration of a proxy, an agent of power that is detached from its portrait (image or representation) embedded in ideology as well as guided by interests but is not a subject. It may be argued that Spivak places the conception of justice as an experience of the impossible, which deconstruction as a form of work reaches through proxy.

Proxy is also another name for agency according to Spivak (ibid: 258), and is hence different from portrait, and her difference with Foucault also stems from this fact. The proxy embodies for her a form of agency or power in pursuit of an ideologically determined interest, which is an option unavailable to an abstract technological notion of power proposed by Foucault. This brings us to another interesting debate on the question of defining the post-colonial subject in India with respect to the relation of theory to experience and vice versa.

The debate between Gopal Guru and Sundar Sarukkai only obliquely meant to deal with Social Justice or Justice as such, and gives a panoramic view of details pertaining to the questions related to Social Justice. Central to this work is defining the role of theory in Social Sciences where an unequal equivalence has forced a division of labour into the 'theoretical brahmins' and 'empirical sudras'. The creation of a certain kind of epistemic practice that is grounded in a non-critical reading/understanding of society and the concomitant aversion to deal with caste as a form of experience that has no more than a pedantic value were among the important reasons behind this division of labour.

Of interest is the coincidence on the role of experience for theory in the Guru-Sarukkai debate and Spivak. Spivak's stand on the subaltern existence of theory as independent of the metropolitan and globalised view of the subaltern as an agent bathing in the subject of European theory (Spivak 1999: 254) is crucial for extrapolating this debate on how experience becomes theoretical and hence political. She drives home the point amongst others that intellectuals mean neither subjects defined by relations of power (Foucault) nor immanent modes of individual becomings controlled by desire (Deleuze), but positions defined at the cusp of knowledge-and-power societies. If one adds to this Spivak's invocation of Derrida in his definition of justice as the experience of the impossible, many things will become clear to our understanding regarding the diffidence of her critique of post-colonialism in accepting a theory of justice as fairness. The assumption that invocation of justice through categorical imperatives is still capable of reducing the conditions of post-coloniality to originary positions is a vague assumption that dwells on colonialism itself as an imperative.

Dalit literature, meanwhile, has produced a Kafkesque rendering of justice as a form of desire – of escape from the law (Deleuze and Guattari 1975). Its autobiographical version (life-writing, according to Udayakumar (2013)) especially has come to occupy the mediator role in negotiating this desire of escape from the law (of Brahminism) or experience of the impossible, neither of them with a radical alternative. Udayakumar (ibid) has indicated that the experience of stigma, humiliation or shame has a form of singularity or particularity, which through expressing itself overrules historical function as a positive fact. It is a denial of justice that also defies bringing itself to testimony that earmarks the Dalit autobiographies and hence their persistent struggle to become political. He argues that the problems faced by Ambedkar initially in writing a history of untouchability in India, in 1915, where he confessed to the lack of an exact methodology (of the kind used in positivism), is similar in kind to the problems Gramsci felt in writing a history of the Italian subaltern in the 1940s (ibid 2013: 160–1).

Social injustice

This book also is an assemblage of problems which are methodological in derivation relating to social injustices experienced through anti-caste movements, thoughts and epistemology. The challenge of encountering injustice before accepting it into a framework forms the meeting point of these chapters. They do not obey the textbook definition of justice, least of all that of the much-plagiarised definition of social justice. They approach injustice as a social plane of immanence for all forms of relations – political, economic, historic, ideological, etc. The manifold reflections it produces in the form of challenges to freedoms of an individual or of a community has been the undercurrent of modern history in India. These chapters try to locate the vanishing traces of an unjust, impure nation unfazed by challenges to purify itself as the only possible ground for its integrity. This may be thought along the lines of a thin *svaraj*, which exercises not just the liberty principle of thick svaraj, but also equality and where 'hybridity and pluralism appear everywhere one looks, especially down and within' (Rathore 2017: 151). They open up to various interesting areas of Social, Colonial and Post-Colonial theory, apart from throwing open the form in which frameworks of justice are easily deconstructed by themselves when exposed to the realities of the world that is lived in.

The moot question while raising an issue with Social Theory in India on the grounds of injustice is to ignite a discussion on what of justice can be retrieved from the processes of law – government and the courts (legal/procedural justice according to Guru 2008: 230–49) – for a detailed, polemical and theoretical comprehension of the social or the milieu in which forms of injustice are experienced. That caste or forms of experience related to it emerge as the most important in this respect is significant for understanding the arguments in this book. In a way it improvises Guru and Sarukkai's (2012) debate on the emergent grounds for perception of caste. Guru and Sarukkai's debate is a prelude to a larger discourse of minoritarian operations of caste as in movements for caste annihilation, spiritual discourses that implicate castes or the caste system, the discourse of the left for social justice and action, in addition to the liberal and democratic discourses where it had always been treated as merely a remainder of tradition not involved with modernity. A critique of these post-colonial careers of caste has not been seriously attempted frequently, and being one in this direction, this book is certainly inspired by Guru and Sarukkai. For example, the manner in which they have pitch-forked untouchability as a philosophical moot point is worthwhile in discussing how the caste system traditionally understood in India had always kept untouchables out of knowledge as a system. Chapter 6 in this book, for example, discusses the instance of Narayana Guru as an untouchable philosopher in colonial India with a political affirmation for the *avarna* to become philosophical (ascetic).

What stimulates thoughts on injustice, as these chapters would argue, is the absence of a milieu, especially a dissembling of the social that loses meaning without an overbearing structure of the hierarchy. This is as much a result of the disintegration of vernacular myths and languages as an episteme for thought expressed in epistemology of Eurocentric systems of knowledge as it is about the reassembling of the social from the margins, outliers of modernity.[2] Pandian has observed this as a trail blazed by lower caste engagement with politics whereby 'one step outside modernity is being one step ahead of modernity' (Pandian 2002). The ingenuity of these chapters lies not merely in reckoning a state-of-the-art of caste, but also a statement of interdisciplinarity that defies the derivative essence of discourses related to knowledge systems of the West.

Robert Deliege's contention that isolated cases of injustice remain bones of contention in the absence of a milieu on the reflection of such injustices cannot be compensated with thoughts about annihilating them that also lack a milieu (Deliege 1999: 1–10). These chapters are an attempt to fulfil the latter requirement, which is an uppermost one as reflected in the various discussions situated around caste in the recent past (Guru and Sarukkai 2012; Hardtmann 2009; Deliege 1999). They primarily address a question that is neither theoretical nor empirical, but methodological. It is an experience in reflecting on social injustice from the underbelly of a concept of nation. Therefore, the method in these chapters is to approach this concept from a given, but consciously absented, milieu of impurity in imagining the nation. It is a retrieval of the abstract within the sense of impurity and injustice that has triggered the thoughts defining this volume.

Revolution, action, practice

The Ambedkar-Gandhi debate has been one of the recurrent themes of Indian politics that has brought social justice to the fore time and again, the most recent as commented by Gopal Guru being a 'rush to reconcile' the two extremes of thought (cited in Rathore 2017: 149). Vidhu Verma maintains that the differences between Gandhi and Ambedkar remain as irreconcilable as ever, and she postulates a Derridean notion of justice – or justice as the experience of the impossible for Dalits – to prove her point. The law of Hinduism that encompasses the Dalit as a community being a creation of the Poona Pact, the parameters of a struggle towards creation of a just society for the Dalits remains today as it was in 1932. Inclusive parameters of democracy such as rights or individual achievement do not help the Dalits, in the continued presence of the social stigma arising out of their majority being followers of Hinduism.

Vidhu Verma also tries to interrogate the tradition of liberal thinking on Social Justice from two angles, one that of the drawbacks of the Rawlsian framework and two that of the criticism of the framework of Satyagraha (as a Gandhian notion) in the Indian context. The case of violence against the Dalits illustrates the need for a higher moral sensitivity in registering the violations of justice incurred against them than Satyagraha. This is because they are not merely a political category, but one with a history. The reason for the continued violence against the Dalits, for which caste is not upheld by the courts of the country (the Khairlanji verdict by High Court of Maharashtra 2010), as a sufficient reason has been critically approached in this chapter. Search for a new standpoint that is informed by a direct representation of the oppressed is salvaged by her chapter in contextualising the discourse of Social Justice in India.

Soumyabrata Choudhury's chapter in this book deals with the historic role occupied by the *Bhagavad Gita* in the context of the caste system and Ambedkar's criticism of it. The *Bhagavad Gita* has been called a counter-revolution of Brahminism by Ambedkar, which employed the text for wresting the awareness of an event – Buddhism and its challenge to Brahminism, a revolution in the history of India. The equality principle inherent to Buddhism is re-invoked by Ambedkar through the exemplar of the French Revolution before the Dalits during the Mahad Satyagraha in 1927.

Choudhury's chapter encounters the singularity of this event (the Mahad Satyagraha)and contrasts it with its immanent comparativity with the French Revolution, in the thoughts of Abbe Sieyes and B. R. Ambedkar, and delves into the levels at which the polemic of such comparativity scuttles the colonial claim to caste or its hierarchy as representative of Indian totality. Drawing from the experience of the Haitian Revolution in 1791, he claims there are revolutions that are only inherently comparative and not comparable. He even questions the historic positioning of the untouchable as a subaltern subject with this event (the Mahad Satyagraha). He considers the subaltern as a site of positive affirmation by historians where no class or any such form exists.

Comparison in post-colonial writings has contributed to observation of mimicry, imitation of the metropolis – in the erstwhile colony by a subject in the post-colony. Baidik Bhattacharya (2006) has observed that these are 'belated spaces' of performance where comparison alternates between the metropolis and the periphery or between text and anthropology for the native informant. Baidik Bhattacharya (2016), citing the case of world literature today, argues that genealogy of comparitism as a paradigm has routinely ignored colonial histories to secure both its internal coherence and pure European origin. Choudhury's chapter traces the maturity of this exercise; of understanding the resistance of a subject in the post-colony (figure of native informant, for example) as a polemic against the very globality of knowledge systems of the metropolis, such as Indology, that constituted comparison as a neutral platform for traffic of thoughts. Discourses stemming from Phule and Ambedkar challenge such cognitions of Indian myths and religions that innocently accepted them as of an Aryan stock– the Indo-European.

Michael Dusche exposes the Habermasian framework of rationality to its inherent vulnerabilities in cross-cultural discourses. Referring to the advantages of the method of communicative rationality in social sciences, he distinguishes it from the accurate or predictive rationality of natural or exact sciences. But he then extends it to cross-cultural examinations, where he exposes it to its vulnerabilities on account of Eurocentric notions of culture. He argues how Habermas' views can be restricted by mythical, extra-legal notions of politics in the West. He suggests that it is possible to read Habermas along with experiences of non-Western cultures given that his concept of communicative rationality is derived from a methodological standpoint that permits variables of language and culture in social sciences. He uses the concept of ethopoesis by Foucault to illuminate how certain forms of action based on application of Truth rather than Logic by the ethos or individual being can transform discursive rationality, rather than be restricted to the domain of values or culture. He highlights the Gandhian Satyagraha as a form of ethopoesis, or a form of action that cannot be explained by the forms of rationality defined by Habermas.

He nonetheless opens to wide debate the Gandhian notion of *Swaraj*, approximately translated to a Western audience as autonomy of the lifeworld. Lifeworld, though a category adopted from Habermas, has lost its autonomy, being left with a choice of being modern or anti-modern. A Gandhian option of being non-modern is being offered as a critique to Habermas' theory by Dusche. Dusche's chapter, in exploring the limits of the Habermasian framework, brings Social Justice under the scanner, as it happens to be one of the frameworks which is globally accepted to be akin to the Rawlsian framework (Rathore 2017: 118–21).

Neshat Quaiser's chapter dwells further on the meaning of action in society, especially the limits of post-structuralist frameworks in coming to terms with the idea of justice. It argues with Foucault and Scott on the inevitability or unavoidability of injustice as the structural premise for a discourse of justice. Similarly, it struggles with their, especially Foucault's, refusal of any formalisation of justice, given that modernity has conceived of the courts in much the same way it has conceived of instruments of punishment, such as the prisons.

Neshat's chapter is in conversation with Michael Dusche's chapter, especially on points related to Critical Theory, where the two can be effectively seen to be engaged in a debate on how to pronounce the relationship of Foucault to Critical Theory. This is a Marxian problematic for Neshat, whereas it is a Liberal one for Dusche. Nonetheless, it makes for an interesting debate within the scope of post-colonial social theory to understand how to relate social practices to knowledge itself. His chapter (on a speculative note) definitely defies the rhetoric that *Khap panchayats* could also be counted as parallel practices if the people's courts are counted as parallel practices, because he is raising the issue of the people's courts with respect to a historical moment when the practice of surveillance came to be accepted as the norm of punishment. While it is true that material conditions in semi-feudal countries like India might suggest the Khap panchayat instance to be true in a parallel sense, it actually cannot because of its power to will to exempt itself from history. Nehsat's chapter, instead of making parallel practices sound normative – that is, by delinking it from any exclusionary position to history that it might attempt to – exposes it to its legal liminalities, conditioned by post-colonial inter-subjectivities crafted necessarily out of a complex milieu of communities already lived in.

Philosophy, spirituality, anti-caste thought

Narayana Guru's philosophy, as interpreted by his disciple Nataraja Guru (*An Integrated Science of the Absolute*), that proclaims the centrality of philosophy to the practice of spirituality in India, is a persuasive reading in understanding the role of philosophy in India today. The book comprises two articles focused on the thoughts assembled around Narayana Guru, the twentieth century's leading thinker and reformer of Kerala. The basic attraction in the chapter by Sundar Sarukkai is the profiling of Narayana Guru's philosophy with respect to the Indian paradigm of linking spirituality with philosophy. Sarukkai has left out a discussion of how a non-Brahmin, anti-caste thinker becomes a representative of philosophy in India, which terrain my own chapter attempts to negotiate.

He has put to creative reading the commentary called *An Integrated Science of the Absolute* by Nataraja Guru (2001) to arrive at a philosophical premise which is linked to the Continental (European) philosophy of contemporary times (early to mid-twentieth century) through the works of Henri Bergson and the Structuralists. He points to how the vacuum created in delinking philosophy and spirituality has led to the commercialisation of the latter and a negative attitude towards the metaphysical for the former. While Nataraja Guru's attempt integrates the two, such attempts are few and far between because of a mistaken understanding of the exercise of spirituality in a modern world as totally detached from philosophy.

Sarukkai's chapter concludes that unitive thought of physics and metaphysics – gross and subtle – is the groundwork for understanding both Narayana Guru and Nataraja Guru. A chapter by me attempts to locate this observation in the context of challenge posed to orthodoxy by Narayana Guru in the form of his (lower caste) asceticism. This is an aspect which can be theorised only with difficulty, because of a colonial silencing or absence of a link between the work of reform and the thoughts of Narayana Guru. I have sought to solve the riddle by locating Narayana Guru in the milieu of an ascetic tradition that fought an intellectual crusade against social injustices and also challenged the Brahminical orthodoxy with respect to knowledge by challenging such norms as hierarchy in thoughts as well as devotion. The political society it gave form to in the wake of a spiritual renaissance through education and organisation was conceived in the form of a suspension of iconoclasm and right to deification (Wakankar 2010) akin to the spirit of the Bhakti movement. Yet, given the circumstances of a colonial modernity in which it emerged, the subjectivity it was challenged with deconstructing was that of an anthropocentrism caught between its (Ezhava, the caste Narayana Guru was born into) victimhood as an oppressed caste and parasitism as a vision of the emerging multitudes from within.

Sarukkai's chapter closes with the following lines:

> Ultimately, [Nataraja Guru] is striving for the unification of physics and metaphysics. If we remember the meanings of these terms, the unification he and Narayana Guru are emphasising

> is nothing more than the unity of the world of things and the world of ideas, which is the first prerequisite for a spiritual experience.

This is a valuable departure point for entering into a debate with Sarukkai on the question of humanism or anthropocentrism that underlies Nataraja Guru's interpretation of Narayana Guru. While trying to maintain the most highlighting aspects of both their claims regarding unification of physics and metaphysics to be true, I argue that its supporting base was not the same for Nataraja Guru and Narayana Guru. This also brings out their differences as the multitudes (castes such as the non-Brahmin) in which Narayana Guru's own views were to be extended during his own time find little or no presence in that of Nataraja Guru. The unifying essence of metaphysics and physics, to put it short for Naryana Guru, was not the human self, but a man-machine assemblage or a *Karu*, something that was only virtually human and had an abiding characteristic of multiplying itself generally without an end.

Sarukkai also does not encounter the problem if the question of the Self, which is apparently discoursed at length in the Thousand Verse of Self Instruction (*atmopadesa satakam*) by Narayana Guru, becomes a turning point in understanding his philosophy or not, because it has been identified as his intellectual passage to *Advaita* (monism) and therefore the road to reception of his philosophy as an Idealist one (Yati 2005; Muni Narayana Prasad 1997). For the programme of social action that he conceived of, including the resolute stand against caste and its eradication, did it not pose anathema is a relevant question. The current definition of its (caste annihilation) movement is drawn from Buddhism, and it is well known that Buddha 'posited no autonomous self' and therefore his teachings 'were radically different from the views set forth in his time'(Macy 1979: 43). How then should one understand the passage to Advaita or monistic philosophy which is centred on the self and its liberation in Narayana Guru, especially when a flourishing Buddhist past is believed to have been cut short by the arrival of Brahminical Hinduism in Southern India, with colonial Travancore where Narayana Guru lived and wrote being no exception?

The peculiarity of his vision is its multiplicity that rises to a level of anthropology of vision, which is articulated through different combinations of matter and form, without arresting knowledge itself to permanency of a subject or its representation in selfhood. It is an anthropology of a man-machine assemblage that underlines his vision, which can only be understood if we are able to identify and develop the fragments of a metaphor called *karu* (a victim, as I argue in my chapter) that is omnipresent in his writings, especially *atmopadesa satakam*. It defies many descriptions, and therefore this vision of Advaita cannot be coupled with those of Vivekananda or Aurobindo, neither of which evoke a metaphor of victimhood in relation to philosophy. Writing about the role of experience in theory, Gopal Guru identifies victim as the site of the objectification of thought, where the tormentor who uses experience as a political condition to maintain domination and the theoretician uses it as a tool for theorisation (Guru and Sarukkai 2012: 72) encounter each other. The exegesis that I have given to Narayana Guru's works is inclined to override the use of self as a metaphor, with which it has often been identified, and reinstate victim as a most definitive trope in them.

The reason to include two chapters on Narayana Guru stems from none other than to delink it from a colonial discourse of Brahminism, which completely surmounted it or silenced its many other contexts. This is a compelling illusion, as the Advaita or Vedantic philosophy has been considered a mainstay for all attempts at social reform in India like the Arya Samajor Brahmo Samaj. It also marked its influence in Nationalist thought, as in the works of Vivekananda and Aurobindo. That Narayana Guru and the movement he founded would effortlessly fall into place once seen as a link in this chain of reformist movements should be understood as a work of post-colonial reason today. Very few, if any, evidences to the contrary can be cited in defence of an alternate argument about his vision within the confines of such a reason.

The impasse thus created can only be solved by evoking the pretext of his aversion to the *Bhagavad Gita*, which in its turn can re-enlighten us to his entire oeuvre in a significant way. Narayana Guru's aversion to the *Gita* stems from a simple reason that it sanctioned a violence which no philosophy (especially the Vedantic) could ever justify. It is interesting to note that Narayana Guru reveals his mind in a friendly conversation to his favourite disciple Nataraja Guru (Devan 2002) and not in any written form. In fact, Nataraja

Guru, Nity Chaitanya Yati and Muni Narayana Prasad – three of the most scholarly commentators on his philosophy – wrote independent commentaries on the *Gita*, whereas Narayana Guru showed no or little interest in it.

S.S. More (1990) has argued that the tradition called *Brahmathraya*– or the trio of *Upanishads*, *Brahma Sutras* and *Bhagavad Gita*– have been conventionally cited as the source of wisdom in India, especially by the Brahmins. He also claims that, of the three, the *Upanishads*, which occupy the most valuable role, has been called the Vedanta and is believed to be condensed in meaning in the form of the *Brahma Sutras*. The *Gita*, as he argues, has been added later on to this retinue, as it can be historically seen as integral to the epic *Mahabharata*. But, a strict allegiance to the three pillars of wisdom had secured for the Hindu orthodoxy its position of power since the time of Sankara through the time of Ramanuja and Madhavacharya up till the present. Bala Gangadhara Tilak's *Gitarahasya* (1915) was an interpolation of a new meaning, that of action into the *Gita* (which was earlier read only in conjunction with devotion (*bhakti*), knowledge (*jnana*)and attendant bodily discipline called Yoga as a means to *moksha*, or liberation) drastically transformed the power attached to this text for a new national audience. It is to this rendition of Yoga as Karma Yoga, a Copernican revolution (More 1990: 37) envisaged by Tilak's *Gitarahasya*, that the rest of the nationalist thinkers, including Gandhi, Vivekananda and Aurobindo, reciprocated with their own commentaries. Despite the persuasion of his disciple Nataraja Guru to comment on the *Gita* at a time when nationalism was ruling the roost, Narayana Guru stuck to an Upanishadic or Vedantic view of wisdom and composed the *Vedanta Suktas* instead. This fact has been insufficiently apprised of in almost all commentaries on Narayana Guru, probably due to its late discovery in the 1970s. It is precisely for this reason that a chapter on his vision as read from a victim's role as a philosopher has been included in this book.

Notes

1 See the chapters by Michael Dusche and Vidhu Verma in this book.
2 See Soumyabrata Choudhury's chapter in this book.

References

Bhattacharya, Baidik. 2006. "Naipaul's New World: Post Colonial Modernity and the Enigma of Belated Space." *NOVEL: A Forum on Fiction*, 39(2), Spring: 245–267, Post Colonial Disjunctions.

Bhattacharya, Baidik. 2016. 'On Comparitism in the Colony: Archives, Methods and the Project of *Worltliteratur*', *Critical Inquiry*, 42(3), Spring: 677–711.

Cavell, Stanley. 1996. 'Comments on Veena Das's Essay; "Language and Body: Transactions in the Construction of Pain"', *Daedalus*, 125(1), Winter: 93–8, Social Suffering.

Das, Veena. 1996. 'Transactions in the Construction of Pain', *Daedalus*, 125(1), Winter: 67–91, Social Suffering.

Deleuze, Gilles and Guattari, Felix. 1975. *Kafka: Toward a Minor Literature*. Minneapolis and London: University of Minnesota Press.

Deliege, Robert. 1999. *The Untouchables of India*. Michigan: Berg.

Devan, Madathil Vasudevan. 2002. 'Guruvinu Gita Pramanamo?', in K.N. Shaji (ed.), *Narayana Guru: Jivitam, Kritikal, Darsanam*, pp. 352–65. Thrissur: Current Books.

Guru, Gopal. 2008. 'Constitutional Justice: Positional and Cultural', in Rajeev Bhargava (ed.), *Politics and Ethics of the Indian Constitution*, pp. 230–49. New Delhi: Oxford University Press.

Guru, Gopal and Sarukkai, Sundar. 2012. *The Cracked Mirror*. New Delhi: Oxford University Press.

Guru, Nataraja. 2001. *Integrated Science of the Absolute*. New Delhi: D.K. Printworld.

Hardtmann, Eva Maria. 2009. *The Dalit Movement in India: Local Practices, Global Connections*. New Delhi: Oxford University Press.

Macy, Joanna Rogers. 1979. 'Dependent Co-arising: The Distinctiveness of Buddhist Ethics', *The Journal of Religious Ethics*, 7(1), Spring: 38–52.

More, Sadananand S. 1990. *The Gita: A Theory of Human Action*. New Delhi: Sri Satguru Publications.

Muni Narayana Prasad. 1997. *The Vedanta Sutras of Narayana Guru*. New Delhi: D.K. Printworld.

Pandian, Mathias Samuel Soundra. 2002. 'One Step Outside Modernity: Caste, Identity Politics and Public Sphere', *Economic and Political Weekly*, 37(18), May 4–10: 1735–41.

Rao, Anupama. 2013. 'Revisting Interwar Thought: Stigma, Labor and the Immanence of Caste-Class', in CosimoZene (ed.), *The Political Philosophies of Antonio Gramsci and B.R. Ambedkar*, pp. 43–59. Oxon and New York: Routledge.

Rathore, Aaksah Singh. 2017. *Indian Political Theory: Laying the Groundwork for Svaraj*. London and New York: Rutledge.

Spivak, Gayatri Chakravorty. 1999. *A Critique of Post Colonial Reason: Toward a History of the Vanishing Present*. Cambridge, MA and London: Cambridge University Press.

Udaya Kumar. 2013. 'Consciousness, Agency and Humiliation: Reflections on Dalit life-writing and Subalternity', in Cosimo Zene (ed.), *The Political Philosophies of Antonio Gramsci and B.R. Ambedkar*, pp. 158–71. Oxon and New York: Routledge.

Wakankar, Milind. 2010. *Subalternity and Religion: The Prehistory of Dalit Empowerment in South Asia*. New Delhi: Routledge.

Yati, Nitya Chaitanya. 2005. *Narayana Guru*. New Delhi: Indian Council for Philosophical Research.

Chapter 1

Ambedkar and Gandhi

Exploring aporias in social justice and practices

Vidhu Verma

Introduction

Since the 1970s, liberal political theory has developed a new approach toward justice that is indispensable in promoting balanced judgement and consideration of equal interests in society. Issues of justice inspired by John Rawls played a prominent role in adjudicating conflicts and legitimising their solutions within the welfare discourse, and increasingly it is accepted that a set of institutions can be so well-conceived and so well-ordered that the latter fit the selves it presupposes (Rawls 1973). One of the many consequences of the liberalism that Rawls proposed was the focus on inherited social inequalities, along with an injustice arising out of individual differences. Subsequently, many philosophers have analysed and contested his famous difference principle, according to which the basic structure of society arranges social and economic inequalities such that they are to the greatest advantage of the least well-off in the representative group.

But democratic societies are confronted with new challenges that Rawls' universal theory is ill-prepared to answer. The idea of the original position makes sense only against the background of a social context; a comprehensive theory makes sense in an abstract situation of rational choice based on capabilities of persons with access to primary goods. Several scholars criticise Rawls' focus on social institutions. His principles of justice are criticised for not addressing the ongoing conversation on justice in a democratic society and the role that an openly ended characterisation of perfectionism can play (Cavell 1990). Back in the 1990s, Sen made a case for 'capabilities' as a more appropriate criterion for assessing individual wellbeing (Agarwal et al. 2006).[1] He argued that diversity meant that people would need different levels of primary goods to do the same kind of things. While opportunities and income are very critical issues of justice, Rawls' strong assumptions about persons in the post-contract situation deflect attention from aspects of structural processes that do not fit into the distributive paradigm and from dominant norms and ideologies that construct social groups as different (Young 1990). Cohen objects that Rawls exempts individual choices from judgements of justice in light of the focus on the basic structure.[2] Sen argues that Rawls' *niti*-centered approach ignores the actual behaviours that make a society reasonably just (Sen 2009). Cavell disagrees with Rawls' attack on perfectionism and instead argues that it is a dimension of the moral life that places particular weight on the 'possibility or necessity of the transforming of oneself and one's society' (Cavell 1990, 1; Mulhall 1997). Given these critiques, it is high time that we relinquish some of the components of the dominant political theory today and begin thinking about politics in a different way if we want to deepen our democratic institutions. With this in mind, I look at a series of issues that are now central to Indian politics to show how looking closely at two major perspectives could offer insights on social justice.

Social justice as a concept has been part of our social imagination and has been one of the core fundamental ideas in our political discourse that has transformed Indian society. Both Gandhi and Ambedkar, with different perspectives, played a crucial role in shaping the public discourse on social justice in anti-colonial thought. But did their assumptions uniquely anchor the tensions that existed within a discourse of justice in the Indian context? Their interest in constructing India's post-colonial legal and political structures had a profound effect on the proliferation of new genres and alternative discourses of framing social and political ideals. Their books, articles and published communications have been the object of various interpretations, which usually seek to understand and respond to social, political, cultural and academic conjunctures related to the deepening of the crisis of the political system. Drawing on these two perspectives, I wish to make explicit that this discussion on justice is different from the debates in Western political theory that are mostly understood as considerations for 'fairness' (Miller 2013: 173–174; 2003: 121). Their reflections on political institutions, concepts used to interpret and organise political life, the relation between aims of ethics and nature of politics are still relevant as they continue to inform our current context.

I also wish to point out that this discussion draws from several distinct but closely related theoretical perspectives. First, social justice in the Indian context is about affirmative action policies of the state, addressing the quotas for groups that have faced historic injustice and disadvantage. Marked by broad welfare managerialism, the state is seen to oversee social policy for the greater good of all while emphasising the disadvantaged position of the scheduled castes, scheduled tribes, and Other Backward Classes. The meaning of distributive justice sometimes overlaps with that of social justice, but I view the former as specifically related to the socialist concern with an appropriate allocation of wealth, power, reward and respect among different classes. These are mostly located within changes in the mode of production debates.[3]

Second, in recent years, it is the perspectives from the marginalities which have changed and contested issues of governance and the classical grammar of social justice. Many scholars argue that the responses to social justice are not only due to variations in the material distribution of power or the way institutions deny social recognition but also result from the changes in beliefs, ideas and norms. These contestations at the boundaries of competing local structures have led to the destabilisation of a statist social justice discourse and have infused it with multiple perspectives and new claims. While the term has come to encompass a variety of claims, it is fair to say that social justice proponents have now used it as an umbrella term to characterise the moral and political claims of marginalised groups, including women, queer groups and people with special needs. Contemporary theories of social justice are about entitlements and discourse of rights that rarely put forward the idea of responsibility and solidarity. Taking this into account, is it possible to think of social justice as a universal ordering device and norm as well as one that varies in meaning according to the context? The question then arises: is the foundational concept open to being socially reconstituted and reproduced even when there seems no way to bridge the gulf between universalism and particularity?

What is suggested in this chapter is two-fold; first, social and distributive justice are more closely related than is often thought, and they show normative principles in slightly different versions in many contexts involving historical injustices, social discrimination, backwardness or disadvantaged positions. Drawing insights from an Ambedkarite approach on group justice, I discuss the potential of a double possibility: social justice as a differentiated and partial notion that might be shaped in various ways to offer cultural, political and social rights for oppressed groups as well as a basis for concrete political action. Ambedkar, with his stress on the particular case of a denial of legal rights for Dalits and on the need to accept plurality and contradiction, is particularly helpful to think about democracy. However, in the contemporary Indian context, the pursuit of social justice inevitably runs up against formidable contradictions, which are impossible to avoid and at the same time impossible to resolve, and so we are ethically compelled to pursue resolutions.

At the core of the difficulties in using the concept of social justice for illuminating contemporary problems is an ambiguity between descriptive and normative uses of the concept. As a description, social justice purports to tell how social institutions in Indian democracy work. But as a normative term, it sketches an ideal picture of the democracy as India could and should be, where the contradiction that Ambedkar had noted in the constituent assembly between political and economic life no longer exists.[4]

In the past 70 years, the Indian state has made significant attempts to classify populations for public policy and promoted affirmative action for the most disadvantaged and discriminated groups. The approach followed by the Indian state in introducing some of the disadvantaged groups, in administrative categories, Scheduled Castes (SCs), Scheduled Tribes (STs) and Other Backward Classes (OBC), should be seen as part of 'governmentality' that has created myriad problems for some of these groups who wish to reframe their histories. All categorical distinctions involve evaluative and normative commitments, which in turn necessitate the exercise of power and reflect the conditions of those who are socially dominant. Recently, there is a discernible shift away from the radical rhetoric that characterised the early Dalit perspectives and a concordant move towards affirming market-based mechanisms for overcoming discrimination and injustice. I argue that political realism works to ideologically translate social justice issues into a question of technical efficacy related to problems of identification of creamy layer, promotions, identification of beneficiaries, etc. This situation where politics is reduced to principles of technocratic managerialism and market efficiency involves a fundamental change in social democratic praxis. The realists' emphasis on the dark side of politics and scepticism about ethical standards to bear on politics is well taken. But realist views of social justice are misleading, as social groups have no such essential properties that define them in static terms. Instead, realist views have their manifestation in identity politics where political mobilisation based on membership in some group is thought to be delimited by some shared experiences or features that define that group. These classifications sometimes ignore the prevalent power structures which continue to build relations of caste hierarchy and sustain them. I argue that the classification scheme of disadvantaged social groups by the Indian state is a strong pragmatic construction, even though the aim of the Ambedkarite perspective is to abolish norms that compel people to act in ways defined by these classifications based on caste hierarchies.

The challenge of empirical sciences: developing a theory of injustice

This discussion on social justice may be questioned on two grounds which it unjustifiably ignores: the first is that the opinions on social justice on grounds of its having consequences that are beneficial will always be contradictory, and the second is that it is unclear to what extent beliefs on social justice in terms of its capacity to enable members to advance their common interests are in line with people's behaviour as political equals in a democracy. These are serious drawbacks to empirical justice research as widespread disregard of popular beliefs of justice raise the question of sources of political legitimacy. David Miller in his work tries to 'discover the underlying principles that people use when they judge some aspect of their society to be just or unjust, and then to show that these principles are coherent'(Miller 2003: ix). But principles being used in different contexts show that social justice presupposes morally bounded societies with restraints on individual liberty led by a state agency. Scholars like Michael Walzer argue that social justice could only be based on a 'complex equality', which is about the distribution of social goods according to different criteria reflecting the specificity of these goods, their social significance and the variety of their recipients (Walzer 1984). In very complex societies, the idea of simple equality is 'neither achievable nor desirable'. Donald explains that

> rather than deriving normative principles that would apply in all cases from either the rights of individuals or the promise of universal emancipation, Walzer insists on respect for the boundaries between social spheres and the negotiation of meanings and criteria appropriate to that particular sphere.
>
> (Donald 1992: 143)

Judith Shklar shifts attention away from principles and distributive contexts and raises the question of behaviour that is equivalent to passive injustice, as 'refusal of both officials and private citizens to prevent acts of wrongdoing when they could and should do so'. She defines it as more than habitual indifference to the misery of others, as it is precisely 'civic failure to stop private and public acts of injustice' (Shklar 1990: 6). She argues that passive injustice encourages the false and arrogant belief that a body of rules can capture the full range of actions that can inspire critiques of injustice. Woozley has taken her argument further by explicitly asserting that injustice is a separate concept from justice and admonishes us for overlooking voices of victims who face injustice (Woozley 1973). However, we become concerned about justice only when injustice is being done, and thus some scholars suggest that we 'adopt a negative approach, discovering what justice is by considering on what occasions we protest at injustice and unfairness' (Lucas 1980: 4). Is injustice merely the failure to be just? Is injustice about violating rules or the principle of justice known and justified before the analysis of injustice? As I argue in this chapter, we can make invaluable judgements on injustice, as did Ambedkar and Gandhi, without having a full-blown theory of justice. The concrete reality of injustice, immersed in a context along with a critical reflexivity of one's position in the social hierarchy, gives a moral framework for developing a theory of injustice.

By addressing these questions, we are raising a more fundamental problem. Within these morally bounded communities, how do we transform attitudes into expressions and embodiments of beliefs with the self and others in a critical manner? Furthermore, how do we translate ideas on social justice into an understanding of differences and engagement in everyday practices? Since the drafting of the Constitution, academic engagement with caste and its cultural forms have increased in various disciplines, and Dalit studies have emerged as a distinct programme with the formal establishment of Ambedkar Chairs and Centres in educational institutions. Teaching equality and justice courses for a better world have meant addressing some of our presuppositions and recognising the epistemologically disadvantaged as one for generating new concepts, knowledge and utopias. Tools of social sciences describe the trajectory of Dalit Studies as historically strained yet steadily improving through legal reforms to yield a more egalitarian society. An aporetic situation around controversial issues shakes our fundamental belief structure about society and others around us.

Due to these problems, I believe that our discussion on social justice represents a distorted application of Ambedkar's approach. Social sciences openly acknowledge the progress made in the pursuit of social justice. They have been a critical resource for understanding the nature and impact of various forms of oppression, even as they have a long tradition of exclusion and marginalisation. They are committed to conveying the complex ways in which caste domination and oppression marginalising Dalits are preserved at the very moment that laws prohibiting discrimination and market-inspired Dalit millionaires are used to profess the declining influence of caste. Hence, even though many questions have arisen about theoretical and methodological limitations of social justice, they have not challenged the standards and practices of some of the normative positions they raise. The aporia asks us to look beyond the mechanical work of teaching and to work through the tensions to give the promise of new modes of subjectivities.

To summarise, I argue that the challenge for the future social sciences which in the past has been more to galvanise the political processes and institutions of social justice deliberations is to now make problematic normative subjectivity of groups of historical discrimination. While such deliberation is acknowledged to be important in effective policy development, this enlightenment function has been designed to settle rather than to stimulate 'contestation and significance of Dalits as a political category with a history' (Rao 2008: 11). The second problem has been the continued reliance on a narrow technocratic orientation in policy analysis that emphasises the efficiency of means to meet the goals laid down by constitutional amendments. Policies of social justice have been about establishing definitions of and assigning meaning to 'transformations of the social realm'. By denying an epistemic privilege to the struggles at the boundaries of competing local structures that question a statist view of social justice, social science scholarship serves to offer ideological support for configurations of power as it does to explain it (Krishna 2014: 139).[5]

Preliminaries

Before proceeding with this discussion, a few conceptual clarifications are necessary. I take the title 'aporias' of this paper from Derrida's landmark essay 'Force of Law: the Mystical Foundation of Authority', where he observes that it is justice that the law sets out to symbolise and represent, and there is no law without the possibility of justice (Derrida 1990: 943). Since justice is impossible, immeasurable and irreducible, it cannot be circumscribed by legal or moral systems. Indeed, justice will always be in excess of the law that marks law's failure, and thus justice remains a disturbing force that unsettles confidence in any particular set of rules.

Derrida's views can act as a helpful supplement to some of our discussions on justice in the Indian context. What one finds in his analysis is an interpretation of justice aporetic: justice is opening up the possibility of ever-greater concrete realisation and yet defers its attainment. Aporia is usually understood 'as the state of impasse, non-passage, or logical contradiction that can never be permanently resolved, a state of the constant dilemma with no general or final solution' (Wang 2005: 45). In Derrida's formulation, because the law is about violation, it constitutes itself only in the way it proposes its own need to be remade. In short, the law comes into being only as abuse that goes on infinitely. In what follows, I intend to use this interpretation to a post-colonial condition in which Dalit subjectivity through a critical and self-reflective lens acknowledges the shortcomings of social justice. Despite laws against untouchability, the notions of impurity, the divisions and classifications it entails, it is an aporia, or in Derrida's words, 'something that does not allow passage' yet can offer us a glimpse of a community that is coming in the future.

One of the central aims of this chapter is to trace and recover the trajectories of thought and practices in Ambedkar and Gandhi, where they could be relocated in the way they addressed questions related to social discrimination, forgiveness and representation. A socio-ethical exploration of some of their arguments could provide substantial inroads for the aporias of justice and the destination of social equality within (un)recognisable reach. In thinking of the aporias of social justice, we need to ask not only what happens to social justice in circumstances of crisis but also how its concept is formed, what tensions and oppositions it contains. The history of social justice entails a protracted debate of Gandhi and Ambedkar that culminates in the Poona Pact, which included scheduled castes as part of the Hindu community. The central research question then focuses on understanding the historical moment and in imagining social sciences with possibilities of moving beyond this impasse regarding emancipatory practices.

Scholars like Nagaraj have pointed out that Ambedkar's 'politics was different from the Gandhian ideology and cultural politics that had dominated the nation', even though he later argues that they transformed each other. The 'imprint' of the Gandhian model of tackling the Harijan question 'merits a serious analysis' (Nagaraj 2013: 360). According to Nagaraj, both plunged into examining the question in a way that 'they cured each other's excesses; they emerged as transformed persons at the end of a very intense encounter' (ibid). If Nagaraj's argument is correct, it vindicates not simply Gandhi's view but the claim that his theory is a relevant conceptual and moral tool to respond to injustice. In this chapter, I argue that this defence of Gandhi is problematic and less effectively responds to Ambedkar's testimonial sensibility.

Without a doubt, for both, the polarised caste culture had to be addressed. We must be sensitive to the fact, at the same time, that we are facing a dynamic and ever-changing political process. The principal contradiction would be only for a short period, as new struggles would appear within the reality they both were studying. Most of their effort was expended in providing critiques of untouchability. What they discovered was a notion of the past not over and done with. Instead of a historicising perspective, which would have led them to view the ancient texts as irretrievable for their use, they focused on liberating people from that polarisation. In what follows, I would argue that the differences stem from competing theories and from the fact that the same terms relate to entirely different concepts (Coward 2003). The question was not whether caste existed – everyone seemed to agree that it did – but how should we remove it? Gandhi did not subscribe to the argument given in 'Annihilation of Caste' that caste system was an inescapable result of Hindu society and religion. While earlier Gandhi criticised the poor treatment of 'Harijans', he stepped back in condemning caste as a social hierarchy and instead suggested ways to improve upon its practices. He argued that inequalities faced by Dalits would be remedied by a change of heart among caste Hindus. In contrast, the complex and enduring character of injustice as a social phenomenon led Ambedkar to include the victims' reasons and his or her sense of injustice.

A useful way to balance these competing positions is to locate them in a rejection of discourses that appeal to a single concept or grand explanatory narrative. To be able to defend his position, Gandhi was dependent upon collective liability for making reparations to those wronged. However, the individual responsibility that he raises in no way implies moral blame since it is based on association and not on individual action. There is another line of argumentation in the writings of Ambedkar that touches on the affective exploration of the oppressed: the focus is on the high level of moral sensitivity needed to grasp the injustice done to them. It is precisely this notion that forms the point of departure for an outline of an Ambedkarite concept of social justice.

Re-framing the debate: tension and paradox

Gandhi's arrival in South Africa was followed by encounters with colonial arrogance and colour prejudice. With the Black Act in 1906, Indians were forced to register and show permits. Gandhi's experience as a 'coolie', though painful, was very different from the humiliation suffered by the subaltern diaspora plantation workers from India; 'coolies' were seen as people from the lowest caste and least desirable in the Indian population and carriers of disease (Natrajan 2013). On his return to India in 1914, he founded the Satyagraha Ashram, where he settled down to campaign against untouchability, which also became a cardinal point of his campaign to unify Hindu society. Gandhi failed to make a partner in the fight against 'untouchability' of Dr B.R. Ambedkar, himself an 'untouchable' but a highly educated one with degrees in law and economics, and who was, like Gandhi, invited to a Round Table Conference (RTC) in London in 1931. It was in the campaign against untouchability that Ambedkar, as opposed to Gandhi, argued that rights of 'untouchables' could not be at the mercy of caste Hindus.[6] Their subordination lies in the social relations and the production processes that cannot be eliminated through mere campaigns.

The differences on untouchability came up during the constitutional reforms proposed by the British government.[7] Ambedkar's presidential speech at the All India Depressed Classes Conference in Nagpur in August 1930 gave the themes central to the struggle of the Dalits: representation, recognition and political power.[8] During these years, Ambedkar demanded separate electorates and reservations for depressed classes in electoral seats and in posts in state and educational institutions.[9] The contrasting views emerged during the RTC and created a major crisis in the political deliberations on the communal award of 1932.[10] In one of his public speeches before the RTC in the plenary session, he argued:

> A patriot and a nationalist in India is one who sees with open eyes his fellowmen treated as being less than man. But his humanity does not rise in protest. He knows that men and women for

> no cause are denied their human rights. But it does not prick his civic sense to helpful action. . . . I am glad, I do not belong to that class of patriots. I belong to that class which takes its stand on democracy and which seeks to destroy monopoly in every shape and form. Our aim is to realise in practice our ideal of 'one man, one value' in all walks of life – political, economic and social.
>
> (Ambedkar 2005b: 598–9)

During the RTC, Gandhi alienated him by offering 'to share the honor . . . of representing the interests of untouchables'. Ambedkar responded icily, 'I fully represent the claims of my community'. He believed that 'untouchables were keepers of their own destiny and deserved their own movement (Ambedkar 2005a: 655–6).[11] In 'A Scheme of Political Safeguards for the Protection of Depressed Classes' submitted to the British government, Ambedkar argued that 'the Depressed classes cannot consent to subject themselves to majority rule in their present state of hereditary bondsmen' (Ambedkar and Srinivasan 2005a: 546). Before establishing majority rule, 'their emancipation from the system of untouchability must be an accomplished fact. . . . The Depressed classes must be made free citizens entitled to all the rights of citizenship in common with other citizens of the state' (Ambedkar and Srinivasan 2005a: ibid). The entire text demands free enjoyment of equal rights, which must be followed by adequate laws to protect depressed classes against discrimination.

In the RTC proceedings in 1931, Gandhi's presentation began with the assertion that the deadlock on the communal question was 'inherent in the composition of the Indian delegation' and that the minorities committee be adjourned (Ambedkar 2005c: 660). But Gandhi also claims that 'untouchability will soon be a relic of our sinful past', as 'conscience of Hindus has been stirred', and the depressed classes must not be given 'special representation' (Ambedkar 2005c: 661). In response to Ambedkar, Gandhi argued:

> I can understand the claims advanced by other minorities, but the claims advanced on behalf of untouchables that to me is the unkindest cut of all. It means the perpetual bar-sinister. . . . I claim myself in my person to represent the vast mass of the untouchables . . .and we do not want on our register and on our census untouchables classified as a separate class. . . . I am

> speaking with a due sense of responsibility, and I say that it is not a proper claim which is registered by Dr Ambedkar when he seeks to speak for the whole of the untouchables of India.
>
> (Ambedkar 2005c: 662–3)

Ambedkar's position on the representation of the Depressed Classes was complex and had evolved over the years (Ambedkar 1989a). In the 'Evidence before the Southborough Committee on Franchise' he presented on 27 January 1919, Ambedkar discussed the question of representation of interests and citizenship rights (Ambedkar 1989c: 256). He claimed that the interests of untouchables 'can be represented by untouchables alone' as 'untouchability constitutes a definite set of interests which the untouchables alone can speak for'. The challenge was to 'find them in such numbers' so that they constitute a 'force sufficient to claim redress' (ibid).

Eight years later, on 25 December 1927, he made history in Mahad, when he publicly burned the text of caste Hindus, the *Manusmriti*, so that the Dalits could drink from the water tank. Despite a legal order that existed to authorise free access to water resources, the upper caste groups in the region had restricted its use. In his presidential speech, Ambedkar explained that the aim was not only to gain access to water but also to break down the social inequalities perpetuated by the caste system. He conveyed some of the goals of the French Revolution – liberty, equality and fraternity – and the dangers of seeking temporary and inadequate solutions (Ambedkar 2013). However, as he had to withdraw the movement, he explained in a note that:

> the untouchables are caught between the caste Hindus and the government. They can attack one of the two. There is nothing to be ashamed of in admitting that today they do not have the strength to attack both of them at the same time.
>
> (Ambedkar 2013a: 3–27)

He also distinguished between a *satyagraha* launched by caste Hindus against the government which had community support and one initiated by Dalits against the caste Hindus that had no support (Gore 1993). He was to continue this position that in the RTC, the supplementary memorandum on the claims of the Depressed Classes for Special Representation (4 November 1931) elaborated that 'the depressed classes shall not only have the right to their own separate electorates, but they shall also have the right to be represented by their own men'. Depressed classes were defined strictly as persons 'belonging to communities which are subject to the system of untouchability' (Ambedkar and Srinivasan 2005b: 671).

The encounter during the RTC with Gandhi, mentioned earlier, did not end there. After the communal award of 1932, lodged in Yerawad prison, Gandhi expressed his determination to starve himself after his return from London. His threat led to withdrawal of the representation for the depressed classes and culminated in the Poona Pact. Ambedkar wrote that the fast was the worst form of coercion to give up the constitutional safeguards (Ambedkar 1991a). For years afterward, the problem of political representation remained chronic, and their differences on untouchability came out in the open. In a chapter called "A Mean Deal," Ambedkar explained why 'everybody felt that Mr. Gandhi was the most determined enemy of the Untouchables' (Ambedkar 1991b, 70).[12] The Poona Pact was a big blow for the Dalit movement, and Gandhi was looked on as one of the enemies of the cause Ambedkar was fighting for. Historians were quick, however, to see this encounter as one where Gandhi was remarkably successful in preventing the emergence of a fatal divide between the caste Hindus and the Untouchable communities, which came to a head in 1932 (Kumar 1989: 137). Others, however, see this event in which separate electorates were withdrawn for the Dalits as one which also recognised them as a political category across British India by providing representation for the Depressed Classes in the central legislature and provincial legislature (Jaffrelot 2003).

The making and un-making of social justice: responsibility, solidarity and forgiveness

The Gandhian era is viewed as a period in which the nationalist movement became multi-class and mass-based and gained politico-moral legitimacy. Within an incredibly short time, Gandhi became the most prominent nationalist leader. One of the challenges that Congress had already surmounted was from the Depressed Classes Conference by passing resolutions that made social justice for members of the depressed classes a 'nationalist priority' (Bayly 2005; Keer 1995). In the first decade of the twentieth century, in some of its regional branches, debates were held about the conditions of the lower castes. Gandhi was to inherit this Congress position on untouchability, which he reinterpreted by locating in the twin ideas of personal responsibility and corrective justice. As a leader working for a national goal, Gandhi argued for removing injustices faced by 'untouchables' because he felt the need to overcome the social divisions in Hindu society into a political force against the British; he argued for pursuing this course of reform without challenging the social fabric of Indian society. Gandhi maintained that the 'achievement of social justice as the common lot must proceed from a character reformation of each individual, from the heart and mind of each Indian outward into society as a whole' (Austin 2000: 31). Significantly, for him, Hinduism contained within itself the solution to the social degradation of untouchability. This emphasis on the caste Hindu's obligations to the 'untouchables' was to emerge in the justification for the latter's political safeguards in constituent assembly debates.[13]

Many scholars view the Gandhian approach on caste polarisation as responsible for driving away the intended beneficiaries (Nanda 1985). The term 'Harijan', a euphemism for 'untouchable', was not radical and neither was 'untouchability', upliftment or temple entry movements solutions – all of these were intended as an expiation of the upper castes' sins. Although this approach was meant to persuade the obstinate upper castes, it showed a limiting nature of the Gandhian perspective. In this approach, the depressed classes were merely objects to be exploited for the political salvation of the upper castes here on earth as much for their spiritual salvation in heaven (Parekh 1989). The scope of the programme was limited to temperance, temple-entry movement, inter-dining, cleanliness and discipline, and no change in their socio-economic much less political situation was intended.

I would argue that this approach was a little more complex, as in Gandhi's words we hear echoes of corrective justice; equality between two parties to a bipolar transaction as opposed to distributive justice, which is in a proportion in which each person's share is assessed. The fundamental question in Gandhi's philosophical writings is to what extent an appeal to corrective justice is to identify the transactional wrong which forms the basis for the claim. Its appeal lies in deontological and not in a utilitarian set of values, so the obligation to reach out to the injured flows from the fact that injurer is responsible for the injury wrongfully inflicted on the other. In the past, Gandhi had already redefined the connection between culpable wrongs and hard penal treatment. The claim that those who committed wrong acts deserved punishment was questioned by Gandhi, as it meant that wrongdoers always deserved punishment. He believed that the degree to which a person was at fault for some act depended in some important part on what the person knew or intended. Given that wrongdoers did not always deserve punishment, and a person could unknowingly commit acts, he believed in an evangelical approach. The disassociation of personal sin from wrongdoing limits what he has to say about actions. The remedy for untouchability must also be sought in rejuvenating social life from within Hindu society. Those who have the gift of a moral power of love, who have the least feeling of enmity, 'through a change of heart' would be able to resolve this problem (Lynch 1969: 132).

If for Gandhi the real mistake of 'untouchability', a moral transaction, was to be corrected by 'solidarity' within Hindu society, it consisted eventually in the ignorance of the injury inflicted on the other. His reflections on the development of the idea of a moral consensus in Hindu society flow from a complex combination of several arguments. The social problem was primarily a moral one to be remedied by nourishing a virtue of charity. The unity in Hindu society also denotes some 'interdependence', 'communion', forgiveness and reconciliation, commitment to the good of one's neighbour, spirit of cooperation and readiness to defend the poor and helpless. These varied interpretations in Gandhi underscore his approach to an altruistic lifestyle and purport to prescribe the moral and political responsibilities of individuals in a network of mutual relationships.

While fluidity characterises the idea of a village republic in Gandhi, a point I take up later, one distinguishing element underlines these various treatments: the placement of 'atonement of sins' at the centre of solidarity. Gandhi insists on converting individual hearts as imperative to a better social order. Gandhi pursues the idea of justice also in 'ahimsa', which is a refusal to do harm; in a negative form it means non-injury, but in a positive form it means the greatest love and charity. He claims non-violence is 'love, compassion, forgiveness'. The idea of love could be traced in its association with the truth: 'True love is boundless like the ocean and rising and swelling within one spreads itself out and crossing all boundaries and frontiers envelops the whole world' (Gandhi 2001: 63).[14] Secondly, love in Gandhi's conception is connected to service. In his words, 'service is not possible unless it is rooted in love, in Ahimsa'.[15] In his words, Gandhi's response to injustice is non-violence. It successfully denounces injustice without harming its perpetrator. Forgiveness is preceded by recognising a wrongdoing, but such an ethical attitude cannot be confused with accepting injustice; there can be no forgiveness without justice, without the recognition that a given offence has wounded our human dignity and self-respect (Fiasse 2008). On closer look, it demonstrates the religious-political nature of the concept of 'solidarity'. This conception in the context of liberal democracy raises various problems for the production of Dalit personhood and subjectivity, and I will argue as follows that it cannot be fully sustained.

The argument for personal responsibility and corrective justice, although effective in engaging people to act in ways that ameliorate suffering, can have negative consequences for those facing injustice: loss of dignity and powerlessness. It lends itself to an approach which positions those with power in the role of the protector and those in need of protection as lacking in such capacities. The latter must respond with gratitude and forgiveness must result. In this way, this approach does not look to remedy the underlying cause of a transactional moral wrong. All this raises questions about whether responsibility and obligation are entirely personal issues independent of social structures. Gandhi prioritises individuals over social structures and insists that whatever social structures may exist are simply products of the evil thoughts and activities of persons within the society, overlooking the historical processes that have created the problems.

Hence, a theory that is useful in promoting corrective justice can be limited and dangerous in reinforcing the legitimacy of past practices. Moreover, a responsibility for injustice is often conferred in a hierarchical fashion, as the conflict between mercy and obligation emerges while discussing village republics. Gandhi presents solidarity as an authentic 'attitude' of community participation and a natural constituent of human existence. The question is: how do barriers between different forms of hierarchy and oppression relent to allow communication about political forms? These problems in the concept of solidarity raise further questions in categorising Gandhi's discourse either as exclusively liberatory or confirming the status quo: To what extent are the Dalits in Gandhi's schema free and autonomous in the face of fixed social positions in caste hierarchies today? Do Dalits in local-based communities in the village have the power to influence what happens around them?

Although my explication expands Gandhi's categories considerably, they are compatible with the principle of corrective justice, which posits that 'one who harms another by wrongful conduct is morally obligated to make amends to the victim'. These have implications for society's collective responsibility for the harmful effects of wrongful conduct and the affects of past societal discrimination against the depressed classes. Thus, if socio-economic disadvantages faced by the ex-'untouchables' were due to social discrimination, then society was obligated to remedy these conditions. More significantly, Gandhi defended the plausibility of a moral obligation that society should assume to remedy the injurious effects of the culpable human action.

This notion of justice is different from compensatory claims arising out of historical recollection of injustices that have to do with identity and contingency. It must be clarified that the claims that Ambedkar would make were not only to make up for the loss of opportunity, dignity and status in society that 'untouchables' suffered at the hands of their fellow citizens, but they were to recognise that this injustice had occurred in Hindu society and that these people were among the victims. Hence, for Ambedkar, these were not only to repair harms; these claims were not only about substantial transfers of land, wealth and resources to rectify the past wrongs. They were about public recognition of past injustices that would help reconstruct a political community based on this idea of radical equality. Even more in his case, the idea of solidarity is important, but that it is not possible to explain along the lines of a deontological, contractual or rationality conception.

The difference between these two thinkers becomes apparent when we recognise that Ambedkar's arguments depict injustice as consisting of serious harms and injuries that are immeasurable. Although historical discrimination is a backward-looking argument, it explains why some groups are still suffering today in independent India. The effects of discrimination in creating a group whose social position has led to adverse consequences for the self-esteem of members of that group means individuals were targeted as representatives of their group. Thus, effects of a major injustice can be perpetuated from one generation to another, unless they are compensated in some way.

Ambedkar: new beginnings and new solidarities

Ambedkar begins to challenge structures built upon the so-called neutrality of an objective reality to argue that systems we have in place represent and reproduce the dominant culture and values in society. His history and position influence, for example, the questions he asks, and in this way, he can forge new epistemologies. By incorporating Dalit lived experiences, emotions and feelings into the knowledge-building process, Ambedkar clarifies:

> that caste in the singular number is an unreality. Castes exist only in the plural number. . . . To illustrate my meaning: while making themselves into a caste, the Brahmins, by virtue of this created non-Brahmin caste . . . while closing themselves in they closed others out.
>
> (Ambedkar 1989a: 20)

Ambedkar questioned the broad understanding of liberal representation espoused by the British rulers and nationalist leaders. He raised the basis of positions as elected candidates for their disadvantaged communities; along with that he questioned the location of certain social groups and their history that made them experience reality differently and develop a distinctive historical experience about it from the dominant views in society, thereby adopting a moral perspective that involves abstracting from their standpoints. But recognising 'difference' was not a mere tool for liberation of these groups. Ambedkar outlined the material and spiritual aspects of conversion to Buddhism due to oppression faced by those in Hindu society. He is of the view that as long as the experience of untouchability has to do with 'social stigma', it could never be 'washed away by right or individual achievement' (Ambedkar 1936).

At the outset then, what begins as Ambedkar's discourse of the 'closed others' and the disenfranchised right seekers becomes a defining aspect of democratic government in the constituent assembly. So the debate in RTC is revolutionary, and it announces a new conception of the citizen, one who is no longer rooted in status and hierarchy, but who asks for a right to politics for all human beings. It is extremely productive for emancipatory politics, as there is a nexus between sovereign political communities and the protection of the 'rightless', in this case, the depressed classes.

Viewed from this angle, Ambedkar's responses to the representation of Dalits and the subsequent conversion to Buddhism gave weight to a theory of social action (Verma 2010). Although he stressed Buddha's attack on caste and the Dalit's historical connection with Buddhism, it should be noted that Ambedkar did not, however, identify the Buddha's message and movement solely as a revolt against the caste system; as clear in the story of the 'going forth', the social concerns were much wider and involved a larger audience. The denial of agency eventually leads him to reclaim or create new idioms of selfhood and subjectivity through conversion (Verma 2010).

In one of his earliest texts, he had described the terms Liberty, Equality and Fraternity that display a temporal thickness, as these concepts reveal themselves as 'not yet'. The unavailability of democracy or justice boils down to the fact that we only understand these through reference to either the past or the future. He explains his idea of solidarity:

> What objection can there be to a fraternity? . . . In an ideal society, there should be many interests consciously communicated and shared. There should be varied and free points of contact with other modes of association. In other words, there must be social endosmosis.
>
> (Ambedkar 1989b: 23; see Zelliot 1996: 159)

By invoking conversion, he builds on the idea of solidarity based on 'karuna' (compassion) shared by all concerned participants. It can be charged that Ambedkar assumes that participants who experience hatred, animosity and injustice will be inspired to forgive and forget. Nevertheless, Ambedkar urges us to recognise the limitations to the need for consensus but instead suggests that we recognise suffering and try to alleviate it. Gandhi errs in contending that solidarity in terms of a universal consensus is relevant in determining our moral obligations to each other. The weight of these claims for solidarity relied on the presuppositions of social action. Ambedkar's thoughts on *manuski*, *maitri* and *karuna* translate the theories of human sociality into concrete systems of living through creating just structures, which care for people, enhance their dignity and foster the common good of society.

Ambedkar did not share the intellectual tradition which believed a good society was constituted around the principle of harmony in village-centred republics and responded harshly to critiques in the constituent assembly. Many members read the draft of the constitution as being hostile to the Gandhian vision and being disrespectful of the Mahatma itself. Seth Govind Das claimed that Ambedkar's remarks on the village as a 'sink of localism, a den of ignorance, narrow-mindedness, and communalism' had caused him and others great pain (Constituent Assembly Debates, 22 November 1948, p. 523). For Ambedkar, villages were 'cesspools', a cauldron of backwardness, tradition and bondage. For these reasons, untouchables had to escape from the villages, and India also had to reject its village past. Ambedkar's idea of praxis was based on a new understanding of Dalit politics, and he offered a very particular definition of dignity that it is not in seeking equality with the brahman; it is about being oneself with all the contradictions of one's way of being, doing and knowing.

Unlike Gandhi, Ambedkar reconstructs the normative principles of acting in solidarity by taking into account negative practices of mis-recognition.[16] His primary concern is to reclaim not only the values of equality and rights of individuals but also the positive forms of association of free individuals. So when the need to give a new doctrinal basis to religion arose, that according to Ambedkar will be consonant with liberty, equality and fraternity, it meant in his words

> a complete change . . . it means new life. But a new life cannot enter a body that is dead. New life can enter only in a new body. The old body must die before a new body can come into existence and a new life can enter into it. To put it simply, the old must cease to be operative before the new can begin to enliven and pulsate.
>
> (Ambedkar 1989b: 78)

This passage evokes the group-connected experience in the contexts of interaction. Pulses of attraction and aversion modulate all interactions, with specific consequences for experience of the body. Hindu religion had defined some groups as different and imprisoned them in the bodies by defining individuals with characteristics as ugly, dirty, defiled, impure, contaminated or sick.

In summary, there are two parts to Ambedkar's argument in his account of social justice. First, Ambedkar realised that changing the behaviour, images and stereotypes contributing to the oppression of disadvantaged social groups is not enough. Dalits were considered as having a separate social and cultural entity, with the most subordinate and polluting status linked to roles allotted to them by the caste system. At the same time, they were included in principle in the Hindu community. From 1933 onwards, the defeat in the Poona Pact over separate electorates meant that either untouchables were at the mercy of paternalism of upper castes or they were incorporated in such a way as to make a 'difference' unnecessary. How were Dalits as a group to become autonomous in politics: by giving up their subordinate identities or retaining their (polluting) identities within the Hindu fold?

In practice, liberal politics in the 1960s was fundamentally about assimilation. I have argued elsewhere that it incorporated people into the nation-state project and ignored special rights. When Ambedkar examined the inequalities of the social sphere, he was arguing against the assimilationist ideals of Gandhi, liberal politics as well as the vocabulary of minority groups; he did not want Dalits to be integrated into mainstream Hindu society or to maintain their cultural distinctiveness. That was the strength of his argument. He did not ask for preservation of their distinct identity. He urged the Dalits to critically reflect on their subordinate position and rid them of that identity. Moreover, they were expected to reject long-standing practices of their groups. But with time, religion, ethnicity and caste continue to play a central role, and Dalit history was deeply implicated in the story of Indian modernity. I argue that Ambedkar's stress on the freedom to choose one's religion reworks conceptions of moral personhood and ultimately of self that throws some light on the impossibility of justice (i.e., of a casteless society within a liberal theoretical frame) (Verma 2011, 2015).

The second important aspect of Ambedkar's arguments fortify claims for the relevance of social structures while creating awareness for what I would call 'testimonial sensibility' (i.e., the trained sensitivity to 'experience' the multifarious signs of a speakers' degree of epistemic trustworthiness). The particular injustice that is to count as epistemic is brought out by Gandhi not being open to the truth of Ambedkar's testimony. The assumption of individual responsibility raised by Gandhi demands a certain level of critical scrutiny from some of its adherents. In Ambedkar's formulation, the injustice arising out of an identity prejudice in which the credibility assigned to him in the RTC and to his testimony is deficient. In Ambedkar's idea of 'solidarity', the virtuous hearer must perceive the interlocutor as trustworthy in what he or she is asserting. While this account explains the phenomenology of everyday testimonial exchange, it also preserves the operation of the critical rationality of everyday testimonial exchanges in the hearer. Instead of relying on revenge, forgiveness and violence, Ambedkar confronts the agential choices opened up by his experience as a Dalit.

Conclusion

This chapter reads the intellectual history of Gandhi and Ambedkar for their interventions on social hierarchies of the caste system. It is also an attempt to consider with the help of various theoretical insights as well as discursive analysis the challenges in the social justice discourse today. I argued that social justice in the Indian context acquires a shared meaning related to struggles against practices of untouchability and aspiration towards equality of opportunity during the nationalist discourse. But as Lefort has argued, a democratic discourse can incite different forms of emancipatory struggles. For Gandhi, including Dalits within Hindu society was a reversal of the structures of sin, which was achievable through conversion of hearts, individuals' sacrifices, forgiveness and acts of charity. But then we fall into the danger of drawing a straight line between individual acts and social structures, overlooking the historical moments that have created ethical dilemmas. By relying on the term 'aporia' is to reach beyond the particular moments of debate and question the categories available in our discourse. A host of irresolvable dilemmas has arisen with Gandhi's approach because its demand for individual responsibility and solidarity lead to an undoing of the problems in which they arise.

In the case of Ambedkar, the social relations in the caste system are antagonistic, for he believes that the association with Hindu society is stopping Dalits from developing their own identity (Wadikar 2007). To make this profound shift in perspective, Dalits must have access to tools that allow them to envision a world that lives beyond caste subordination to imagine what they could become in that alternative space; second, to raise praxis-oriented questions for possibilities for a collective struggle to overthrow the structures of discrimination, they need to find ways to adequately represent these testimonies of personal and collective suffering beyond realities of victimhood.

In post-colonial India, abolishing untouchability also cemented 'untouchability as a legal effect', as a category or practice that acquires visibility in the public domain in the constituent assembly. At the beginning of this process, the public space of citizenship was the domain of equality, while in the private sphere no questioning of social inequalities in everyday practices took place. Since then, thousands of cases of caste violence and atrocities and the generation of statistics about them suggest the story of the failure of our understanding of social justice. The continuation of caste violence against Dalits in liberal institutions despite legal rights reveals the merger of these institutions with that of exclusionary politics. Notwithstanding the changes in social sciences and active state intervention in this regard, non-state socio-cultural practices continue to exclude Dalits. The High Court in July 2010 reiterated that caste was not the reason for Dalit killings in Khairlanji (Bavadam 2006). As dynamics of Dalit emancipation threaten to upset the traditional rural order, the idea of reconciling Gandhi and Ambedkar's solutions to address the caste issue seems far from a possibility. The violence and brutality against Dalits continue in vast areas of the country. In response to these challenges, Dalits critics and writers are reviewing Indian literary traditions and histories that establish the structures of exclusion while also posing the question of representation of Dalits in the post-colonial context as a critical issue. Both flexible and extensible, political identity tropes continue to influence these new claims.[17] The aporia of social justice highlights the general impasse in the question of Dalit identity. The concern both to accommodate difference and preserve the analytic and political force of theories of oppression specifically drawn from the standpoint of the oppressed is the main challenge today.

Notes

1 Very simply, the distinction between the capabilities approach and the primary goods approach is that capability theorists focus on the ends as a measure of justice whereas the latter focus on the means (i.e., fair distribution of resources as a measure of justice).
2 A coherent account of these arguments can be found in G.A. Cohen (1995).
3 On Indian debates, see Alice Thorner (1982).
4 See B.R. Ambedkar, Constituent Assembly Debates (CAD), 25 November 1949.
5 This involves an engagement with the social location of concepts and their involvement in a wider cultural field of power relations. Studies of marginalised groups now challenge mainstream assumptions by seeking to locate the subject in his or her own understandings.

6 I use the term 'untouchable' as Ambedkar used it in the 1920s to create the idea of an oppressed minority in India. He tried to eliminate regional identities in order to create a heterogeneous group of people outside of Hindu society.

7 A Royal Commission under Sir John Simon was appointed by the British in 1928. Subsequently, representative Indians were called to London at a Round Table Conference. Dr Ambedkar and Diwan Bahadur Srinivasan were invited to represent the 'untouchables'.

8 Ambedkar endorsed dominion status and argued for salvation for the depressed classes through education and through helping themselves. See Keer 141–3; Khairmode, 1958. vol. 3: 358.

9 The main arguments in this section are drawn from the first and second sessions of the RTC in 1930–1931 under chairmanship of the Prime Minister Ramsay MacDonald and are also from the deliberations of the Minorities Committee. See Ambedkar (2005a: 503–672).

10 MacDonald announced the communal award on 16 August 1932. Based on the findings of the Lothian committee, the communal award established separate electorates and reserved seats for minorities. It provided for the depressed classes to vote in both general and special constituencies.

11 The document on political safeguards for depressed classes was presented as an appendix to the report of the sub-committee in the RTC. He tried to impress on Gandhi his point that the Congress had not so far done anything tangible for the depressed classes, and Mr Gandhi was under a delusion imagining that the depressed classes were solidly behind him. See 'Ambedkar eventually left without convincing Mr Gandhi', *Times of India*, 15 August 1931; See Ambedkar (2005b).

12 It was in the wake of the controversy over the Poona Pact that Gandhi founded the Harijan Sevak Sangh in 1932. The following year he relaunched his journal *Young India* as *Harijan*.

13 See, for example, Patel's speech (at the first meeting of the advisory committee 27 February 1947) that they had a 'special responsibility' and 'special obligation' for the protection of the interests of the minorities. The mission was to satisfy 'every one of them'. See B. Shiva Rao. vol. 2. 2006b: 66.

14 See Gandhi, *Young India*, 20.9.1929. in Gandhi (2001).

15 See Gandhi, *Young India*, 20.9.1928.

16 I borrow this from Axel Honneth (2008).

17 For some of these epistemic breaks on the ambiguity for the Dalit thinker, see Khare (1984): 'He considers his group to be simply neither Hindu nor outside Indian civilization; neither merely consensual nor entirely alienated'.

References

Primary sources

Ambedkar, Bhimrao Ramji. 1936. *What Path to Salvation? Speech, Bombay Presidency Mahar Conference*, 31st May. Translated by Vasant W. Moon.

www.columbia.edu/itc/mealac/pritchett/00ambedkar/txt_ambedkar_salvation.html (accessed on 22 August 2017).

Ambedkar, Bhimrao Ramji. 1989a. *Castes in India: Their Mechanism, Genesis and Development*, 1916, SW. Vol. 1, 3–22. Mumbai: Education Department, Government of Maharashtra.

Ambedkar, Bhimrao Ramji. 1989b. *Annihilation of Caste*, with a Reply to Mahatma Gandhi, 1936, SW. Vol. 1, 23–96. Mumbai: Education Department, Government of Maharashtra. Reprint.

Ambedkar, Bhimrao Ramji. 1989c. *Evidence Before the Southborough Committee*, 1919, SW. Vol. 1, 247–78. Mumbai: Education Department, Government of Maharashtra.

Ambedkar, Bhimrao Ramji. 1991a. *Statement on Mr Gandhi's Threat to Fast Unto Death Against the Prime Minister's Award Granting Separate Electorates to the Untouchables*, SW. Vol. 9, 311–16. Mumbai: Education Department, Government of Maharashtra. Appendix 4.

Ambedkar, Bhimrao Ramji. 1991b. *What Congress and Gandhi Have Done to the Untouchables*, 1945, SW. Vol. 9, 1–387. Mumbai: Education Department, Government of Maharashtra.

Ambedkar, Bhimrao Ramji. 2003. *Constituent Assembly Debates* (henceforth CAD). Official Report. New Delhi: Lok Sabha Secretariat. Fourth Reprint.

Ambedkar, Bhimrao Ramji. 2005a. *Proceedings of the Round Table Conference: Federal Structure Committee and Minorities Committee*, 8th Sitting, 1st October 1931, SW. Vol. 2, 654–9. Mumbai: Education Department, Government of Maharashtra.

Ambedkar, Bhimrao Ramji. 2005b. *Proceedings of the Round Table Conference*, 1st Session, 8th Sitting, 19th January 1931, SW. Vol. 2, 596–8. Mumbai: Education Department, Government of Maharashtra.

Ambedkar, Bhimrao Ramji. 2005c. *Proceedings of the Round Table Conference*, 1st Session, 9th Sitting, 8th October 1931, SW. Vol. 2, 659–63. Mumbai: Education Department, Government of Maharashtra.

Ambedkar, Bhimrao Ramji. 2013a. *Why the Satyagraha Was Suspended*, 3rd February 1928, Bahishkrit Bharat, SW. Vol. 17. Mumbai: Education Department, Government of Maharashtra.

Ambedkar, Bhimrao Ramji. 2013b. 'Mahad Satyagraha Not for Water But to Establish Human Rights', in *Dr Ambedkar and His Egalitarian Revolution*, SW. Vol. 17, 3–50. Mumbai: Education Department, Government of Maharashtra.

Ambedkar, Bhimrao Ramji and Srinivasan, Rao Bahadur R. 2005a. '*A Scheme of Political Safeguards for the Protection of Depressed Classes in the Future Constitution of a Self-Governing India*', Appendix to Report of Sub-Committee No III on Minorities, 31 December 1930, SW. Vol. 2, 546–56. Mumbai: Education Department, Government of Maharashtra.

Ambedkar, Bhimrao Ramji and Srinivasan, Rao Bahadur R. 2005b. *Supplementary Memorandum on the Claims of the Depressed Classes for Special Representation*. Appendix II, 4th November 1931, SW. Vol. 2, 669–72. Mumbai: Education Department, Government of Maharashtra.

Secondary sources

Agarwal, Bina, Humphries, Jane and Robeyns, Ingrid (eds.). 2006. *Capabilities, Freedom and Equality: Amartya Sen's Work From a Gender Perspective*. New Delhi: Oxford University Press.
Austin, Granville. 2000. *The Indian Constitution: Cornerstone of a Nation*. New Delhi: Oxford University Press.
Bavadam, Lyla. 2006. 'Dalit Blood on Village square', *Frontline*, 23(23).
Bayly, Susan. 2005. *Caste, Society and Politics in India From the Eighteenth Century to the Modern Age*. Cambridge: Cambridge University Press.
Cavell, Stanley. 1990. *Conditions Handsome and Unhandsome: The Constitution of Emersonian Perfectionism*. Chicago: University of Chicago Press.
Cohen, Gerald Allan. 1995. *Self Ownership, Freedom and Equality*. Cambridge: Cambridge University Press.
Coward, Harold. 2003. *Indian Critiques of Gandhi*. Albany: SUNY Press.
Derrida, Jacques. 1990. 'Force of Law, the Mystical Foundation of Authority', May Quaintance (trans.), *Cardozo Law Review*, 11: 920–1045.
Donald, James. 1992. *Sentimental Education*. London: Verso.
Fiasse, Gaelle. 2008. 'Forgiveness and the Refusal of Injustice', *Proceedings of the American Catholic Philosophical Association*, 82: 125–34.
Gandhi, Mohandas Karamchand. 1928. *Young India*, September 9.
Gandhi, Mohandas Karamchand. 2001. *India of My Dreams*. Ahmedabad: Navajivan Publishers.
Gore, Madhav Sadashiv. 1993. *The Social Context of an Ideology: Ambedkar's Political and Social Thought*. New Delhi: Sage Publications.
Honneth, Axel. 2008. *Disrespect: The Normative Foundations of Critical Theory*. Cambridge: Polity Press.
Jaffrelot, Christophe. 2003. *India's Silent Revolution: The Rise of the Lower Castes in India*. London: C Hurst and Co.
Keer, Dhananjay. 1995. *Ambedkar: Life and Mission*. Mumbai: Popular Prakashan.
Khairmode, Changdev Bhavanrav. 1958. *Dr Bhimrao Ramaji Ambedkar*. Vol. 3. Pune: Sugava Prakashan. Presidential Address, All India Depressed Classes Conference, pp. 546–54.
Khare, Ravinder. 1984. *The Untouchable as Himself: Ideology, Identity and Pragmatism*. Cambridge: Cambridge University Press.
Krishna, Sankaran. 2014. 'A Postcolonial Racial/Spatial Order: Gandhi, Ambedkar and the Construction of the International', in Robbie Shilliam,

Alex Anievas and Nivi Mandchanda (eds.), *Confronting the Global Order*, pp. 139–56. London and New York: Routledge.
Kumar, Ravinder. 1989. *The Making of a Nation*. New Delhi: Manohar.
Lucas, John Randolph. 1980. *On Justice*. Oxford: Oxford University Press.
Lynch, Owen. 1969. *Politics of Untouchability: Social Mobility and Social Change in a City of India*. New York: Columbia University Press.
Miller, David. 1999 [2003]. *Principles of Social Justice*. Cambridge, MA: Harvard University Press.
Miller, David. 2013. *Justice for Earthlings: Essays in Political Philosophy*. Cambridge: Cambridge University Press.
Mulhall, Stephen. 1997. 'Promising Consent, and Citizenship: Rawls and Cavell on Morality and Politics', *Political Theory*, 25(2): 171–92.
Nagaraj, Doddaballapura Ramaiah. 2013. 'Self Purification Versus Self-Respect: On the Roots of the Dalit Movement', in R. Raghuramaraju (ed.), *Debating Gandhi: A Reader*, pp. 359–88. New Delhi: Oxford University Press.
Nanda, Bal Ram. 1985. *Gandhi and His Critics*. New Delhi: Oxford University Press.
Natrajan, Nalini. 2013. *Atlantic Gandhi: The Mahatma Overseas*. India: Sage Publications.
Parekh, Bhikhu C. 1989. *Gandhi's Political Philosophy: A Critical Examination*. Palgrave Macmillan.
Rao, Anupama. 2008. 'Who Is a Dalit? The Emergence of a New Political Subject', in Manu Bhagvan and Anne Feldhaus (eds.), *Claiming Power From Below: Dalits and the Subaltern Question in India*, pp. 11–27. New Delhi: Oxford University Press.
Rawls, John. 1973. *A Theory of Justice*. Oxford: Oxford University Press.
Sen, Amartya. 2009. *The Idea of Justice*. India: Allen Lane and Penguin.
Shklar, Judith. 1990. *The Faces of Injustice*. New Haven: Yale University Press.
Thorner, Alice. 1982. 'Semi-Feudalism or Capitalism? Contemporary Debate on Classes and Modes of Production of India', *EPW*, 17(49): 1961–8.
Verma, Vidhu. 2010. 'Reinterpreting Buddhism: Ambedkar on the Politics of Social Action', *EPW*, XLV (49): 56–65.
Verma, Vidhu. 2011. *Non-discrimination and Equality: Contesting Boundaries of Social Justice in India*. London: Routledge.
Verma, Vidhu (ed.). 2015. *Unequal Worlds: Discrimination and Social Inequality in Modern India*. New Delhi: Oxford University Press.
Wadikar, Shailaja. 2007. 'Silent Suffering and Agony in Mulk Raj Anand's Untouchable', in Amar Nath Prasad and Rajiv K. Mallik (eds.), *Indian English Poetry and Fiction: Critical Elucidations*. Vol. 1, pp. 144–55. New Delhi: Sarup and Sons.
Walzer, Michael. 1984. *Spheres of Justice: A Defense of Pluralism and Equality*. Basic Books.

Wang, H. 2005. 'Aporias, Responsibility and the Im/possibility of Teaching Multicultural Education', *Educational Theory*, 55(1): 45–59.

Woozley, Anthony. 1973. 'Injustice', *American Philosophical Quarterly*, Monograph no. 7.

Young, Iris Marion. 1990. *Justice and the Politics of Difference*. Princeton: Princeton University Press.

Zelliot, Eleanor. 1996. *From Untouchable to Dalit: Essays on the Ambedkar Movement*. New Delhi: Manohar.

Chapter 2

Ambedkar and other immortals

A note on comparative politics and incomparable events[1]

Soumyabrata Choudhury

I

A mosaic of citations:

a The French Revolution gave rise to two new principles – the principle of self-government and the principle of self-determination. . . . The hope of humanity was centred on the fructification of these principles. Unfortunately after the lapse of nearly 140 years these principles have failed to take root. The old regime has continued either in all its nakedness or by making sham concessions to these two principles. Barring a few countries, there was neither self-government nor self-determination in the world.[2]

b Do not let yourselves suppose that the Satyagraha Committee has invited you to Mahad merely to drink the water of the Chavadar Lake of Mahad. It is not as if drinking the water of the Chavadar Lake will make us immortal. . . . We are not going to the Chavadar Lake merely to drink its water. We are going to the lake to assert that we too are human beings like others. It must be clear that this meeting has been called to set up the norm of equality.

I am certain that no one who thinks of this meeting in this light will doubt that it is unprecedented. I feel that no parallel to it can be found in the history of India. If we seek for another meeting in the past to equal this we shall have to go to the history of France on the continent of Europe.[3]

So will we build a comparative political perspective on something which takes place on the continent of Europe and something else somewhere else? Make a table of similarities and differences, neighbourhoods and strangeness so as to produce a scale of comparison regulating the *limits* of what is comparable? Locate a common terrain called 'politics' and duly cut off other contextual exoticisms?

It is not difficult to derive this common task and terrain of politics by a kind of negative inference from the prior citations: since the old regime continues (at least when Ambedkar is writing in the first half of the twentieth century), the 'common' of politics must be to oppose this regime. What issue can there be with this shared orientation which prescribes the limits and imperatives of the task at hand? None except the naive objection that the apparently *universal* prescription of politics is actually prescribed by *history*. That is why the French Revolution 'gave rise to two new principles' and whoever 'thinks' of the Mahad Satyagraha in the light of its true meaning cannot doubt that it is 'unprecedented'.

It is indeed a naive objection not because the provenance and power of the universal are obvious to the sophisticated mind but due to the historical element itself, which in the said prescription, is unprocessed, if not errant. Such processing will require the loosening of the strait jacket and the blurring of the sharp predicate 'historical' in a presupposed 'historical time', which forever precedes that which is unprecedented. The problem is the opposite: what is the *historicity* of the new, the unprecedented that erupts out of and into historical time, where political fulfilment is tied to the prescription of an emancipatory, even redemptive, horizon to that time? I think that is Ambedkar's problem – and one shouldn't get too upset with an eschatological insinuation in Ambedkar's philosophy of history. The point is that the historicity of the new, which the French Revolution articulates as 'new principles', in the element of so-called historical time, *erupts* as an emancipatory prescription breaking that time into two, one part useless, archaic history of the 'old regime' (which continues!) and the other a zone of 'raw' time of a new event of politics and not an emancipatory political programme.

Of course, it can be objected that Ambedkar's problem is not the 'original' event of the French Revolution; his interest is indeed in the 'repetition' *planned* for the Mahad Satyagraha.[4] In response to this, one must look once more at Ambedkar's words in their context(s). It is true that in one context – when Ambedkar was a member of the Governor General's executive council between 1942 and 1946 – the French Revolution is, as it were, already resolved and fulfilled into the new, modern principles of egalitarian politics.[5] The Revolution is now a *paradigm* for this politics. Against this paradigm, the world is evaluated and judged; its emancipatory exigencies and programmes are prescribed. If the old regime continues in most of the world, it is not as a paradigmatic option any more, it continues merely *empirically*. The time of the world pre-Revolution has been drained and denuded to an empty shell; the time of post-revolutionary *history* is full and consequential. Such is the mode of historical resolution and indeed of eschatological fulfilment of the 'event' of the French Revolution.

It is the other context of the Mahad Satyagraha of 1927, the other section of the mosaic that reveals a strangely different and 'raw' design of the temporalisation, not of a presupposed historical time surging from 'empty' to 'full' (or the opposite process) but of the *event itself*. Yet Ambedkar does not praise the event itself, the event *as* event at all! If event is the happening of what happens, the unfolding of its material sequence, then Ambedkar doesn't encourage the overvaluation of the prohibited act of drinking water from the Chavadar Tank at Mahad. 'It is not as if drinking water of the Chavadar Tank will make us immortal'. What superb contempt for that very symbolic-ritual meaning of the Mahad Satyagraha taken at face value which makes it an upsurge and transgression against the Brahmanical order! This cutting down to size of the redemptive pretensions of the 'event' with a single stroke of enunciation which cuts to the bone of the matter, parallels Ambedkar's lowering of stakes on the Temple Entry evaluation.[6] The parallel lies in the structural result that both 'events' fluently, too easily re-insert themselves into the Hindu totality albeit in a kind of dialectically emancipated form through the transgressive acts(s) and moment(s) of negativity. The totality itself is not, and must not be, emancipated because that would mean its *dissolution* into something unrecognisable as Hindu – that is Ambedkar's point of demystification of the so-called event.

And yet the Mahad Satyagraha is 'unprecedented'. Its time is not the mere fulfilment of the reformist promise of 'other' Hinduism(s); neither is it the dialectical 'solution' of a Hindu 'problem', and by that token, of Indian History which 'corrects' the economy of wrong relations between historically finite and biologically mortal 'subjects'.[7] No, if the Mahad Satyagraha is indeed 'unprecedented', then the question to ask is, what takes place there such that *someone* is made immortal? An unprecedented if raw and excruciatingly recent immortality? It seems to me that Ambedkar is tracking a different political and conceptual thinking of the event from the expected one, a thinking tied to a differently immortalist philosophy of history.

In grasping this difference of thinking, one must resist two temptations that seem to serve the thought a bit too well: the first temptation develops from the as if immediate saturation of the event – the Mahad Satyagraha – by its ritual-symbolic meaning mentioned earlier. As if to this immediacy of the great ritual transgression corresponds an *immediately* immortal subject this points onwards, trangressively purified of its erstwhile impure imputations as it were. And to this immediate and inflamed 'Untouchable' subject of history strangely corresponds the *immemorial* 'Hindu' subject, whose permanent truth was always the highest stake in this double game of historical emancipation and vicarious immortality. Strange really that the latest vicar of 'Hindu' truth is the *new* immortal/immemorial, the Untouchable!

The second temptation not to fall into is the *revolutionary* one. It asks the people of the Mahad Satyagraha, as much as us at this inscrutable distance, that we believe that the continuum of history is *already* breached; that *modern* politics already includes us in its epochal embrace; that the new immortal is already fulfilled in an *exemplary* instance of time. By this axiomatic logic, the breach in 'Hindu' history, hollowed out by the Mahad transgression, is only the *vicarious* functionary of the revolutionary immortality of the modern 'idea' of politics already inaugurated somewhere else. So if the Mahad Satyagraha is 'unprecedented' only with strict reference to *Indian* history, then such newness is also parasitic on a greater 'modern' continuum of time. This temptation of a parasitic immortality must also be resisted along with the autochthonous one.

I suggest we carry out a 'test' of the event vis-a-vis Ambedkar's declaration during the Mahad Satyagraha along the three following lines: first, if, according to what Ambedkar says, the true meaning of Mahad lies not in *describing* the action of drinking water from the Tank but *declaring* that the people are here to assert that they – the Untouchables – too are human beings like all others, then is this local declaration also the local, almost *isolated*, birth of a new and *generic* idea of equality?[8] The test is whether the Mahar declaration merely cites and applies an available 'modern' discourse and doctrine of equal rights or does it supplement, intervene and create a new *performative immortality* for a historical idea torn from the time of the 'old regime'?

Now the second 'test': it is the test of the *thought* of the event, understood in both directions of the genitive. Let's recall what Ambedkar says: 'I am certain that no one who thinks of this meeting in this light will doubt that it is unprecedented'. But the declarative – or performative, if you will – light of the Mahad Satyagraha is nothing if not the light of thought – *that* is what makes it an immortal light. It is the thought of the 'norm of equality', generically prescribed by the event, which makes it as much the thought of the event in the sense of coming from the latter's disappearing crystal in the shape of an inextinguishable light. Then the question is, *who* will think this thought of the event as an evaluation, a 'test' of the event's irreducible newness? Who will be made immortal by thinking a new and immortal thought? What are our options? On this question of the so-called subject of the event, to my mind, we have three options to consider – the militant subject, the spectatorial subject and the discursive subject. Let me explain:

a The militant *decides* to commit to the thought of the event and thereupon bears it so as to follow through with at least a part of its consequences. To do so, first of all, she must wager that there *is* such a thought and show, to use Alain Badiou's word, a kind of 'fidelity' to it.[9] The militant is *anyone*; yet she is always someone who raises the stakes of a localised isolate, which the event is, to the immortality of a 'truth'. Nevertheless, the 'composition' of the immortal is extracted from the 'atomic' composition of the isolate: the militant is a rare, fiery and material cross-section of historicity cut from the passage between atomicity and immortality, between event and truth.[10] In another style of expression, one might call the militant the bearer of the *trace* of historicity. *Whoever* will have declared that *some* people had declared that they were equal as anyone else because *no one* will have been unequal, is a militant. Hence the partisan and generic declaration of the Mahar *thought*, which is itself declared as the unprecedented scission between the Untouchable and the Hindu, is essential to the condition of the 'test' of militancy.[11]
b The militant subject clearly acts in the present so as to enforce therein *another* present. It is as if she impregnates the present with a future anteriority ('*will have been*') so as to deliver a new, raw and revolutionary eternity to the time of the present in the present. The *spectatorial* subject, in contradistinction, takes a step away from the present.

In a short text, written in the last decade of the eighteenth century, called 'The Contest of Faculties', Immanuel Kant proposed the figure of the spectator as a locus of the *thought* of the just-concluded – and endless – French Revolution as significantly different from how the 'actors' of the Revolution were led to think about the event from within the thickness of its present element (Kant 1979). The spectator, quite enigmatically, saw and thought about the Revolution in its *absence*. Here absence is not a pure void; rather, what is involved is an operation of extracting from the partisan activities of the militants of the Revolution a *sign* of that 'disposition' or 'tendency' of which the 'actors' are not only possibly unaware but *against* which their localised interests often lead them to act. According to Kant, such a disposition signified by the French Revolution, against the bloody and partisan revolutionary *actuality* and despite it, is humankind's disposition to a kind of universal 'progress'.[12] The Revolution must be absented from itself to be inscribed on the surface of 'thought' in the form of a sign and in the mode of a virtual event, or, if you will, a 'permanent virtuality' (Foucault 1997: 97). The spectator is not the one who 'sees' the Revolution enacted in history from the sidelines – there is no voyeurism of the event! – but the spectator is a kind of 'virtual humankind' which contemplates the Revolution *in its absence and as a sign*. While the militant has the dust of history in her mouth and is moved to further thresholds of passionate interest and incalculable decision, the spectator responds to the incorporeal 'event', to the revolutionary 'virtuality' with a neutral 'enthusiasm'.[13] Indeed, with all the bloodshed and the heartbreak, the French Revolution is still a (no)thing of contemplative splendour and 'shows' that humankind is progressing!

c So might one say that irrespective of its empirical unfolding, the Mahad Satyagraha of 1927 is an event in the sense of a *sign* that signifies that Indian history is progressing? That the 'norm of equality' Ambedkar speaks of is an index of approximation, a step towards the *horizon* of emancipation subtending Indian history as part of *universal history*? Unlike the 'militant' philosophy of history that *interrupts* the present with another emancipatory present – the norm of equality sounding the sweet clamour of this interruption – 'the universalist' idea of progress is marked by stages or, shall we say, *traces* of historical discourses along a narrative path of emancipation. Now to institute the 'test' of discursive subject vis-à-vis the event, one must

> test whether it is possible carrying out the relativising operation of freeing the traces of discourse from the global narrative so as to present them as a scatter of *discursive* events. Which implies asking the question whether it is possible to distribute the truth-effects of discourse according to a logic of egalitarian analogy (between discourses) rather than by the logic of subordination to a transcendentally regulative horizon such as 'universal progress'. This double test is oriented to finally examining the problem of the subject whose 'truth' will be woven from the fabric of discourse, replacing the transcendental regulation by universal history with the immanent regularities of discourses and their historicity. It seems to me that given these operational conditions, the deontological status and *name* of the subject will now be the *decision* of the professional archivist and scholar. It will be the historian's greater hazard to balance a scholarly, nay, scholastic, Kantianism and a disciplinary heterodoxy, if not militancy, under whose shadow she will, for instance, name the Mahad subject not progressive or humanist, not Mahar, not even Untouchable but with the analogically rationalised and 'true' name hitherto dispersed over the dust of the archive, which is 'subaltern'.[14]

We are really down to the question of whether Ambedkar was militant, universalist or scholastic? Or, one among the long and weary list of permutations . . . militant universalist, scholarly militant, scholar-universalist, militant scholar? Before plumbing for one of the options, let's look at what Ambedkar says at Mahad once again. He says that the water of Chavadar will not make us immortal. The meeting is to 'set up' the norm of equality. In this it is an unprecedented . . . event. If one wants to *think* about it and find an 'event' to equal it, it will be found in the history of Europe (not India), i.e., the French Revolution. Notice that nowhere does Ambedkar say that the Mahad Satyagraha *emulates* the French Revolution. In fact, a little later – we will come to this in the next section – he will say that the 1927 movement can't even be called 'political' in the constitutive sense of the French Revolution, which doesn't mean that the Mahad intervention and 'social' character make the 'event' any less unprecedented. But neither does Ambedkar say that the Satyagrahis are entirely autochthonous forces sprung from a secret source of the earth of 'culture' hitherto buried in the time of Indian history, but the key to whose release remains elementally *Indian*. Like

Jyotiba Phule before him, Ambedkar's 'test' here and elsewhere is always to ask the question: what is the *real* experience of the breach of Indian history? Vis-a-vis the real experience of the Untouchable over millennia, who experiences the lightning-flash of the cleaving and voiding movement of the history of that experience?[15] Again, the questions resonate: is it the militant, the universalist, the archivist . . . or the Untouchable herself who *makes* the militant decision, *universalises* the decision to the scale of an act of generic humanity and *writes* her act into the flesh of the historical breach while vigilantly guarding the key to the code of reading the breach, thus incarnating in one immortalised scholarly body the historiographer and the archivist?

It seems to me that in the background of these questions ranging from extreme minoritarian punctuation to epic crescendo, Ambedkar proposes something precise at Mahad as a way of making the event *thinkable* instead of either imitative or inscrutable. According to Ambedkar, one can think of the Mahad Satyagraha as *equal* to the French Revolution. One can think of them as equal *analogically*; at the same time, one *must* think of them as equal and *incomparable*. The analogical schema first: by virtue of their respective institutions of the 'norm of equality', Mahad and the French Revolution become analogous. But the comparison gains its real efficacy from the analogy of *truth-effects* that attaches to their respective discursive ensembles. If Ambedkar is not making the trivial point of similar forms of institution but that the two conjunctures are traversed by comparable truth-effects despite vast *differences* of the institution of historical discourses, then the further significance of this analogical schema lies in its common function in both cases that it consolidates the history beyond and against the old regime in the name of a new regime of truth-effect(s). So 'norm of equality' is not simply a formal statement joining the two cases in an unequal synchrony of 'events' – first French Revolution, then after a lag, the Mahad Satyagraha of 1927 – plugged into a shared teleology of universal human progress; 'norm of equality' is the *power* of truth attached to that statement henceforth to be *equally* enjoyed by whoever utters it. By an analogy of enjoyment of true speech under the 'new regime', Indian history, from 1927 onwards, is equal to any other. The job then is not to take one's assigned historical place in an abstract schema of universal emancipation but to live an *equal* historical life of truth while analogically consolidating institutions and discourses of that life.

Now the imperative of an 'incomparable' thinking: in the foregoing schema, we saw the analogical productivity of truth. However, for it to pass between events and histories and invest subjects and identities, truth must also be anonymous. That is why despite the differential 'state of institution' of the 'norm of equality' in different societies, as a truth the norm must itself possess an egalitarian and anonymous permanent 'virtuality' for *all*.[16] This means that an immanent Kantianism of discourse persists, and the *experience* of equality is intelligible only when supported by the anonymous web of discourses. The equality and anonymity of true discourses is the condition for all 'modern' political experience. However, what breaches the old regime is the *actual* declaration of equality. And if it, indeed, is the declaration of a *breach*, then the breach cannot be an effect of discourse; its anonymity is not global and virtual but local, here and now, the localisation of the here and now unto a void of all discourses.[17] Yet there is a *real experience of the breach* – that is the wager of an unprecedented thought.

No sense, no discourse, no anonymous profundity of analogies-in-depth must precede what is 'unprecedented'. Ambedkar submits, in my view, to the imperative and wager of this new, raw and almost naive thinking. Yet to make *thinkable* what *must* be thought, he undertakes the comparatist gesture. But this time the gesture is not analogical. It cannot be since any analogy between the experiences of breach between regimes of discourse, power and truth is totally void. What is the comparatist gesture then if not analogical? I will say that instead of seizing comparable attributes and relations which can't exist between breaches of regimes, the gesture is *absolute* and *egalitarian*. It seizes the fact that in each case there *is* a breach, there results a *void-material* of historical time with which intense historicities are woven. That there *is* a declaration of equality in the French Revolution and in Mahad, strictly speaking, an *absurd* declaration in each case with no discursive support, is what unites them across an abyss. All subsequent discursive consolidation in history that will translate one 'event' into another must, everytime, translate in a necessarily absurd language, the fact that the abyss itself is untranslatable (Benjamin 1969: 69–82). That the gesture of comparison is absolute is because it seizes an experience which is *untranslatable* in each case; that it is egalitarian is because it seizes, in each case, an experience that *is* untranslatable. At the end of the first section, let me translate (!) this thesis centred on the spatial image of the abyss as the (non)place of incommensurable egalitarian contact, of absurd effective comparison into some considerations on the *time* of such contact and comparison.

In this schematisation of the 'tests' of the event we encountered, broadly, three temporal perspectives. The first perspective, which is militant, with an eschatological twist (whose unravelling I hold back), not only explodes out of the continuum of time a present time of the event, but it also explodes out of the present *another* present. This other present was called 'historicity' as opposed to the *historical* continuum.[18] The grammatical mood of the historicity of a new present is a peculiar future anteriority whereby the 'norm of equality' will have been *true* and *unprecedented* every time it is declared, whether in the history of Europe, at Mahad or anywhere else it is being declared *even as I write.*

The second perspective is universalist but with a view on the event as *sign*. The word 'perspective' is indeed apt here, unlike in the militant case where the event's immanent thickness absorbs all perspectival partialities rendering the time of the event 'perfect', at the same time ruining all hermeneutic binding of the event into meaning. Conversely, the universalist hermeneutic binding of the event – or a hermeneutic universalism of the same – avoids this 'zone of indistinction' (Agamben 2005: 2–3) between perfection and ruination. It seems to me that the hermeneutic of the event as sign is the contemplative synthesis to be performed by the spectatorial subject. The spectator 'absents' the thick void of the event into a virtual staging of signs. This is not a theatre where we hear the hoarse cry of triumph and the tender entreaties in defeat coming from the battleground of history; instead, a *dispositio* of pantomime *stretches*, with a kind of wispy gestural violence, the pure, thick void of the event into a tendency of time, a horizon of futurity, a 'sense of history'.[19] Though I have to say that in this scheme, the sense and the spectacle are not brought *from* the theatre of history; they play *upon* the surface of thought, which has gone absolutely still with the shock that a sign of history's sense and orientation has *just* fallen to the spectator's contemplation. The subsequent enthusiasm that 'the event shows, history tends to progress!' doesn't disturb any of the stillness brought upon by the inaugural shock, it is a still enthusiasm as opposed to the militant and performative intervention in the first case.

Of course, the affective metaphysic above is only possible on the condition that the spectator read signs, purvey discourses. Which means, she is confronted with the *logical time* of symbolic systems and makes something of this encounter as a 'subject'. Unlike Kant's epochal spectator in the age of enlightenment – and not the enlightened spectator – the discursive subject cannot read the protocols of *one* type of discourse as the entire horizon of historical sense and hermeneutic realisation. In the first place, she is subject to *several* temporalities of time, and the resolution of this heterogeneity can only be that she *decides* to become the militant of some one time (of discourse) as against every other that she *does* belong to. How to arrive at this decision? Not by wagering the present as its immortal – and ruined – other, not by diagnosing the present unto its permanent if slight futurity . . . by what then? It seems to me that historians of the Subaltern School and some post-colonial writers take an impressive archival path to a fork on the road: a direction towards the genealogical constitution of the present and another towards the present as an exceptional event of the new. Further, it seems, in their admirable writings, they would perform the leap – which is a leap between history and politics – between the two constitutions of time. Because the merit of their work is precisely to show the relentless saturation of history by discourse, yielding a complex of logical times *and* the limits of symbolic representations of historical force – of revolts of time – the only way out of the impasse is to convert it into a conjunctural *passage*. History passes into the present of revolt through the force of its own internal repressions and dominations such that the subject of revolt is the correlated passage from an unconscious *historical* virtuality locked in discourse to a flash of counter-conduct and event-driven 'consciousness'. I think these writers have provided enough reason for one to say that what they occasionally call 'consciousness' *is* event (Chatterjee 2013: 73). *At the same time*, they would archivally support the historicity of 'consciousness' with 'another' history which is marginalised and buried, subaltern and interstitial. There is a 'messianic' solution to this equivocation. It is that the will to recuperate the subjugated documents of the past comes from the decision in the present to make the 'tiger's leap' from the torn present to the unredeemed past.[20] The scholarly will to 'another' tradition of indigenous-subaltern egalitarianism of a historical society comes from the entirely unprecedented declaration of equality in the present irreversibly separated from the past. I think this threshold of *absolute* separation prescribes the task of writing a history of relative proximity to the present threshold, a history of relative and 'graded subalternities' opening onto the *chance* of the present in whose alien element it is declared that all humans are absolutely equal.[21] It is the historical scholar's (unavowed?) decision on the chance of the present to mobilise the past as a history of subalternity relative to the norm of equality *and* as a history of the subaltern in the image of the absolute and immortal equal. In my view, the chance of the present, apart from prescribing the impossible genealogy of its 'separate' being also prescribes a separated eternity. Exactly at the cusp of an irreversible present, a time of reversible and aleatory eternity obtains where Ambedkar will experiment with myriad constellations all his life – constellations of one thought and one thought only![22]

II

'If we seek for another meeting in the past to equal this we shall have to go to the history of France'. Ambedkar's first temporal perspective is that of the present – not which is analysable into a causal depth of the past or reversible into a comparative perspective. Everything must begin again with the Mahad Satyagraha in December 1927.[23] That's the unstated *world-historical* stress on 'this' when Ambedkar says, 'we seek . . . in the past to equal *this* [emphasis mine]'. *This* unprecedented event is an *event* by virtue of being unprecedented. Which means that when Mahad in 1927 forces a caesura in the nominal continuum called 'Indian history', it as much hollows out a section from the continuum of continuums, the name of the time that nominally includes all times, i.e., from 'world-history'. The impasse of Indian history is an impasse of *all* history and *any* politics. Hence, the subsequent passion that will 'seek' within the hollow the 'equal' of this very hollow in any history!

Ambedkar's second temporal perspective is born of the irreversible world-historical position of Mahad – let's call it the perspective of 'eternity', more exactly, *reversible*, *aleatory* eternity. Eternity of a temporal hollow of history, it, nevertheless, obeys not the laws of history but the *play* of eternity (Ambedkar 1987: 371). According to such 'play', the French Revolution is an equal of Mahad – that is Ambedkar's comparatist thesis. What does the thesis imply? Once we agree that the event is a conjunctural effectivity based on *nothing*, on the nothing, the hollow that intervenes between the old and the new regimes, it remains for one to see how the event – Mahad – owes no *debt* to the temporalisation of historical time. Eternity is the state of debtlessness, an effective ideality which manifests the reversible perspective that no event owes a debt to another, that there is no *history of events*: Mahad and the French Revolution are gleaming historicities without any history temporalising them.

In *Krishna and his Gita*, Ambedkar, when discussing B.G. Tilak's apotheosis of the *Gita* in the rival context of the Buddhist revolution in Indian history, says that the *Gita* is a counter-revolutionary textual institution. And with the reference to Tilak's 'ingenious' argument against Buddhism's precedence over the *Gita*, Ambedkar generalises 'with them it is a matter of honour that counter-revolution should not be shown to be indebted to Revolution'.[24] Counter-revolution doesn't want to be seen to have borrowed from the *time* of the revolution and would present itself as an *eternity*, but it is a false eternity. Because counter-revolution would institute a *debt of eternity* and temporalise it as a 'history of debt'. The debt which encodes history is the one the future must pay to the 'monument' of the event (such as the *Bhagavad Gita*). On the other hand, the meaning of 'revolution' that Ambedkar gives to Mahad and, through it, to the French Revolution is that the Revolution as event interrupts the debt of the past (the old regime) and *does not* prescribe any new debts. The event is the effectivity of the hollow, the nothing that voids the time of the historical continuum – an effectivity which can also be seen as the real experience of a defaulting not just on behalf of the past debtors but also on behalf of the very element of the credit that *is* the time of history.[25] The counter-revolution trembles before the breach of debt and quickly attempts to re-impose it even if in the guise of a *revolutionary* debt.[26] It is as if the 'subject' is held within a heightened sense of obligation to the 'monumental' event borne by none less than the 'ímmortal', who is indifferent to the vicissitudes of historico-mortal time *and* none less than the 'partisan' who is entirely enveloped by the interest of a historical aggrandisement. The counter-revolutionary 'subject' is dual – immortal and wounded to death, indifferent and driven by passionate interest(s), sovereignly eternal and adversarially tied to the revolutionary episode. The subject of the revolution, or the 'event', if you will, is double: In the element of a ruined historical temporalisation, she is wounded to immortality. In a milieu of interests and passions, she is moved to withdraw her stakes. Not to forge a separate eternal world but to expose an *operator of separation* in the time of the world which itself doesn't belong to any form of historical time. Such an operator, an evental operator, gives itself to be thought while resisting given forms of 'historical' thinkability. I would like to suggest that Ambedkar performed two gestures of such defaulting 'alien' thought – the aleatory thought of comparison and the forcing thought of constitution. Let us take them briefly, one by one, and with that end this note:

a *The Comparatist Gesture*: In the preface to his *Gulamgiri (On Slavery)*, Jyotiba Phule already makes a gesture which doubles comparison with stating that which is exceptional and incomparable. According to Phule, the legendary Purshuram from ancient Indian texts is seen to be a more fiendish and inhuman character than other such 'world-historical' fiends as Nero, Alaric and Machiavelli (Phule 2008: 5). The extent of the genocide of those who belonged to the land by Purshuram to establish an alien Brahmanisation, in Phule's view, is unprecedented on a comparative world-historical scale. In a homologous gesture he, in this text, will hear a resonance between the great emancipator of this land from Brahmanism, Baliraja that is, with the Great Redeemer born in the West.[27] The point is, Phule, while making these comparative statements with a global sweep, *isolates* and *localises* the birth of the comparison in the historicity of the so-called Brahmanical insinuation in non-Aryan indigenous India. It is an exceptional – and exceptionally – brutal birth that must still be re-inserted into the history of the world, or more exactly, *any* history.

What is remarkable is that this conjunctural risk of comparison which someone like Phule, and then Ambedkar, must take belongs, chronologically speaking, to the same age as Indological knowledges and orientalist comparativisms. The terribly complex economies of discourse instituted by and as these comparativist knowledges, apart from taking as their objects such specific domains as religion, mythology, grammar, etc., institute as if a global abstract object – object of objects – which is 'comparativity' itself.[28] The world has suddenly become commensurable in terms of structural and philological 'globalisation'. At this very instant of global intelligibility, an equally instantaneous birth takes place, which is *literally* exceptional to the structural 'world-order'.[29] The Indian Untouchable, as much as the American slave, are literally exceptional to the abstract order which knowledge(s) hold in commensurable, egalitarian(!) reserve on a world scale. But Phule, Ambedkar later, and someone like

Toussaint L'Overture in Haiti nearly 100 years before, are not interested in holding in counter-reserve an alternative 'subaltern' local incommensurable tradition and temporality.[30] On the contrary! They will have, instead of being the guardians of local exceptions *to* the world, excepted the *world* from its own arche-global philosophy of history, its world-historical arche-tecture. For L'Overture in Haiti at the end of the eighteenth century, for Phule at the end of the nineteenth century and Ambedkar, round the corner in the twentieth century, the task is to *force* comparison out of the very crack of comparativity and its historic-philosophical power to declare concrete and singular *world-historical events*. Or rather, their declaration *is* the instantaneous historicity of events, their incommensurable comparativity.

But once declared in this difficult element of historicity without any possible philosophy of history, the French Revolution, the French Revolution of Haiti, the Mahad declaration of the French Revolution–the event(s)–are released into a playful eternity. The play consists in the fact that the event joyfully defaults on both the historical conditions from which it is born and the rousing inheritance of events from which it is supposed to draw its revolutionary credit. There is no *order* of events with structural relations and homologous properties. Unlike the scholarly perspective on 'comparable' social and cultural objects which gives them a kind of graded or hierarchical equality – so close to Ambedkar's thesis on caste! – the equality of events is the equality of their *chance* if treacherous birth. The play of chance is as much as the play of their aleatory (non)time rather than the time of history to which they 'belong'. In this eternal (non) time of play, there are *gratuitous* metrics of thought that are supplemental to the event *in* history.[31] Thus gratuitously, the French Revolution serves as a metric of thought for 'measuring' the Mahad Satyagraha *just as* the Mahad Satyagraha will have served as a metric for the French Revolution in the (non)time of eternity. Just as Ambedkar will have been the immortal lighting up the path for the revolutionary French thinkers of 1789 in a reversible egalitarian eternity.

b *The Constitutional Gesture*: Will Ambedkar have inspired Emmanuel Joseph Sieyes? Will, for instance, Sieyes' pamphlet *What Is the Third Estate?* have been inspired by a text like *Who*

Are the Shudras?[32] One the one hand, even by our reversible parameter, that is unlikely: because while Ambedkar, in tracing a history of the formation of the Shudras, as a kind of minoritisation of a minority – in the same way that the formation of the Brahmin is the majoritisation of another minority – would like to *void* this category and begin history from a clean slate, Sieyes would *affirm* the 'third estate' as the sovereign constitution of a numerical majority.[33] The erstwhile Shudra will have become indiscernible from any other social group in a revolutionised egalitarian society, while the third estate will have expunged the nobility and the clergy. And yet, at another level, in the further sections of his speech at Mahad, Ambedkar precisely draws a comparison between the Mahad declaration and the 'expulsive' proclamations of equality by the French National Assembly in January, May and June 1789.[34] What is the significance of this comparison? It is that the exercise doesn't take place with the specific *nature* of social difference between Indian and French societies in view – in which case the caste system and the division of estates would be fundamentally irreconcilable – but from the perspective of the *totality* of society, which in both cases needs to be dismantled.[35] In Ambedkar's words, the *intensity* of the inequalities is comparable, not their analytic constituents.[36] Which can only mean, the intensity is being challenged by *another* intensity, the intensity of the events(s) at hand. From this point of view, the difference between the 'third estate' and the composition of the shudras and ati shudras becomes 'minor'.[37]

Let me open a brief aside here: it seems to me that Ambedkar and Sieyes occupy an analogous position as logicians and pamphleteers occupying the edge of an event. They are equally the exemplars of a logical and polemical *culture*. This means, the two figures are engaged in war of discourses, Ambedkar with Gandhi, among others, Sieyes with Thomas Paine and others, and then, at the cusp of a historical mutation, riding a lightning flash, the two extract out of the situation of discourse, a *true* proposition that universalises itself out and beyond the crucible of time. In following these protocols of *war* and *truth*, Ambedkar and Sieyes impart an ethical lesson, too. You must be able to sustain a robust, even extreme polemical culture, disabusing yourself of all illusions of natural consensus, to reach such a threshold which yields a new truth which becomes the operator of a new *separation*, rather than consensus.[38] Though with very different historical modalities, they arrive at the same 'separator', call it the 'third estate' or the 'comprehension' of shudras and ati shudras (Aloysius 2009: 65).

But the differentiations have comparable and *different* consequences for the 'new regime' as it unfolds in each case: it has been pointed out by astute commentaries, including ones by Christophe Jafferlot and O. Herrenschmidt, that Ambedkar's decisive thesis on 'graded system of sovereignty' regulating Indian caste-society is based on the crucial value of *minimal difference*.[39] Everything is arranged such that in the least difference between two rungs of a hierarchy, there is the reflection of the *maximal* functioning of the hierarchy *itself*, of sovereignty *itself*. In simple terms it means that between two lowly placed castes (jatis) in the system, where one is *nearly* the same as the other from the point of view of the apex of the pyramid, there might obtain a relationship of nearly *absolute*-Brahmanical subordination. The system is so dense and labyrinthine with this weaving of minimal absolute difference that it appears, to borrow an expression from medieval Christianity, as if one has one's foot on the neighbour's head.[40] Surely it is a matter of immense comparative interest to see Sieyes, in the years following the Terror, at least up to Napoleon's empire, repeatedly, nay, obsessively *constituting* the French Nation as a system scissored by ghosts of great pre-revolutionary forces (the Estates), now in the global form of revolutionaries and counter-revolutionaries, Thermidoreans and Jacobins, republicans and monarchists.[41] No more the voiding declaration of 1789; instead, the constitutional gesture that 'forces' the event to convert the egalitarian and popular 'immortality' of an instant into a perpetual and historico-mortal republican hierarchy! Peculiarly, this constitutional path forged or forced, out of revolutionary history culminated, after 1799, in the wake of Napoleon's coup, in a system of gradual, or *graded*, election (in the political sphere) and promotion (in the non-political bureaucratic sphere).[42] Erected on an *absolutely* egalitarian base, Sieyes, to solve the problem of the base splitting into the old regime of hierarchy of discrete estates *and* the new (perverted) regime of binary hierarchy of ruling class and the governed, constitutes a system of dense and minimally articulated differences where every political candidate and bureaucratic aspirant would have to go through each stage of the system to be elected or promoted to the next stage. An excruciating step-by-step promenade across the staircase up to the apex proceeds by strangely mobilising yet replacing the static architecture of death where everyone has their foot on their neighbour's head and everyone dies on the floor they are born in.[43]

Is it any surprise then that B.R. Ambedkar, in an essay from the 1940s called *A Plea to the Foreigner*, in his addresses to the Constituent Assembly of the new republic, on several other occasions considered the Constitution to be an absolutely essential and essentially 'forced' document?[44] Unlike Sieyes, Ambedkar did not, *could not*, accept the presumption of equality in the historical constitution of India's political constitution.[45] Which also meant that there couldn't be the presumption of a *natural* meritocracy corresponding to political democracy. Rather, the issues of equality, democracy and meritocracy must be *forced*. The reason for this asymmetry seems to be as delicate as it is brutal: while Sieyes, a resolute anti-Jacobin if not conservative, *belonged* to the revolutionary sequence following the 'event', Ambedkar, while carrying the immortal void of an event in his heart and his writings, was *abandoned* to a counter-revolutionary history. In retort to this abandonment, Ambedkar, no Jacobin himself, nevertheless, puts the constitution to a 'forcing' test; it is the test of political and administrative *reservations* for real unequals, also called 'minorities'.[46] Indeed, it seems to me, that reservations are a debt that counter-revolution must perpetually pay to the revolution that it tried to swallow up and which got stuck in its throat. Only when it will have breathed out and released its immortal anathema counter-revolution will it also have realised that the event never prescribed any debts in the first place!

Notes

1 This chapter is taken from the collection of essays by the same author titled *Ambedkar and Other Immortals* (2018), published by the Navayana, New Delhi.

2 See the selection G. Aloysius (ed.), *Ambedkar on Nation and Nationalism* (New Delhi: Critical Quest, 2009), p. 62. This extract from Ambedkar is from the period when he was Member of the Governor General's Executive Council (1942–6).

3 Ibid, p. 64. This passage is from Dr Ambedkar's speech at Mahad, 1927, cited from Arjun Dangle's book *Poisoned Bread*.

4 For a substantiation of the 'plan' of the Mahad Satyagraha, its historical division between two phases, the exigencies of violence and the policy of restraint (not retreat) – though without any comparative perspective with the French Revolution – see Eleanor Zelliot, *Ambedkar's World: The Making of Babasaheb and the Dalit Movement* (New

Delhi: Navayana, 2013), pp. 74–82. While Gandhi's great name 'Satyagraha' is usually applied to Mahad, one must remember that Mahad is a part of the history of 'Conferences', which are intellectual as well as militant assemblies of the Untouchables. One must also recall the fact that Ambedkar at an earlier conference at Nipani in 1925 called the 'Satyagraha' (he used the word) at Vaikam in Travancore on the Ezhuva castes' demand to use a Temple road, 'the most important event in the country' (p. 77) at that time.

5 While in what is to follow it will be parts of the Mahad address that will be discussed at length, Ambedkar's references to the French Revolution in the later period (to be found in Vol. IX of Ambedkar's works brought out by Government of Maharashtra) is crucial. It demolishes the axiomatic complacency of 'we moderns' that 'we' are, unproblematically, living in the new regime. Ambedkar reminds us that insofar as caste exists, the old regime continues. And yet, we cannot not *also* live and think in the element of the new regime, which is incessantly 'impurified' by the old in the name of a *pure immemorial* order, not a spatio-temporal or historical regime at all.

6 Elsewhere, I have dealt with the metaphysical maintenance of 'totality' as the support of Hindu society, in conservation *and* change, as an essential stake of Gandhi's position(s) against Ambedkar's insistence on 'annihilation' of totality. Historically, of course, the Temple Entry question is tightly grouped with the Poona Pact and the debate following the publication of *Annihilation of Caste*. I would hazard that unlike Gandhi's engagement with this historical continuum when he *consolidates* a certain body of social, political, metaphysical prescriptions, Ambedkar seems to issue a single prescription *against* history: expose the spurious time of totality!

7 Ambedkar himself said that fundamentally caste is 'wrong relation'. This is an acute assertion of a logician of historical structures and not of a phenomenologist of intolerable 'experience' or an exorcist of bad 'substance'. But we must equally ask the fundamental question whether Ambedkar thought the wrong relation was correctible, without intervening in if not voiding the structure. We will, in the coming pages, touch upon this question, Ambedkar's thesis on a graded system of sovereignty/slavery and the conclusion on the 'relative' Hindu against the absolute one. The Hindu always exists *relatively* while claiming a fictional absolute status. This is Ambedkar's riposte to Gandhi after the latter's repudiation of Annihilation of Caste. See Babasaheb Ambedkar, 'Annihilation of Caste', in *Writings and Speeches*, Vol. 1, ed. Vasant Moon (Bombay: Education Department, Government of Maharashtra, 1989), p. 89.

8 It is not difficult to recognise that the phrase 'generic equality' denotes an effort of thinking the idea of equality without recourse to evaluating equality through equal empirical predicates and attributes in subjects. Generic equality is the thesis 'There is equality' and not 'X=Y' ('=' standing for 'equal to') in this or that respect (with reference to predicates, p 1, p 2 . . .). Clearly generic equality or axiomatic equality (though they are not the same) is a condition for empirical programmes of equality but

does not depend on the latter. Moreover, in Ambedkar's own extremely subtle constructions or 'theorems' on practical equality, we see why equality, generically speaking, is a good axiom. See ibid, p. 58.

9 See Alain Badiou, *St. Paul: The Foundation of Universalism*, trans. Ray Brassier (Stanford: Stanford University Press, 2003). 'Fidelity' is the English translation of Alain Badiou's French translation of St Paul's use of the Greek word '*pistis*'. The common translation of Paul's word is 'faith'.

10 The proposition incipient here is that the 'thought' of equality, which is an 'immortal' thought, is entirely immanent to, and is a kind of sub-set of the real elements of the 'local set' or the actual atoms of the isolate. This condensed idea is inspired by and a conscious misapplication of Alain Badiou's sub-section 'Real Atoms and the Postulate of Materialism' from the section 'Atomic Logic' in his *Logics of Worlds*. See Alain Badiou, *Logics of Words: Being and Event II*, trans. Alberto Toscano (London: Continuum, 2009), pp. 250–1.

11 According to this architectonics of immanence, one doesn't have to choose between a Mahar movement, a Mahar-led Untouchable movement or a purely Untouchable movement for characterising the event(s) of this period. The Mahar is one of the discernible names of the 'real atoms', the Untouchable the *immanent* general name of the particular atomic names – and the name of the immortal, ontologically *indiscernible* from the historical atoms, . . . Dalit? Only insofar as Dalit 'discerns' the immortality of a mortal and oppressed world.

12 On an interpretation of Kant's diagnostic based upon the sign of the present and a possible event-philosophy, I, very provisionally, refer the reader to Soumyabrata Choudhury, *Theatre, Number, Event: Three Studies on the Relationship of Sovereignty, Power and Truth* (Shimla: IIAS, 2013), pp. 169–70.

13 For another use of the word "enthusiasm" as the subjective passion of the revolutionary and the objective milieu of the Revolution, one can go to the sumptuous prose of Jules Michelet and his history of the French Revolution in the middle of the nineteenth century. For this comparison, see Soumyabrata Choudhury, op. cit., p. 154, note 73.

14 It is important to note that between Antonio Gramsci's usage of the term 'subaltern' as a kind of non-unified 'group' rather than strata or class transforms to an *affirmative* usage by the historians of the Subaltern School. But the real delicacy of the challenge is to maintain this powerful affirmation at the level of this fundamental socio-historical *weakness*. See Antonio Gramsci, *Selections From the Prison Notebooks*, trans. Quentin Hoare and Geoffrey Nowell-Smith (New York: International Publishers, 1971), p. 52. The relevant section is cited, with interesting effect, by Gayatri Chakravorty Spivak in a recent polemic against Vivek Chibber's *Postcolonial Theory and the Specter of Capital*. See Gayatri Chakravorty Spivak, 'Postcolonial Theory and the Specter of Capital', *Cambridge Review of International Affairs*, 27(1), 184–98, doi:10.1080/09557571.2014.877262.

15 It is true that Phule, unlike Ambedkar, who wants to wipe the slate clean with reconstructing *and* voiding the history of the Shudra, calls

the *shudras* and *atishudras* aboriginals of the land. But even this aboriginality, this autochthony, to be rendered its due, demands a completely new and revolutionised thinking *in the present*. This thinking Phule calls 'education' for which the British system of learning, which is a contingent *chance* of history, will provide the organon. Thus, according to Phule, the British policy of spreading their learning among the Bhatts is to implement an insipid policy of educational 'trickledown'. The Bhatts don't know how to use the organon; they have no use of it! See Jotirao Phule, *Slavery* (New Delhi: Critical Quest, 2008). The preface is written in English by the author, and the remaining Marathi text is translated by Maya Pundit.

16 At this stage though, it is speculative to determine the concept of 'all'. One can restrict the idea to the fact that the 'all' here is neither a numerical count of everyone nor an alibi for something like a higher unity subsuming particular 'ones', such as one God or one Universe/World, etc. The 'all' then becomes 'one-all'. But as effect of the analogical and virtual programmes of discourse, the 'all' is also a negotiation of virtualities.

17 In other words, there is no local 'knowledge', strictly speaking, supporting a declaration of equality, no local, hidden egalitarian tradition to be mobilised. This was Ambedkar's early wager against recommencing the cult of Cokhamela among the Mahars as an emancipatory kernel for the future. Willing to pay the price of foregoing the shelter of the great name of Cokhamela on this occasion, on another he will mobilise the name 'Buddhism' as a kind of *paleonymy*, not a referent, of the new moment of conversion. See Eleanor Zelliot, op. cit., pp. 52–7.

18 See the last part of the second study of Soumyabrata Choudhury, op. cit., pp. 142–5. The section is called 'What is a historical multiplicity? A concluding note on torsion'.

19 The word 'sense' here imitates the French '*sens*', which means both meaning and direction. The point of historicity against history is the same as the event without sense against a 'sense-time'.

20 This image is from Thesis XIV of Walter Benjamin's 'The Concept of History'. Let me express my thanks to a reading of Walter Benjamin close to my concerns, which were greatly clarified by this reading. See Aniruddha Chowdhury, *Post-Deconstructive Subjectivity and History* (Leiden and Boston: Brill, 2013), pp. 87–118.

21 'Graded subalternities' is another case of conscious misapplication – this time of Ambedkar's thesis. There is some obvious resonance with Ambedkar's alternative expression 'graded slavery'; however, the real significance of this coinage is a differential saturation of the social field foreclosing *any* politics as opposed to the image of the subaltern who is *excluded* from political subjectivity as constituted by the *absolutely* dominant class.

22 I mean this in a precise sense. The 'only' thought is the *principle* of thinking itself, which is neither a prescription of habit nor an ordinance of law. Thinking is the same thing as *responsibility*, and it always precedes every institution of religion and law. Caste itself is an enunciative apparatus of law and (Hindu) religion that prohibits thought in the sense of a 'free responsibility'. Exactly in this sense the thought of the

French Revolution – liberty, equality, fraternity (Ambedkar will add the Marathi word *Manuskhi*, humanity) – must be the 'free responsibility' of another society in another age. See Babasaheb Ambedkar, 'Annihilation of Caste', in *Writings and Speeches*, Vol. 1, pp. 75–6. Notice in this section that the Kantian-sounding Ambedkar *thinks*, he doesn't *obey*.

23 Beyond all fetishism of the Book, whether to be venerated or burnt, the act of burning the *Manusmriti* on 25 December 1927 at Mahad must be taken as an absolute beginnings of thought as a right, a potency and as an affirmation at the exact point of its historical, enunciative and ontological capture. We must remember that at this fragile point of absolute beginning, the demand for a full right of thought is as much a minimal upsurge of a *trace* of thinking from the ashes of a Book, nay, book. See Eleanor Zelliot, op. cit., p. 80. Also of interest is the fact that the idea of burning the *Manusmriti* was G.N. Sahasrabuddhe's, a Chitpavan Brahmin. In the constitutive imagination of my thesis, the Caste-Hindu participates in symbolic acts of solidarity to the fullest degree; the Dalit draws the minimal *real* consequence for thought from such action. Ambedkar's refusal to *think* the event at the level of mere transgression in 1927 must be joined to the question of how to think the burning of the *Manusmriti*.

24 That is why counter-revolutionary thought, while espousing a pure transcendent authority, must *enforce* this transcendence in the element of historical time. This enforcement can be analogical through schematic parallels between transcendental and earthly authority, or it can be 'mysterious' through the force of decision arising from a void, beyond all immanent legitimacy. In all of this, counter-revolution will not admit that the void is an ontological break-out of and from the time of the world in the world which is sometimes called "revolution". This double structure is to be found in the thought of such diverse figures as Joseph de Maistre, Carl Schmitt, B.G. Tilak, etc.

25 The most vivid example of such fundamental defaulting on the very system of credit and debt that encodes historical time can be seen in the refusal to pay *tithes* to the Church during the French Revolution. To not pay taxes to the Church was to default on the inheritance of a powerful social and cultural identity, to effect a crack in the *corporate* form of the Church and to interrupt the time of political descent from the old regime. See Soumyabrata Choudhury, op. cit., pp. 202–8.

26 It is fascinating to see how counter-revolution responds to revolutionary violence and interprets it not as a means to a new historical society but as a *sign* that chaos, in the name of revolution, is here that someone forgot to pay his debt to the true authority, which is a mystery and a transcendence. There will always be blood, but the question is whether its quantity is equal to the debt owed to the true sovereign whose tax-collectors (blood-collectors?) are the One King, One Culture, One Tradition, etc. . . . whether there is uneconomical blood as price for revolutionary arrogance that there could be immanent constitution of sovereign truth. So the task is to use revolutionary-Jacobin blindness to a greater transcendental illumination, to prescribe a peculiar 'revolutionary' debt of eternal Tradition. See ibid, p. 143 for the substantiation

of this point through an analysis of Joseph de Maistre's polemic against the French Revolution.

27 Ibid, p. 47.

28 A masterly representative of this exposition of "'Indo-European' comparativity" is Georges Dumézil, *Mitra-Varuna: An Essay on Two Indo-European Representations of Sovereignty*, trans. Derek Coltman (New York: Zone Books, 1988). In a sense, we can say the notion of 'Indo-European Culture' corresponds to and constitutes a neutral object 'comparativity itself' – and from this utterly objective, cold premise, the political critique of orientalism must begin.

29 This, I will say, is the birth of 'comparative politics', which, to all measures of comparativity itself, is an impossible idea because it is exceptional and generic at the same time. Conversely, it can be shown that global orders of knowledge-discourses are deployed as *political* exigencies in the face of exceptional 'events'. Susan Bayly persuades us that 'orientalist' policies of the British government and global notions of Indian caste system, are not uniquely or even inherently knowledges of a biased (Eurocentric) type but the specific and unified political response *forced* by the 'event' of 1857 Revolt (among other exceptional moments in history). See Susan Bayly, 'Western "Orientalists" and the Colonial Perception of Caste', in *Caste in Modern India*, ed. Sumit Sarkar and Tanika Sarkar (Ranikhet: Permanent Black, 2014), pp. 47–87.

30 For a related but different view on the question bringing together Marxist and several post-colonial literatures, see the chapter 'Passages of Sovereignty', in *Empire*, eds. Antonio Negri and Michael Hardt (Cambridge, MA and London: Harvard University Press, 2001), pp. 67–204.

31 Might we call this gratuitous procedure a Dalit 'snobbism', a leisurely thought of glacial constellations with a certain militant *disinterest* in the sound and fury of the world as it exists? I have written on this point with reference to the Ambedkar-Gandhi debate in the essay 'Ambedkar Contra Aristotle: On a possible contention about who is capable of politics'. The essay is available in Bengali and Hindi translations (*Charchapad*, August 2013 and *Pratiman*, January–April, 2014 respectively) and forthcoming in the *Journal of Humanities and Social Sciences*, IIAS, Shimla.

32 See 'What Is the Third Estate?' [1789], in *Sieyès: Political Writings*, ed. Michael Sonenscher, (Indianapolis: Hackett, 2003), and Babasaheb Ambedkar 'Who Were the Shudras?', in *Writings and Speeches*, Vol. 7, ed. Vasant Moon (Bombay: Education Dept., Government of India, 1990).

33 On the Estates-General in 1789 and the doubling of the vote of the third estate as a reflection of its majority, see Georges Lefebvre, *The French Revolution: From Its Origins to 1793*, trans. Elisabeth Moss Evanson (London and New York: Routledge, 2007), pp. 98–111.

34 In his Mahad speech, Ambedkar builds a qualitative comparison between the estates of the old regime in France and Hindu caste-division in terms of corporate hierarchy of society and points out that at this point (1927), a political comparison is not possible. That is because the *numerical* intervention of converting the major magnitude (the third estate) into a sovereign 'quality' (new regime) is not on the agenda of

any Indian 'National Assembly'. Remember one of the leading slogans of the revolutionary conjuncture in France was 'The Nation is the People Assembled'! See the rest of Ambedkar's speech extracted in G. Aloysius, op. cit. pp. 64–6.

35 'The thing to bear in mind is there is great similarity between the French National Assembly that met on 5 May 1789 at Versailles and our meeting today. The similarity is not only in the circumstances . . . but also in their ideals. That Assembly of the French people was convened to reorganize French society. Our meeting today too has been convened to reorganize Hindu society'. Ibid, p. 65.

36 Ibid, p. 65.

37 "[L]ike the Hindu Society, the French had a class of Brahmins and another of Kshatriyas. But instead of three different castes of Vaishya, Shudra and Atishudras, there was one class[the third estate] that comprehended these. This is a *minor* [emphasis mine] difference". Ibid, p. 65.

38 Very cryptically put, this polemical culture is nearly wiped out in our times. Is it ironic, or is there a logical explanation, that in times of habitual and neurotic sensitivity to the 'hurt' that we threaten each other with, the 'we' is itself a matter of consensus rather than a function of real separation? I think the essential thing lacking is the *promise* of a new truth born out of separation, a truth of which as yet we know nothing – instead, we live and rage in the consensus that we know everything.

39 See Christophe Jaffrelot, 'Analysing and Ethnicizing Caste to Eradicate it More Effectively', in *Caste in Modern India*, Vol. 2, ed. Sumit Sarkar and Tanika Sarkar, p. 322.

40 For this extraordinary and continuous modulation of minimal difference into dense graded hierarchy in the age of Meister Eckhart and Latin Christianity, see Rainer Schürmann, *Broken Hegemonies*, trans. Reginald Lilly (Bloomington and Indianapolis: Indiana University Press, 2003), pp. 298–318. It is to be noted that here is a model of ontological hierarchy of being subject to God in the mode of ontological loans/credit distributed from a hegemonic/sovereign source to every being of the hierarchy. If the sovereign turns away, the entire hierarchy collapses and the world of beings is annihilated. So debt is necessary, productive and empowering in the structure of graded sovereignty with clearly two articulations of the sovereign: the Singular Sovereign-Creditor-Hegemon and the plural system of Social Sovereignty of *all debtors*. Subtract the Christian God from the system and you get Hindu caste-society at a pinch!

41 For a complex historical account of these forces, see Michael Sonenscher, *Public Debt, Inequality and the Intellectual Origins of the French Revolution* (Princeton and Oxford: Princeton University Press, 2007), pp. 22–94.

42 Ibid, pp. 77–9.

43 See Arundhati Roy's interview in *Outlook* magazine in the wake of her introduction to a new annotated edition of Ambedkar's *Annihilation of Caste*. Interview taken by Saba Naqvi. *Outlook*, 10 March 2014.

44 See Babasaheb Ambedkar, 'A Plea to the Foreigner', in *Writings and Speeches*, Vol. 9, ed. Vasant Moon (Bombay: Education Department, Government of Maharashtra, 1991). Also the speeches to the Constituent Assembly on 4 November 1948 and 25 November 1949 – where Ambedkar, unhappily, insisted that the Constitution must impose a code of necessity on an area which was intrinsically *contingent*, that is, 'administration' (instead of legislature). See Ambedkar's speech on 4 November 1948 to the Constituent Assembly in *Writings and Speeches*, Vol. 13 (Bombay: Education Department, Government of Maharashtra, 1994), pp. 60–1.

45 See Ambedkar's speech to the Constituent Assembly on 25 November 1949. He ends with a threnody where he clearly laments the utter absence of equality in Indian society against which the axiom of political equality must be constituted, nay, *forced*. Actually, even this formulation must be modified because the point was to force generic equality through a political constitution. See Constituent Assembly Debates, Vol. XI, pp. 977–81.

46 For an alternative path of history which wouldn't end up with the impasse Ambedkar lamented on the eve of the new republic, the latter had attempted, from the days of the first Round Table Conference and the Communal Award of separate electorates to the 1947 document *States and Minorities*, to develop an emancipatory political arithmetic instead of depending on an analogon of the exceptional 'event' which reservations was in the Constitution. In an improvised discussion at the Centre for Studies in Social Sciences, Kolkata on a different paper by me on a connected issue, Partha Chatterjee strikingly suggested that seen in this light, reservations was analogous to something like dictatorship of the proletariat on the way to true communist equality.

References

Agamben, Giorgio. 2005. *State of Exception*. Kevin Attell (trans.). Chicago and London: The University of Chicago Press.

Aloysius, G. 2009. *Ambedkar on Nation and Nationalism*. New Delhi: Critical Quest.

Ambedkar, Bhimrao Ramji. 1987. 'Krishna and His Gita', in Vasant Moon (ed.), *Writings and Speeches*. Vol. 3, pp. 371–91. Bombay: Education Department, Government of Maharashtra.

Ambedkar, Bhimrao Ramji. 1989. 'Annihilation of Caste', in Vasant Moon (ed.), *Writings and Speeches*. Vol. 1, pp. 80–120. Bombay: Education Department, Government of Maharashtra.

Ambedkar, Bhimrao Ramji. 1990. 'Who Were the Shudras?', in Vasant Moon (ed.), *Writings and Speeches*. Vol. 7, pp. 245–95. Bombay: Education Department, Government of India.

Badiou, Alain. 2003. *St. Paul: The Foundation of Universalism*. Ray Brassier (trans.). Stanford: Stanford University Press.

Badiou, Alain. 2009. *Logics of Words: Being and Event II*. Alberto Toscano (trans.). London: The Continuum Publishing Corporation.

Bayly, Susan. 2014. 'Western "Orientalists" and the Colonial Perception of Caste', in Sumit Sarkar and Tanika Sarkar (ed.), *Caste in Modern India*, pp. 47–87. Ranikhet: Permanent Black.

Benjamin, Walter. 1969. 'The Task of Translation', in Hannah Arendt (ed.), Harry Zohn (trans.), *Illuminations*, pp. 69–82. New York: Schocken Books.

Chatterjee, Partha. 2013. 'Subaltern Studies and Capital', *Economic and Political Weekly*, XLVIII(37), September 14: 73.

Choudhury, Soumyabrata. 2013. *Theatre, Number, Event: Three Studies on the Relationship of Sovereignty, Power and Truth*. Shimla: IIAS.

Chowdhury, Aniruddha. 2013. *Post-Deconstructive Subjectivity and History*. Leiden and Boston: Brill.

Dumézil, Georges. 1988. *Mitra-Varuna: An Essay on Two Indo-European Representations of Sovereignty*. Derek Coltman (trans.). New York: Zone Books.

Foucault, Michel. 1997. 'What Is Revolution?', in Sylvere Lotringer and Lysa Hochroth (eds.), *The Politics of Truth*. New York: Semiotexte.

Foucault, Michel. 'Politics of Truth', in Sylvere Lotringer and Lysa Hochroth (eds.), *The Politics of Truth*. New York: Semiotexte.

Gramsci, Antonio. 1971. *Selections From the Prison Notebooks*. Quentin Hoare and Geoffrey Nowell-Smith (trans.). New York: International Publishers.

Jaffrelot, Christophe. 2015. 'Analysing and Ethnicizing Caste to Eradicate It More Effectively', in Sumit Sarkar and Tanika Sarkar (eds.), *Caste in Modern India*. Vol. 2, pp. 322–52. Ranikhet: Permanent Black.

Kant, Immanuel. 1979. *The Conflict of Faculties*. M.J. Gregor (trans.). New York: Abaris Books.

Lefebvre, Georges. 2007. *The French Revolution: From Its Origins to 1793*. Elisabeth Moss Evanson (trans.). London and New York: Routledge.

Negri, Antonio and Hardt, Michael. 2001. *Empire*. Cambridge, MA and London: Harvard University Press.

Phule, Jotirao. 2008. *Slavery*. New Delhi: Critical Quest.

Schürmann, Rainer. 2003. *Broken Hegemonies*. Reginald Lilly (trans.). Bloomington and Indianapolis: Indiana University Press.

Sonenscher, Michael (ed.). 2003. *Sieyès: Political Writings*. Indianapolis: Hackett.

Sonenscher, Michael. 2007. *Public Debt, Inequality and the Intellectual Origins of the French Revolution*. Princeton and Oxford: Princeton University Press.

Spivak, Gayatri Chakravorty. 2014. 'Postcolonial Theory and the Specter of Capital', *Cambridge Review of International Affairs*, 27(1): 184–98.
Zelliot, Eleanor. 2013. *Ambedkar's World: The Making of Babasaheb and the Dalit Movement*. New Delhi: Navayana.

Archival reference

Constituent Assembly Debates, Vol. XI, pp. 977–81.

Chapter 3

Parallel praxis

History-domination-resistance-ideology-theory[1]

Neshat Quaiser

> I began to develop a practical and polemical view of philosophy. . . . I established a close link between philosophy and politics
> (Louis Althusser)[2]

Introduction

Situating within the theories of domination, social classes, state and resistance to modes of domination, this chapter examines, first, the discourses that amount to justifying the exploitative relations of domination, inevitability of 'power' and conditions of subjugation, particularly with reference to Michel Foucault and the scholars of his school of thought such as post-modernists; and second, the ways in which the conceptions of transformative praxis and social classes have been influenced by other theoretical traditions such as Althusserian, post-Althusserian, post-Marxist, neo-Marxist and post-modernist, which have privileged ideology and discourse, in varying degrees, as the structuring principle for shaping social life, social groupings and social movements detached from any social determinants. This chapter argues for a linking of ideology, discourse and consciousness to social and historical base (without undermining the relative significance of culture and agency), where critical praxis for a true radical social transformation is located.

Social practice in this chapter is used in the sense of Marx's conception of praxis, which is in opposition to both the way western Marxists, including practitioners of Critical Theory, used the term in which all sorts of practices were included – an all-encompassing category where subjective actions were privileged – and also to the traditionally viewed Aristotelian conception where theory and practice were treated as mutually exclusive domains.

Marx's conception of praxis is inalienably linked with revolutionary transformation, where theory and practice are united to produce change of a fundamental nature and is characterised by conscious human intervention to make a new history and subject. This conception of praxis enables a subject to tread in a zone simultaneously outside while being within Althusserian 'hail' (Althusser 1971: 123) where, with critical subjectivity, ultimately the element of being outside the 'hail' prevails. In Habermas praxis is related to his commitment to the goal of political emancipation through self-knowledge or self-reflection. Insights gained through critical self-awareness are emancipatory in the sense that at least one can recognise the correct reasons for her/his problems (Habermas 1989). Habermasian self-reflection, however, is not sure of producing predictable desired results. Paulo Freire's notion of praxis, despite having been closely identified with that of Marx, ". . . differs only in degree, but not in kind, from the system which he so eloquently criticizes (Taylor 1993: 148; for critique of Paulo Freire's critical pedagogy and praxis see, Gur-Ze'ev 2005, 2010; Morgan and Alexandre, 2018).

This chapter, in addition to an Introduction, is divided into five parts with sub-sections. Part I outlines the notion of parallel praxis; Part II discusses various approaches to parallel practices; Part III presents ten cases illustrative of varying range, types, forms and historicity of parallel practices not only from the Indian subcontinent but also a case from Africa and Europe as well; Part IV, with reference to cases presented in Part III, discusses the concepts of history, people/subject/public/classes, popular justice and people's court and everyday resistance; and Part V contains a detailed concluding remarks.

I. Parallel praxis: against immanent teleology

The phenomenon of parallel practice seems to characterise societal existence. It has quite succinctly been pointed out in the form of a question: 'Was "human" history the history of *man* or the history of *men*?' (Le Goff 1990: 1). Le Goff provides the answer that Lucien Febvre had offered: '*Men*, the only object of history'. This fine historical distinction points to a difference in the social practices arising out of social contradictions, differential cultural practices and societal-historical heterogeneity.

The dynamics of oppositional practices characterise social space(s) and places. Dominance of one set of social practices – as they historically evolve – over the others is marked by a set of oppositional practices of those who do not agree with it. Agreement or disagreement is not determined by one's volition but by the historical/ahistorical structural location of social forces/human agency. However, all types of oppositional practice and practice against established rule may not necessarily be regarded as parallel praxis. Parallel practices, at the surface level, refer to those practices which are against the dominant power and the hegemonic rules – projected as natural – of the few against many and which are ahistorical. They challenge expectations of conformity to the relations of domination sustained through a system of superordination and subordination. So, parallel here is not something that is similar to something else. Thus, parallel practice of dominating class/group in terms of relations to means of production and control over it is not parallel in this context, for they through counter parallel practice become dominating power, reinforcing relations of domination.

Two distinguishing features of parallel practice could be identified: firstly, parallel practice is parallel for its practitioner stands up parallel to power that has come to decide her/his material and spiritual surroundings and the meaning of her/his social existence. For, the powerless does not like this fact of others deciding her/his social existence as it goes against the characteristics of his/her historical social being. So, in whatever manner possible – at a given time and space – he/she thinks, plans and attempts to defy that power. What is this dislike, defiance? How does this get constituted? Does parallel practice take place simply through and against a practice of dominance? It is, we argue, essentially a *necessity*. This necessity is social-historical. In other words, to be dominated/subjugated in a particular social formation is not necessitated by the natural characteristic of that formation. For, no mode of production/historical stage is internally based on injustice and exploitation. For instance, advanced production forces during capitalism. What is this? It actually and truly signified a development in the long journey of human cognition, human experience in interaction with nature and with one's own human self, shaping the transformative human agency that resolutely fought the feudal system in the course of its development of human cognition. How does this then become an exploitative capitalist system? It is not because of the advanced forces of production but because of its control by certain classes. Thus, exploitation and oppression are not the *inevitable* characteristics of a social formation. Social agencies involved with conflicting interests then become important. For instance, within the structure of capitalism, there exist two opposite forces – one to demolish it and the other to preserve it. Thus, a social formation cannot be regarded as a structure in itself. Secondly, although various parallel practices such as rebellion, revolt, movement, collective spontaneous actions, revolutions and everyday invisible, local, micro, spontaneous resistance, back-stage talks and linguistic disguises etc. are distinct – in terms of form and range and particularly in terms of time and space that give them specific touch – from each other, a thread runs through all such practices. This is the thread of shared experience and its recognition within situations of inequality of power and production. This is the thread of ideology – at times very thin and fragile and at times strong enough to become an integrative force. And that is how dialectical linkages between the indigeneity and universality of social practices are established.

Parallel practices intend to create a parallel social space within the given hierarchically structured spaces and constantly contest their dominance in order to finally replace them by new ones. These parallel practices create parallel spaces in almost all domains of social life and in various forms. At the very outset, it may be pointed out that the contestation to dominance is not simply to get immediate relief, but the underlying assumption of all parallel practices – be it small or big, collective or individual, spontaneous or organised – is to get rid of the system that perpetuates the relations of domination. These parallel practices in different stages of society were *necessary* responses to different systems of stratification, hierarchical orders, relations of domination, class divisions and patterns of production and consumption of capital and culture. In other words, power is not located merely in discourse. We wish to contest Scott who, following Foucault's concepts of power, discipline and panopticism, argues that subordinate groups have 'a self-interest for conspiring to reinforce hegemonic appearances' (Scott 1990a: xii). For, even if they 'conspire' to escape immediate retribution due to existing seemingly enduring hegemonic appearances, this act of 'conspiring' itself can be regarded not just as ways to resist but also how these are ingredients/constitutive elements of large historical protests/resistance crossing the boundaries of immediacy, i.e., resistance is not destined to be localised. The debate, therefore, is epistemologically grounded within the contexts of Marxist theory of knowledge and that of Foucault's explanatory models of history and archaeology. Ultimately, parallel practice is linked with the production of knowledge and not governed by utilitarian motives. Parallel practice, therefore, is not immanent critique determined by immanent teleology.

II. Approaches

Systematic study of oppositional practices of marginalised people has received very belated attention from scholars despite Marx's pioneering work. Perspectives such as social movement, popular culture, everyday resistance and everyday life have been employed within the social sciences to study these practices.

The social movement/collective action approach which studies large-scale mass mobilisations and actions and mass upsurges that take place generally either to reform or change the system has dominated the scene. Instances of these are explained either in terms of a tension-release mechanism in which protest, rebellion etc. are perceived as unrestrained responses to stress or in terms of 'breakdown' of social order in the face of societal strain due to rapid social change (Smelser 1962) and which need counter-action to restore the social order. The breakdown theory views movement as an abnormal act. Some scholars have questioned the breakdown theories by highlighting the 'structural factors' (McAdam 1988: 125–54) such as 'political opportunities', 'absence of repression' etc. to explain the emergence of movements. This view heavily depends on the state rather than perspective of historical necessity to explain the movement. However, social movements have also been studied by Marxists from dialectical and class perspectives, as an organised collective endeavour by the dominated people to challenge the system that perpetuates oppression and exploitation. A third stream, represented by scholars such as George Rude (1964) and E. P. Thompson (1988) and others, has approached the problem differently. Of these scholars, Thompson is significant for our purpose, as we shall discuss below. The characteristics of this stream in the analysis of collective action have been enumerated by Tilly (1981: 15) as (a) definitions and beliefs of the participants being taken seriously; (b) attempts being made to connect the action with interests, grievances and aspirations of every day; and (c) attaching great importance to the social structures which link the actors to each other as well as to their rivals, enemies and exploiters. We shall have occasion to further discuss this approach as follows.

The cultural approach has emerged with the advent of studies of popular culture or Cultural Studies since the late 1950s with Hoggart (1954) 'as a starting point'. Under this approach, practices of marginalised people are often studied. As a result, we have studies of 'everyday' practices, 'invisible' practices, 'offstage' discourse, 'linguistic disguise', practices against the 'established rules' and attempts to write 'history from below' and the 'politics of everyday'. Various contending schools of thought in this regard have emerged. Annales historians, Marxists, phenomenologists, constructivists and post-structuralists/post-modernists have attempted to explain in their own ways the phenomenon of what we have called parallel practice.

Outside the Marxist fold, the early American studies of the practices of marginalised people – or what has been called popular culture – were focussed on the media. Some of them studied fads and fashions in modern urban life. By the mid-1960s, some scholars wrote empirical and descriptive accounts of everything: 'from fast-food restaurants to rock-n-roll' while others attempted to study 'commercial language in popular culture' for an understanding of contemporary usage of language. Later, constructivists-phenomenologists made serious efforts to explain how ordinary people could 'break the hold of political institutions over their imaginations' (Mukerji 1992: 1492–3). The popular culture perspective seems to be inadequate for an understanding of parallel practice in its totality. Not simply because it continues to 'romanticise' folk and primitive virtue of ordinary people (Burke 1981), but because there is much more to the whole thing. It would be useful to remember what Stuart Hall (1981: 234) had to say against the background of the early chaotic focus of popular culture studies. He said: 'the structuring principle of the "popular" . . . is the tensions and oppositions between what belongs to the central domain of elite or dominant culture, and the culture of "periphery"'. However, the whole problem is how do the tensions and oppositions get crystallised, what form will they take? There appears to be a general tendency to 'romanticise' the folk, primitive, everyday practices, offstage talks and linguistic disguises and what is popular. We would argue that the popular does not necessarily represent subaltern consciousness. Much of the 'popular' in fact reinforces relations of domination.

Symbolic Interactionism and studies of sub-culture and deviances under its influence emphasised the key role of a labelling process in the maintenance of social order. This perspective failed to uncover the real motives behind labelling.

Phenomenologists emphasised the 'living world' representing the result of the mental and emotional activity of individual subjects. This perspective viewed everyday life in terms of intersubjective consciousness, i.e., an individual's own personalistic reflections (Berger and Luckmann 1979) that are devoid of one's historical situatedness. They did not explain the ideological and the political control over common people and how this works, could be broken and what next. They asserted that no object could exist without the subject, thus critical historical collectivity of parallel practices is individualised.

For Pierre Bourdieu (1984), the differences in cultural consumption are much more significant than differences in cultural production. He focuses on uncovering the specific logic of cultural goods, central to which are the ways and means of appropriating cultural objects. For Bourdieu, culture is the main source of class stability. His fundamental aim in this regard is to look for mechanisms by which domination has been sustained and reproduced across generations. No more than this. It is for this reason that the human practice cannot free itself from the impenetrable prison of habitus. As a result, for Bourdieu, resistance by the working class is not something to be celebrated; rather, it is a trap for reproducing the class system.

On the other hand, 'certain similarity exist' between Foucault and early Annales historians and these scholars were looking for anonymous rules governing collective practices and all scholars participated in displacing the individual "subject" from the history' (Hunt 1989: 7).

Post-modern turn[3]

With the emergence of postmodernism as an influential theoretical framework, postmodern scholars paid attention to the studies of social movements and parallel practices as well. However, there is a great deal of confusion and vagueness about what postmodernism is. Bauman, however, perhaps captured the spirit when he wrote that postmodernism "does not seek to substitute one truth for another, one life ideal for another. . . . It braces itself for a life without truths, standards and ideals" (Bauman 1992: ix).

They broadly argued that the meta-narratives – modernism, Marxism and fascism all clubbed together – are located within the abstract universal metatheories that draw from the totalising enlightenment modernity. It pleaded for heterogeneity and interpretation as key analytical categories in our understanding of truth and social reality. Contextualisation of moral-legal positions thereby is insisted upon – feminists or gays, for example, would demand interpretation of moral-legal values from their vantage perspectives, and for that to happen a multiple view of truth is needed.

Contextualisation theory made them limit both the sources and causes of social inequality and particularly resistance to the immediate and the local. In other words, 'everyday pursuits' can be grasped 'only in the local network' (de Certeau 1988: ix). Thus, with regard to parallel practices postmodernism is fraught with serious philosophical problems and contains contradictions, as its notions of heterogeneity, pluralism and truth are constituted by the view that social reality is permanently fractured and fragmented – a ". . . slippery space of Postmodernism [where] anything goes with anything, like a game without rules. Floating images . . . maintain no relationship with anything at all, and meaning becomes detachable. . . . Dissociated and decontextualized, they slide past one another failing to link up into a coherent sequence. Their fluctuating but not reciprocal interactions are unable to fix meaning" (Gablik, Suzy quoted in Callinicos, 1989: 12). Thus, nothing can be concretely grasped and postmodernism would be liable to participate in the 'choreographic occultation' (Quaiser, 2016) of relations of domination. By postmodernist logic, victims of exploitation and oppression should have allowed themselves to be ecstatically consumed by the almost mystical waves of the fluid state of existence in which it is impossible to assign any responsibility on anything – dominant agrarian castes, classes and state for egregious exploitation and oppression.

Marxists

Within the Marxist tradition, the whole corpus of writings on revolutionary parallel practices since the time of Marx and Engels provided a basis for a parallel analysis of history, class, class relations and consciousness, movements, culture and capital. Emphasis, for obvious reasons, was on open revolutionary activities, to which we shall return in the following sections. In Marxism, praxis is not confined to political alone but is rooted in the principle of universal negativism, a social necessity. It is a free, self-creative activity through which humans create themselves and their historical human surrounding. The concept of praxis in Marxism is rooted in its conception of philosophy. Mao, while criticising the subjectivism of a dogmatist and empiricist view of relation between knowledge and practice, emphasised the importance of theory for revolutionary practice, pointing out 'the dependence of knowledge on social practice, that is, the dependence of knowledge on production and the class struggle' (Mao 1975). And it would be erroneous to think that the domains of culture are in dichotomous relations with production and class.

The most significant turn within the Marxist theory of society, class and parallel praxis came with Louis Althusser. He was critical of the determinant 'final instance' role of the relations of production and argued that society consists of 'instances' with equal influence. Althusser developed his theory of levels or instances and argued that:

> the unity of a structured whole containing what can be called levels or instances which are distinct and 'relatively autonomous', and co-exist within this complex structured unity, articulated with one another according to specific determinations, fixed in the last instance by the level of or instance of the economy.
>
> (Althusser 1970: 97)

Thus, for Althusser structures are composed of economic, political and ideological. This theory contained new implications for transformative parallel practices. Nicos Poulantzas emerged as the most powerful representative of post-Althusserian Marxist tradition with the publication of his book *Political Power and Social Classes* in 1968. In the light of the emergence of various service sectors in Europe of 1960s and 1970s, which gave rise to various middle class theories, Poulantzas argued that the Marxist concept of social classes be re-defined. Moreover, like Althusser he too attacked Marxist 'economism' and 'class reductionism' which became the basis for his emphasis on the specificity and autonomy of the political, which was the hallmark of the Mao's thought, to which people like Althusser and Poulantzas were greatly attracted. Poulantzas agreed with Althusser's theory of instances and levels (1973: 69) but later introduced certain conditions for this (1978: 16–20). Poulantzas in a way paved the way for the post-Marxist thinking within the European left of which Ernesto Laclau and Chantal Mouffe (1985) were the most prominent representatives.

Poulantzas, however, "never went so far" as post Marxists "either with respect to the theoretical detachment of ideology and politics from any social determinations, or with respect to the political detachment of socialism from the working class" (Wood 1998: 25). Laclau and Mouffe denied the role of working class in effecting socialism and also the role of production relations in shaping the politico-ideological realisation and argued that ideology and discourse shape social classes and movements. This thinking had serious implications for social movements. For example, theorists of New Social Movements too have seriously questioned Marxist perspective for its grand theory and methodological holism in the context of collective action. In this new approach, a fundamental shift is from class to social – involving all sections of society and taking up the issues, which were subsumed under and not taken up by the old social movement (Touraine 1984; Laclau and Mouffe 1985). Here the concepts of *social* and of *people* are crucial. Touraine's emphasis on all sections of society and Laclau and Mouffe's insistence on citizens and people and seriously questioning the 'ontological centrality of working class' for any social movements may remind us of the Enlightenment's concept of people that privileged goodness of all people, closing its eyes to the emerging class divisions in European societies in the wake of the industrial revolution, and it would be worth remembering Didero's tirade against the 'paradoxes of Enlightenment'.

From within the Marxist camp, both in the domain of theory and political practice, a growing realisation has been visible that it is necessary 'to stretch Marxist categories further and further' to include the civil rights movements, the women's movement, environmental, gay and lesbian movements, communalism etc. within its paradigm of social change, for it had 'little to say about the cultural radicalism and politics of identity' (Epstein 1990; Habermas 1986, 1985). Even the conventional Communist parties in both Western and non-Western worlds have learned lessons from the experiences of twentieth-century Marxist theory and practice and have been forced to take up issues which were traditionally outside the ambit of their political thinking or had not been paid adequate attention to, for it was thought that once the socialist revolution is achieved, these super-structural aspects will automatically disappear. Any discussion on parallel practice from Marxist perspective today cannot afford to ignore these contexts. The project of the Frankfurt School and its critical theory of society began with the task of restoring Marxism to its original spirit in the face of orthodox, mechanistic, Stalinist dogmatic Marxism. Despite its original claims and its critique of culture industry and of the socio-economic causes of the rise of fascism and the claim that theory must be a weapon for social transformation, it never aligned with the working-class movements. Consequently, the Frankfurt School did not die its natural death; it was yet again massacred and annihilated in the streets of Paris when the time of the test of its claims once again arrived.

E. P. Thompson is particularly important for what may be called the seemingly new Marxist thinking with regard to class practices. Thompson (1988) made a distinct shift from the 'orthodox' mode of Marxist thinking and heralded a new type of historiography, i.e., social history – history from below. Culture and resistance outside the organised worker-peasant movements, hitherto grossly neglected, gained prominence within this tradition of scholarship. Thompson seriously questioned the old base-superstructure perspective of 'economic determinism' as the only valid method in the analysis of history, social life, class and class relations. This perspective emerged out of the debate within the Communist Party Historian Group. Thompson (1988), Hill (1975) and others emerged as the product of this new thinking, seriously questioning the crucial role of ideology in the articulation of an argument against the oppressors. For Thompson, 'making' of a class 'owes as much to agency as to conditioning'. Thus, he does not see class 'as a "structure", nor even as "category", but as something which in fact happens . . . in human relationships'. Therefore, according to him 'class-consciousness is the way in which these experiences (class experiences, largely determined by productive relations) are handled in cultural term: embodied in traditions, value systems, ideas and institutional forms' (Thompson 1988: 8–9). He was subsequently accused of advocating voluntarism and idealism (Trimberger 1984). It is, however, important to note that Thompson differentiates clearly the 'class experience' and cultural 'handling' of such experience, which is different in emphasis from that of Williams (1961), whose emphasis is on 'the culture of the period' in the form of 'structure of feeling' (Easton et al. 1988: 24). With reference to language and class, Stedman Jones (1983) is critical of Thompson for assuming 'a relatively direct relationship between "social being" and "social consciousness" which leaves little independent space for the ideological contest within which the coherence of a particular language of class can be reconstituted' (see Hunt 1989: 6). Historiography of popular culture under this new thinking focussed primarily on the heroic deeds of people's history dating back to pre-capitalist periods, and in the words of Schwartz (1982: 91) 'histories of the later nineteenth and the twentieth century tend to be emptied of such imaginative reconstructions of cultural formations in comparison with those of the earlier periods'. A further look at this approach reveals that the absence of an attempt to study contemporary cultural situations; serious questioning about the role of ideology and agency; analysis of language in terms of its expression; romanticisation of folk, primitive, micro, spontaneous virtues and acts of people; emphasis on mode of power instead of relations of production in the analysis of social relations seem to be characteristic features of this approach.

Foucault and history

The writings of Michel Foucault have exercised considerable influence on the contemporary scholarship in studying the power relations concealed or revealed in everyday transactions at off and on the work situations, in the family, in school and in other areas of social life. Foucault (1980a: 81) believes that 'to think in terms of totality has proved a hindrance to research'. He favours 'an autonomous, non-centralised kind of theoretical production'. His tirade against 'tyranny of globalising discourses' is not simply against the 'functionalist coherence or formal systematisation' (ibid: 83), but has something definitively to do with his notion of history with reference to an understanding of present and past. This notion of history focuses on 'local, discontinuous, disqualified, illegitimate knowledges' uncritically as the only source of authentic knowledge. For an understanding of Foucault's view of history, theory and knowledge, the concept of genealogy is also important, for which he heavily relied on Nietzche. His Genealogies reject any view of history as a 'unitary body of theory which would filter, hierarchies and order them in the name of some true knowledge and some arbitrary idea of what constitutes a science and its objects'; thus, Genealogies are 'precisely anti-sciences' (ibid), and therefore he is also against Marxism as 'it could effectively be a science' (ibid: 84) and argues curiously: 'At the deepest level of Western knowledge, Marxism introduces no real discontinuity' (Foucault 1980b: 261).

What emerges is an almost uncritical acceptance of everyday, illegitimate, obscure, local, what is not part of the grand narrative as the only authentic and legitimate sources of knowledge. For him, 'Nothing in man – not even his body – is sufficiently stable to serve as the basis for self-recognition or for understanding other men' (quoted in O'Brien 1989: 35).[4] For the study of power, Foucault looks for 'technologies of power'. For him power is a 'strategy attributable to functions (dispositions, manoeuvres, tactics and techniques). Power does not originate in either the economy or politics, and it is not grounded there'. He did not locate power either in the state. Instead, he sought 'the most unpromising places' – that is 'feelings, love, conscience, instinct – the interstices of power' – to understand it (O'Brien 1989: 34–5, 37). Foucault insists: 'We must cease once and for all to describe the effects of power in negative terms: it "excludes", it "represses", it "censors", it "abstracts", it "masks", it "conceals". In fact, power produces; it produces reality; it produces domains of objects and rituals of truth. The individual and the knowledge that may be gained of him belong to this production' (Foucault 1982: 194). His analysis of power may be right in terms of oppressive/exploitative structures of power controlled and manipulated by the dominant classes/groups, but the problem is that he sees this as the only truth, almost an absolute truth, and in turn he formulates a totalising theory and leaves almost no scope for self-conscious intervening individual subject(s). Individuals, in his theory, seem to be condemned to be a plaything in the hands of history – an oppressive process, and they cannot make any history. His insistence that an individual cannot produce knowledge of the world outside, of himself, and of this cage of 'power' itself, negates the role of a labour-performing, self-creating individual that produces his historical surroundings and knowledge of this surrounding and of himself in interaction with this surrounding that has the potential to demolish the oppressive 'power'. In other words, Foucault is interested only in the study of 'power' and not at all in the forms of resistance to that power, which from the Foucauldian perspective appears to be impossibility. This thinking is also the structuring principle in his analyses of the concepts of Discipline and Panopticism, as we shall discuss in section IV. Marx, on the other hand, has the promise to encompass human experience in terms of human cognition and its development within the contexts of material conditioning and philosophical cognition. Marx's epistemology is not universalistic in the sense that it precludes specificities of time and space, but contrary to popular belief in certain traditions of scholarship, it insists on a creative and informed interaction, inter-linkages and reciprocity between the general and historical processes and how the two are intrinsically interlinked. Similarly, the past, present and the (anticipated) future form a chain. Unlike Foucault, Marx's epistemology is rooted in commonly shared human experiences of those who are faced with relations of domination and held out the promise of resistance. In order to grasp Marx's epistemology, one would know that Marx demonstrated how and why 'commodities and commodity-exchange must engender the opposition of commodity and money . . . thanks to the property of value immanent in commodities' that led to 'transformation of money into capital . . . based on the purchase and sale of labour-power' (Althusser 1970: 151). It was thus Marx's theory of surplus value that brought about his epistemological *break* with classical economics and that privileged the notion of structure with specific meaning in Marx (Godelier 1978: 335). The significance of Marx's epistemology, however, is that it contains possibilities to travel beyond the confines of Western capitalism and economy as viewed in the narrow sense and has the promise for different times and spaces.

III. Ingredients of history and modes of resistance

In this section we present a few cases (A1, A2, A3; B1, B2, B3, B4; and C1, C2, C3). These cases – not covering all dimensions though – are illustrative of a varying range, types, forms and historicity of parallel practices. This is followed by a discussion on certain theoretical issues involved in the debate in Part IV. The discussion would also focus on the supposed dichotomy between the everyday, invisible on the one hand and organised, open, ideological parallel practices on the other hand. These dichotomies, we argue, are not mutually exclusive.

A1

> This ungrateful king does not recognise even the goodness of this good man (Bodhisatta) who save his majesty's life. How can we profit from this king. Seize the Tyrant.
>
> (Saccamkira Jataka 1895: 180)

A2

That he may not in future go on playing the part of a thief, we will kill this wicked king, and beat the king with sticks and clubs till he died.

(Padakusalamanava Jataka 1957: 306)

A3

While I was in the Gaboon, old King Glass died. The tribe had grown tired of their king. They thought, indeed, that he was a most potent and evil-disposed wizard, and, though the matter was not openly talked about, there were few natives who would pass his house after night. When he became ill at last everybody seemed very sorry; but several of my friends told me in confidence that the whole town hoped he would die; and die he did. . . . During the days of mourning the old men of the village busied themselves in choosing a new king. This is also a secret operation. . . . It happened that Njogoni, was selected. . . . As he (Njogoni) was walking on the shore on the morning of the seventh day he was suddenly set upon by the entire populace, who proceeded to a ceremony, which is preliminary to the crowning. They surrounded him in a dense crowd, and then began to heap upon him every manner of abuse that the worst of mobs could imagine. Some spat in his face; some beat him with their fists; some kicked him; others threw disgusting objects at him; while those unlucky ones who stood on the outside, and could reach the poor fellow only with their voices, assiduously cursed him, his father, his mother, his sisters and brothers, and all his ancestors to the remotest generation. . . . Amid all the noise and struggle, I caught the words which explained all this to me; for every few minutes some fellow, administering an especially severe blow or kick, would shout out, 'You are not our king yet; for a little while we will do what we please with you. By and by we shall have to do your will.' . . . Njogoni bore himself like a man and a prospective king. . . . He kept his temper, and took all the abuse with a smiling face. When it had lasted about half an hour, they took him to the house of the king. Here he was seated, and became again for a little while the victim of his people's curse. Then all became silent; and the elders of the people rose and said solemnly, (the people repeating after them) 'Now we choose you for our king; we engage to listen to you and to obey you'.

(Canetti 1973: 411–12)[5]

B1

The native soldier in full dress wore a ludicrous and almost pathetic air of uneasiness and rigidity. His clothes hung on him as though he were a very angular wooden frame. Whether from consciousness of the figure, which he cut in his red tunic, or from an instinctive fear of the contamination contained in the Christian cloth, the sepoy was no sooner dismissed from parade or relieved from guard than he hastened to doff every shred of the dress provided by Government. Clad in the unprofessional but more congenial costume of a very scanty pair of linen drawers, he might be seen now seated over a pile of rice or a huge bannock, cooked for him by the women of his family; now, performing the copious ablutions, the obligation to which constitutes the single virtue of his national religion; now, submitting the crown of his head to the barber for a periodical shave; now, perchance, discussing with a circle of comrades the probability of the Emperor of the Russians joining with Brigadier Nepolein and the King of Roum in a scheme for destroying the power of the East India Company.

(Trevelyan 1992: 13)

B2

RaisMian, a Zaminder of Bahadurpur once beat up a Nankar peasant Mathura Dhupi with shoes on a flimsy excuse. The peasant meticulously planned and after a few days while the Zamindar was relaxing alone, the Nankar peasant suddenly reached there and beat him up severely with a pair of shoes. Before the perplexed landlord could summon help, the Nankar had fled. His family and belongings were already aboard a train to Assam and he too joined them and fled the land after having taught the landlord a lesson.

(Bhattacharjee 1986: 33)[6]

B3

The Shepherd's family knew where my gifts had come from, but nobody made any reference to my thieving. I found out that the people did know how to use fresh vegetables, which are more important in the Italian diet than meat, and I also began to realise how irrelevant to the poor are the laws made by the rich. Once I had defied them, I became trustworthy.

(Greer 1987: xv)[7]

B4

That was September, 1992. Around our area (village Mandawli – Fazalpur in Delhi) lots of new housing societies were coming up. One fine morning we find that Sarkar (Government) in collusion with housing society people have started digging up the road leading up to the main village market. This was happening at the Engineer's building side. How could they do this? This is two hundred years old road. This news spread like wild fire. Within no time about five hundred people gathered. We stopped the whole digging up operation. In fact, the DDA has sold that side of the road to housing society people. But look at these housing society people. They are also like Sarkar. Why did they buy it? The case is still on. But now the matter is almost settled.

(an active participant, 1994)

C1

In first week of October 1972, he (Comrade Ganeshi) formed a small squad and on 29th November began the landlord annihilation campaign. And revolutionary committee came into being. Comrade Ganeshi was Chairman. Under the leadership of Revolutionary Committee four guerrilla squads were established. And then Chaunri Revolutionary Committee was formed which included the adjoining areas. Under the leadership of Revolutionary Committee of crop grown of four bigha land belonging to the landlord of Ekvari was seized. A broad united front of poor, landless and middle peasants came into existence under the leadership of poor landless peasants.

In the month of March 1973, began large-scale crop seizure campaign. The poor oppressed people started joining the campaign. Knowing of the crop seizure campaign the said landlord of Ekvari thought of selling his land and fleeing from the village. The Revolutionary Committee came to know of this plan immediately and on a piece of two and half yard cloth the Revolutionary Government's directive was written. It read: 'This land has been seized by the Revolutionary Government. Anybody who will step on this land will be awarded death sentence'. On 5th April, around 50 persons raising slogans hoisted this festoon on this piece of land. Seeing this both of landlords who wanted to buy this land and the one who wanted to sell could not dare to enter that village.

(North Bihar Area Committee Report 1978)[8]

C2

In this village there was a girl who was raped, who then committed suicide. We organised a people's court in the village; and the culprit was given a thorough beating, first by the squad members, and then by the women of the village. The villagers also fixed a fine of Rs. 60,000 to be paid to the family of deceased.

(Bhaskar 2002)[9]

C3

'After the movement was launched, peasants stopped fighting each other and refused to become witness in legal cases against fellow tenants. Musclemen got scared of peasants. Women were liberated from bondage. Begar and Nazrana were stopped. Peasants started going to Mosque and their children started attending schools' (Mohammad, Undated: 2–3).[10] 'When peasants came to know of the attack by the Khans (the big landlords) they got together and returned fire in their self-defence. Faiz Mohammad and Faizullah Khan from Khans' side were killed. Peasants gheraoed the Khans and took two commanders of PakhtoonZalmai (young pakhtoon brigade) in their custody'.

(Report 1973: 22)

IV. Foucault, Scott, history and resistance

Discussion in this section, with reference to cases presented in section III, is centred on the philosophical foundations of everyday resistance perspective in the light of the prior discussion, particularly the ideas of Foucault and Scott, as Foucault resists talking of resistance, in Scott we find extensive debate on resistance from a Foucauldian perspective. If Foucault on the one hand displays pessimism for the possibility of resistance to the powers of ideologies and ideological structures – something that the Foucauldians are not comfortable with – Scott, foregrounding the supposed dichotomy between everyday invisible privileging 'local' and 'discontinuous' on the one hand and open-large-scale forms and codes of resistance, dubbed as ideological, linear grand explanatory models, on the other hand, petrifies the fact that they are not mutually exclusive, but there is a dialectical complementarity between the two.

This perspective fails to examine the idea of replacing the orders of control, exploitation and oppression that remains active beneath the surface of everyday resistance and practice. People seem to be content with everyday resistance that does not threaten the system's persistence and continuation, for the assumption is that 'most subordinate classes are, after all, far less interested in changing the large structures of the state of law' (Scott 1990b: xv).

The cases cited in Part III help us develop the argument presented in the preceding section and would be carried forward in this and the subsequent section. Though divergent in types and forms, a thread of ideology, culture and human agency runs through all the instances. There is a well-articulated sense that injustice is being done and is not to be accommodated, accepted and maintained. Instead, it is to be done away with in whatever manner possible, for it is not unavoidable or inevitable. It is not taken as a fait accompli. Forms of resistance may vary according to situations and circumstances, but the idea to do away with the structures and relations of domination is common to all forms. At times subordinate, powerless people seem to accept things as they are. But truly, they don't.

People/subject/public/classes

The first three instances (A1 to A3) relate to king and people/subjects, alternating as subjects and members of what may be called 'public'. This raises the question, when do the subjects become members or assume the characteristics of public? There is an instructive notion regarding the emergence of public in these cases. All three cases refer to simultaneity of obeying and disobeying. The Jataka instances refer to the structuring principle of king-subject relationship, where an efficient king must protect and follow Dharma. Obedience of his subjects to him depends on this. If a king does not successfully emerge as the protector of Dharma, then the subjects act as public and think they have the right to remove him. The argument makes one way of its contradictory nature. For, the obedience and to be a king and to rule are enshrined in Dharma. Then who will decide whether the king is following the principles regarding ruling a kingdom according to Dharma? Reference to people rising against the king is commonly found in the ancient Indian texts. There is much controversy on the question of interpreting the term 'people', whether it refers to priests, nobles or common people (see Ghoshal 1959; Kane 1946). However, active participation of ordinary people or public in the organisation of resistance against the king in the ancient and medieval ages is not uncommon. This can be seen from another angle – the angle of public. In the case of Gaboon, the insults and blows that the king-designate is subjected to before his formal crowning have been interpreted by Canetti (1973: 418) as 'an intimation to what awaits him in the end. As he submits to them so he will submit to his ultimate fate. His death is anticipated'. However, this is/may not simply be a reminder of natural death. This could very well be interpreted as public demonstration of otherwise constantly present hatred against the king. A link between such behind-the-back talks of hatred against the king and its open/public demonstration even under the cover of ritual and the intense anti-colonial and democratic struggles in Africa cannot be ruled out. It is worth remembering the observation that Canetti makes in the given context: 'It is not for a European of the 20th century to regard himself as above savagery. His despots may use more effective means, but their ends often differ in nothing from those of these African Kings' (ibid: 411).

The next four instances (B1 to B4) are the cases of sustained tactics of resistance, occasional spontaneous individual protests and occasional spontaneous collective protests leading to organised collective actions. The native soldier's attitude toward the Christian clothes and his discussion with comrades about the probability of the emperor of the Russians joining with Brigadier Napoleon and the king of Roum to destroy the power of East India Company had much to do with what happened in 1857 in the form of Mutiny also interpreted as the first war of independence. Similarly, the Nankar peasant's beating of Zamindar cannot be placed correctly without taking into account the open Nankar rebellions in the 1920s and 1930s. And the spontaneous collective *gherao* by the villagers of Mandawli-Fazalpur led to the formation of an organisation resulting in settling of the matter. These cases contain ingredients of history.

Foucault, popular justice and people's court

The last three instances (C1 to C3) refer to organised revolutionary politics. They indicate a central role of ideology and of agency in bringing about radical social transformation. The people's court is a case of reconstruction of existing ideological structures. Foucault in his discussion with Maoists on popular justice argues: 'the court is not a form of popular justice but rather its first deformation'. According to him, as far as popular justice is concerned, the court's 'historical function is to ensnare it, to control it and to strangle it by re-inscribing it within the institutions which are typical of a state apparatus'. With reference to setting up of a court in the wake of the Paris Commune, he observes: 'this form was imposed in an authoritarian manner. Can we not see an embryonic, albeit fragile form of the state apparatus here?' He is not against popular justice but seriously questions the 'neutrality' of the court in delivering the popular justice and sees it as 'a way of resisting popular justice'. His emphasis is on formal structure, the old form: 'Judges behind the table' etc. (Foucault 1980a: 1–3). He is, therefore, 'against the people's court . . . designed to synthesise, to replace, all other forms of struggle against the judicial system' and 'this seemed to re-legitimate a form which drags along with it too much of the ideology imposed by the bourgeoisie' and thinks: 'the masses will discover a way of dealing with . . . those who individually or collectively have harmed them . . . without involving the form of the court which . . . is to be avoided' (ibid: 28). Foucault's engagement with the issue raises certain serious questions relating to crime, punishment and neutrality of the court. Even by the logic of his otherwise brilliant analysis of medieval and bourgeois judicial systems, who defines what, for whom and at what point in time remain central questions. The way the crime, criminal and court have been defined and made to function and perceived by the dominant classes has also sought to construct the public perception of crime, criminal and justice. Crime and justice have been defined and projected as a naturally natural universal category. So, how *critical* the 'popular justice' is needs to be critically examined. What *people* accept *popularly* might be something that reinforces their subjugation. Popular could very well be uncritical reinforced by tradition, customs and powerful caste and class constellations. People in people's court are those who do not constitute the dominant economic, social and cultural groups, and *popular* here relates to these groups. So, the notion of popular justice cannot be neutral. His insistence on the neutrality of court, therefore, prevents him from seeing that popular justice is not only popular but popular partisan against the enemies of people. He seems to be suggesting that law per se is coercive. His views on people's court in fact are intrinsically linked with his concepts of discipline and punish, panopticism and prison. In his discussion on Bentham's Panopticon – 'the architectural configuration of the new mechanism of power' – where the observer is unseen, the inmate 'must never know' he is being seen, and yet the inmate 'must be sure' that he may be seen and observed (Foucault 1982: 201). Thus, those subjected to observation and conscious of their visibility 'conspire to produce their own subjugation' (Smart 1985: 111).

What is this complicity of prisoners in their own subjugation? Do the prisoners consider their status as prison inmates as just and legitimate, for it is unavoidable and inevitable thereby to be endured, or do the prisoners really believe that they truly deserve what they have got as they really have committed *crime/sin*? Foucault's understanding of complicity is intrinsically linked with his concept of power and structures of power, which is inevitable, invincible, leaving no scope for any resistance, as discussed previously. Thus, to be prisoner/inmate/subjugated appears to be inevitable, unavoidable. So, the primary purpose of the Discipline, the Panopticism and prison is that there is no question of any (prison) revolt. The panoptic mechanism is extended beyond the boundary of prison – 'throughout the social body' and 'become a generalised function' (Foucault 1982: 207). His reliance on ancient and Middle Ages and the early bourgeois periods to develop his concepts of power and discipline prevented him from looking into the twentieth century and the more contemporary oppressive/revolutionary situations. It is, however, not the reliance on earlier periods but his understanding of history and power that prevented him from seeing aspects of resistance to power and relations of domination even in pre-modern periods. Resistance and disobedience have been an integral part in history in all times, spaces and situations. Gluckman in the context of tribal Africa notes: 'The possibility of rebellion is something that King, subordinate rulers, and subjects have to take into account all the time. Thus we have to see "rebellion" as an ever-present, persistent and repetitive process influencing day-to-day political relations'(Gluckman 1963: 36; see also Gluckman 1968). Silence is not to be taken as complicity, we would argue. Mathura Dhupi (case B2) took the beating *silently*, but he acted when he could.

Mathura Dhupi's act of beating the Zamindar either as part of the Nankar movement of the period or independent of that was a celebration of his non-acceptance of something, which was not part of his real human self. This raises the principal question: can the content of the old form, structure, for instance court, be changed? We argue that the alternative ideology can change the nature and content of the old form. Foucault has pointed out two images of Discipline: one, 'the discipline blockade, the enclosed institution' and the other being 'the discipline mechanism . . . a design of subtle coercion . . .' marking a 'historical transformation' (Foucault 1982: 209). Architecturally or conceptually, people's court as opposed to the court set up by the state represent neither of the two images. It is open, transparent – not open and public display of coercion and oppressive power – but a display of power that demolishes 'power'. It is a celebration of intervening self, breaking the boundaries of 'power' cloaked in bourgeois democratic legalistic conceptions of right and wrong. People's court actually challenges the forcible appropriation by the 'power' structures of the right to define the social practices in their own way. Foucault chooses not to see and uncover the other of the double logic – the essence of people's court, instead confines only to the panoptic vision of the structure – the panopticon and taken for granted automatic transference of its mechanism to people's court. The philosophical logic of transference is such that it is invariably *induced*, and the central question is under what circumstances change takes place or who effects change. In his analysis of panopticon, Foucault suggests the complicity of subjugated in their own subjugation, as if it is inevitable, and ignores the elements of rather invisible parallel practices that can be produced even in panoptical conditions and how they can become constitutive elements of larger open, visible movements. Thus, people's court can emerge as the organised expression of alternative discourse of individual/collective action. In this changed form, it is an expression of people's popular partisan natural justice against its enemies. It symbolises the power of collective being. The question is further discussed in the following section.

Scott's theoretical astigmatism

The arguments bring out sharply the problem of open revolt versus everyday forms of resistance and of agency. James Scott (1990b) ardently advocated the everyday forms of resistance against open, organised revolt and of agency. In his one-sided enthusiasm to valorise and establish the primacy of 'everyday forms of peasant resistance' and attempts to demolish the Marxist theory of peasant revolt, Scott attempted to prove the futility of open, large-scale, organised revolts and revolutions. He is to a great extent right when he says that the 'most subordinate classes throughout most of history have rarely been awarded the luxury of open, organised, political activity'. But the postulate is epistemologically not correct as it denies the possibility of potential, and the arguments marshalled by him to support the statement are not historically tenable. According to Scott, 'such activity was dangerous, if not suicidal' (for peasants). Furthermore, 'most subordinate classes are, after all, far less interested in changing the large structures of the state and law'. Having attributed such views arbitrarily to peasants, Scott comes to the agency of change. According to him, 'formal organised political activity . . . is typically the preserve of the middle class and the intelligentsia; to look for peasant politics in this realm is to look largely in vain'. To him, 'it is also . . . the first step toward concluding that peasantry is a political nullity unless organised and led by outsiders' (ibid: xv).

The whole argument suffers from a serious theoretical and practical astigmatism. It is an attempt to dislocate the oppressed as historical agency of change and to nullify the historical evidences of peasants' and proletariats' self-organisability and 'interest' in 'changing the large structures of the state of law'. Scott ignores definite linkage between the microcosm and macrocosm. More importantly, he utterly fails to see (or purposely, selectively ignores to see) everyday resistance as constitutive elements of open revolt and revolution, to replace the structures of oppression and exploitation. Moreover, open revolts do not always follow a chronological, linear order or evolution and may not also yield desired results. However, from individual to collective, from spontaneous to organised, and from offstage to onstage and vice versa are logical corollaries of objective necessity and mark the process of perfecting the art of becoming a declared rebel.

From his discussion on ideology and action (ibid: 37–41; and chapter 8), it is clear that Scott, in addition to Foucault's concept of power, heavily relies on the continuous utility of moral economy and more importantly on Bourdieu's (Bourdieu 1977) concept of 'euphemisation' of economic power. From the theoretical arguments advanced by Scott and detailed empirical accounts given by him, it is obvious that according to him the peasants are content with their 'off-stage comments and conversations, their proverbs, folk songs and history, legends, jokes, language, ritual and religion' (Scott 1990b: 41). However, the question of how these everyday forms of resistance could be or get converted into organised collective action to replace the existing oppressive structures does not bother him. The questions of subordination by the elite and opposition by the subordinate classes have been seen from the viewpoint of 'elite values' and 'peasant values', and the nature of values is determined by the tradition that upholds the moral economy, so dear to Scott. Manoeuvrings without harming the given social order seem to be the only legitimate and correct forms of resistance. He seems to be following Moore (1978), who associated inevitability with the perceptions of just and the legitimate, arbitrarily attributed to subordinated classes (Scott 1990b: 322–3). Moore, for instance, observed: 'what is or appears to be unavoidable must also somehow be just' (Moore 1978: 64). Justification of this comes on the grounds that if this is not considered so, then for some victims 'suffering' and 'pain might be intolerable' (ibid: 458–9). This is very much consistent with Moore's position on the peasant movement in the Indian subcontinent, where he pointed out the factors of docile character of Indian peasantry and the caste system that prevented the peasant discontent from developing into overt forms of class collective actions (Moore 1968: chapter VI). Scott on the surface seems to disagree with Moore in some respect but actually follows the internal logic of his argument. Bourdieu observed that because 'the dispositions durably inculcated by objective conditions . . . engender aspirations and practices objectively compatible with those objective requirements, the most improbable practices and excluded . . . as unthinkable'. Furthermore, social agents are inclined 'to make a virtue of necessity, that is, to refuse what is any way refused and to love the inevitable' (Bourdieu 1977: 77). Therefore, accommodating to even adverse 'social relations of production' and continuous endeavour to 'redefine them to their advantage' (Scott 1990b: 306) seem to be a fait accompli of the existence of subordinate classes.

Bourdieu used the concept of euphemisation, upon which Scott heavily relies, to analyse 'the reasons for the pre-capitalist economy's great need for symbolic violence'. The system was apparently based on mutual exchange, but Bourdieu accepts that this is 'just one way' of 'getting and keeping a lasting hold over someone . . . created and maintained by exchange'. Thus, in the process, overt violence or symbolic violence are 'censored, euphemised'. Domination must be disguised under the 'veil of enchanted relationship'. Therefore, euphemisation is the 'only way in which relations of domination can be set up, maintained, or restored'. Thus, the oppressed classes are totally unable to tear the 'veil of exchanged relationships' (Bourdieu 1977: 191). No wonder that Scott found this concept convenient to employ in his analysis of contemporary modes of domination. He, however, utterly failed to recognise that everyday forms of resistance decisively contribute to the constitution of organised collective action, over a long or short span of time, to reconstruct and replace the wider structures, which sustain the relations of domination by new just ones. It seems, he carries with him that proverbial Procrustian bed to field and cuts the facts or 'transcripts' meticulously to size to fit the bed. It would be interesting to reproduce an anecdote that Jain (1991) has provided:

> He (Scott) reminds me of a very bright D. Phil student of social anthropology at Oxford – An American – who said, 'if one pushed the informants hard enough, one could find a lot more about' to which my simple response as her supervisor was to ask, 'Does one really *push* informants in the field?'

Gramsci had said: 'Spontaneity is not sufficient for revolutionary struggles; it never leads the working class beyond the limits of the existing bourgeois democracy. The element of consciousness is needed, the ideological element' (1978: 287–8). However, it would be useful to note that having been fully aware of the conservative nature of folklore and popular morality, Gramsci noted that there would also be a 'series of innovations, often creative and progressive, spontaneously determined by the forms and conditions of life in the process of development' (Davidson 1984). The spontaneous, we argue, is not necessarily unorganised. Spontaneous acts were cumulative expressions of accumulated experiences within relations of domination.

Apparent silence, quiescence, servitude, meekness, passivity, submission, acceptance of the position as preordained, etc. are known peasant responses to the feudal system of superordination and subordination. We have argued previously that to accept this phenomenon at its face value is dangerous to any analysis of the internal dynamics of social relations. Beneath the calm surface lies the uneasy lull, always finding a way out to the surface. Zones of silence closely border the zones of violence. The implicit, the inherent violence finds expression in many ways. Class collective actions are the overt, declared, announced and organised expressions of this implicit violence. There are other ways through which this invisible violence finds expression, i.e., get declared. Largely, it remains invisible, dormant and undeclared. Those experiencing the similar situations can only feel it within. It is invisible because it goes unnoticed, not considered of much significance, considered impulsive, foolish, does not get recorded, and largely unstudied. But this invisible disagreement, discontent and those who execute them – the invisible challengers – contribute immensely to the making of history.

Running away from the lord secretly, abusing the master in his absence, beating the lord in privacy in a fit of anger – even with shoes or otherwise – developing a liking for a woman in the landlord's household, or having an intimate relation with the master's woman in total secrecy etc. are in fact acts against the relations of domination and are not only the basic ingredients and constitutive elements or a collective action, but also, and more importantly, collective in themselves as they are the acts, though invisible otherwise, against the collective domination, where one is robbed of even the intrinsic human qualities like to love somebody or live a life with dignity. In other words, situations of inequality of power are not considered 'unavoidable', 'inevitable' and thus 'just' (see Quaiser 1991).

V. Conclusion: ideology, class and praxis

The rapidly changing economic and political global power structure; fast transforming technological, social, cultural and religious landscapes; emergence of 'new middle classes' and disintegration and increasingly weakening of socialist camps and Marxist movements; rising identity politics and movements, which have also prompted to philosophically privilege essentialism indiscriminately, though many of these could be justified are some of the contexts for the emergence of post-Marxism and post-modernism, prompting a radical rethinking on the parallel practices.

The most significant theoretical response of this rethinking has been to question the theoretical-practical validity of the traditional Marxists paradigm of social movements, particularly involving exploited and oppressed subaltern agrarian classes and the working class, and also other labouring poor.

The response has been articulated by foregrounding theoretical formulations such as: the 'ontological centrality of the working class' (Laclau and Mouffe 1985) as obsolescent; firm conviction that there is 'no social location or analytical position from which the truth value of a text or discourse may be judged' (Scott 1990a: xii); 'local, discontinuous, disqualified, illegitimate knowledges' as the only source of authentic knowledge (Foucault 1980a); social agents are inclined 'to make a virtue of necessity, that is, to refuse what is any way refused and to love the inevitable' (Bourdieu 1977: 77); Foucault's argument that power does not originate in either the economy or politics or in the state (see O'Brien 1989; 34–5, 37); Marxism dubbed as totalizing ideology; open-large-scale forms of resistance regarded as ideological, linear grand explanatory models; middle class 'outsider' leadership of peasant movements; structures of power, considered inevitable, leaving no scope for any resistance; etc. These questions relate to serious theoretical formulations relating to history, knowledge, subjugation and social practices and need serious examination. In the following discussion, an attempt is made to address these questions with a focus on ideology, class and parallel practices.

Consciousness is constitutive of the labour process. Ideology, in turn, may also progress with the changing spatio-temporal situation of material and social production. In such a situation, it contributes crucially to the further growth of social consciousness to be manifested in higher forms, resulting in unexpected small, everyday and collective action. However, the objective conditions need not always result in necessary subjective output.

Since the spatio-temporal situation of production and social relations produces multi-class/groups situation, ideology, therefore, refers to that set of ideas through which a given set of people acquire a particular meaning of a given situation and their lives vis-à-vis that situation. Particular meaning here refers to the meaning as the objective requirement, internal logic of the situation and creative human intervention. Hence, with the change in the structure of the situation, ideological perception also has the potential to get transformed. Thus, it is ideology through which base, production relations, ideological forms and social relations acquire new meanings.

In the sphere of cognition of social realities and practice, ideology operates at two levels: firstly, ideology, as Marx pointed out, distorts, misrepresents and conceals social contradictions and produces 'inverted world consciousness' in the interest of the ruling class as a necessity for the exploitative system. A much-quoted and referred statement in *The German Ideology* tells us: 'If in all ideology men and their circumstances appear upside-down as in *camera obscura*, this phenomenon arises just as much from their historical life-process as the inversion of objects on the retina does from their physical life-process' (Marx and Engels 1970: 47). This is, however, a one-sided view of ideology. We could view ideology, from the corpus of Marxist knowledge and epistemology itself, also not only as an all-encompassing process of hegemony and occultation through and against ruling class ideas but as the structuring principle of all ideas in the society. We could view ideology as the product of practical and rational knowledge of the structural conditions realised by those who seek to mitigate the relations of domination. This conception of ideology seeks to unfold and unmask the social contradictions and presents these in their reality and, more importantly, unmasks their true nature with reference to the conflicting interests of various classes operating in the society at a given stage of history. What is most important to note is that in this process the exploited people generally discover the cause of their exploitation and strive for conscious struggle, in varying forms, to change the situation in their own favour by removing contradictions. This comes as a necessity due to internal contradictions of the system, containing conflicting classes and class interests.

Class-consciousness plays a crucial role in the further sharpening of class conflict and parallel practices. Hence, Marx had argued that the exploited people acquire class-consciousness by grasping the contradictory nature of the system, which produces monopoly, misery, oppression, slavery, exploitation, and, at the same time, with this grows revolts of the working class by the very mechanism of the process of capitalist production itself. However, it must be noted that this 'grasping' and 'revolts' may not always necessarily manifest themselves in such overt or visible forms. In other words, everyday forms of resistance not only are not devoid of class-consciousness, but they are constitutive elements of organised collective action.

The reality is that in ideological forms, 'men become conscious of social conflict and fight it out' (Marx 1977: 21). They desire and strive to build alternative structures by reconstructing the existing ones and by creating new ones. Thus, for instance, against the existing court of law there came people's court; bourgeois and feudal notions of justice and democracy acquired new ideological and practical meaning and were transformed into weapons of agitation and struggle. Such a reconstruction of ideological forms would be preceded and followed by a serious of unexpected everyday, small, spontaneous, collective parallel practices. However, it does not always follow a chronological order. It may often be latent, dormant and subtle. These are necessary constitutive elements of any collective action. It is in this sense that base and superstructure acquire new meanings through ideology; for example, the emergence of people's court or literature as expressions of alternative discourse.

Marx and Engels and others have explained sustenance of the domination of ruling-class ideology in terms of control of the means of material production and distribution of ideas. A question which has arisen is that:

> since the working class does not control the means of production and distribution of ideas, it is hard to see how the ideas of the subordinate classes come to be produced at all; the dominant ideology turns out to be the only ideology.
>
> (Benton 1981: 163)

This has been explained by the theory of the unity of opposites. Thus, Lenin had said: 'The proletariat is the child of capitalism' (Lenin 1975: 86). This, however, poses that pertinent big question which the theory of ideology is consistently faced with, i.e., 'if ideology is an instrument to rationalise the ruling class interest then how come the exploited, the oppressed also believed in it?' In classical Marxism, this phenomenon has been characterised as false consciousness, focussing the cheating of the subordinated class by the ruling class. Another way of looking at the phenomenon of false consciousness has been proposed. That is, it 'applies to the ruling class itself, ideology being a socially determined occultation of the actual motives of class behaviour' and that 'it is the inability of even the exploiters to overcome the limits imposed upon their vision of the social being by their class location' (Merquior 1979: 11, 13) (for a further critique of this view, see Quaiser 2016). Merquior's whole interpretation is rooted in Marx's analysis of the petty bourgeoisie in his *The Eighteenth Brumaire of Louis Bonaparte*, as he cites this text in support of his arguments that the petty bourgeoisie did not act on 'self-conscious class interest' (Merquior 1979: 11, 13). But the trouble is that in his interpretation, the petty bourgeoisie comes to represent the ruling class or exploiters as a whole, which is not tenable. How can this be resolved?

Gramsci often quotes Marx's famous passage in which he refers to legal, political, philosophical – 'in short, ideological forms in which man becomes conscious of this conflict and fight it out' to support his interpretation of ideology as the all-encompassing superstructural sphere in which man acquires consciousness of their contradictory social relations. Hence, ideology becomes, according to Gramsci (1989: 377), 'the terrain on which men move, acquire consciousness of their position, struggle etc'. Hence, a parallel ideology of labouring people develops due to the system's own contradictions. Though Gramsci's notion of hegemonisation of consciousness is too rigid to be accepted in its fullness.

Entering the debate on the question, Althusser (1971) developed his theory of the Ideological State Apparatuses (ISAs). Having pointed out the defects in the Marxist theories of state, he elaborates the role of ISAs in the reproduction of labour-power and of social relations in general as the constitution of individuals as subjects and their interpolation into positions in the system of social relations. Each individual becomes constituted as a subject with respect to his or her beliefs and ideas and his or her relationship to the social system through participation in material practices governed by material rituals, which are themselves defined by the material ideological apparatus (ibid: 158). What emerges out of the arguments advanced by Althusser is that of one-sided determinism of ISAs in shaping and controlling an individual's social relations and perceptions. Later, he considered the family to be the most powerful state apparatus – the most '*frightful, appalling, and horrifying of all the ideological State apparatuses*' (Althusser 1994: 104).[11] Theoretically he seems to be somewhat undermining the role of advancing forces of production in generating class-consciousness. Abercrombie, Hill and Turner pointed out that in Marxism, 'the capacity of the ISAs and other socialising institutions to determine class consciousness, especially corporate consciousness, has been greatly exaggerated' (Abercrombie et al. 1983: 66). It is in this context that they have criticised Therborn (1980) for being 'not sufficiently indeterminate'. Therborn, according to them, has overstated the most prominent role of ideology in constructing human subjectivities.

Human subjectivities are not constituted by ideologies in the sense Therborn has perceived, as ideologies themselves are constituted or *caused* by objective historico-structural conditions with classes of opposing persuasions. In other words, ideologies are not *external* to the evolving human consciousness, but they grow together, simultaneously. Hence, there is a *complementarity*. Therefore, there is an emphasis on the reconstruction and reconstitution of the self.

Marx, as opposed to Manheim, located the class interests and class struggles, and thereby class ideologies in economic concreteness. Class ideologies, in fact, 'are inscribed in the relations of production' (Therborn 1980: 61). In contrast to Marx, Bourdieu (Bourdieu 1977) and Foucault (1978) perceived consciousness as being embedded in the practical constitution of everyday life, whereby the subject is constructed by external socio-structural forms and ideology for them is the coercive dimension of society and culture (Comaroff 1985: 5).

Bourdieu explains this approach through his notion of habitus, which is a 'system of durable, transposable dispositions . . . as principles of the generations of and structuring of practices' (Bourdieu 1977: 72). 'The principles embodied in this way are placed beyond the grasp of consciousness, and hence cannot be touched by voluntary, deliberate transformation, cannot even be made explicit' (ibid: 94). If one goes by Bourdieu's argument then, human consciousness seems to be perpetually banished from its natural abode. Contrarily, the possibility of the reconstruction of the world of the oppressed is implicit even in silence. Actors of resistance cited in III of this chapter and in other similar situations were not 'doomed to reproduce their word mindlessly without its contradictions leaving any mark on their awareness' (Comaroff 1985: 5), but instead they attempted to reconstruct the world that they perceived in their own interest. Thus, any study of ideology with reference to parallel practice and class 'is to study ways in which meaning (or signification) serves to sustain relations of domination' and means and ways employed to mitigate the 'systematically asymmetrical power relations' (Thompson 1984: 4; see also Eagleton 2007).

For an understanding of ideology and parallel practice, it is necessary to grasp the dialectical relationships between expected and unexpected practices. Ideology is not merely an epiphenomenal social reality. It is not merely a reflection of material life but is also consciously constructed. It is not simply illusory but also capable of unmasking. It can contain the strong possibility of opening up 'the passage from the realm of necessity to the realm of freedom' (Timpanaro 1980: 101). It can be endowed with demystificatory and liberating power. It is objectively caused and subjectively realised.

These considerations presuppose a critical conception of ideology as opposed to its neutral conception. Hence, ideology is not only a critique of relations of domination but also the celebration of the parallel practices against the relations of domination.

To conclude, the authors of parallel practice refuse to get 'destroyed'. They command the language by giving it a new meaning and refuse that it is the language that should speak and the 'authors' go into oblivion. For they and those in similar situations make the constituency of audiences, readers and practitioners of their own texts. For, after rejecting the given meanings of dominance, they write their own texts of parallel practice.

Notes

1 A very small part of an earlier version of this chapter under the title 'Some Reflections' was published in *Seminar*, November 1994. This is an expanded and revised version. I thank late professor Satish Sabarwal, among others, for offering comments on this version.

2 Louis Althusser, *The Future Lasts a Long Time and The Facts. Tr. Richard Veasey* (Vintage, London, 1994), p. 169.

3 Whatever the debate and differences of fundamental nature, one thing is sure: that the arrival of post-modernism and early subaltern historiography did act as an eye-opener and energised and shook the tired, placid, self-contented, feel-protected social scientists of all hues including Marxists. They were forced to look at things taken for granted afresh and engage in lively debate even from within.

4 Critiquing the writings of Indian members of post-structuralist avant-garde, clearly Foucauldian, on Third World literature, Aijaz Ahmad wrote that in such theories 'to speak of a stable subject position was to chase the chimera of the "myth of origins"'; see Ahmad (2001).

5 This quotation is from Paul Belloni Du Chaillu. 1861. *Explorations and Adventures in Equatorial Africa*. London: John Murray.

6 Bahadurpur is in the Sylhet district, now in Bangladesh. The incident took place in the early 1920s and is narrated by the author, a leader of the Nankar peasant struggle of that period.

7 Reflections on her experience in a coastal village in southern Italy in the year 1965.

8 *North Bihar Area Committee Report*, Communist Party of India (M-L). No print line. 1978.

9 Eturnagaram village in Bhupalapally district in North Telangana, India.

10 Ishaque Mohammad, who was founder and President of Mzdoor Kisan Party of Pakistan, was reflecting on peasant struggles in the NWFP in the late 1960s and early 1970s.

Ishaque Mohammad, *Shumali Hasht Nagar Mein Muzara'aonka Masla* (Karachi, Undated).

11 Emphasis in original.

References and further reading

Abercrombie, N. et al. 1983. 'Determinacy and Indeterminacy in the Theory of Ideology', *New Left Review*, 142, November–December: 55–67.

Ahmad, Aijaz. 2001. 'Literary Theory and "Third World Literature": Some Contexts', in *In Theory: Classes, Nations, Literatures*. New Delhi: Oxford University Press.

Althusser, Louis. 1971. 'Ideology and Ideological State Apparatuses', in *Lenin and Philosophy and Other Essays*. London: New Left Books.

Althusser, Louis. 1994. *The Future Lasts a Long Time and the Facts*. Richard Veasey (trans.). London: Vintage.

Althusser, Louis and Balibar, Etienne. 1970. *Reading Capital*. London: Verso.

Barthes, Roland. 1977. '"The Death of the Author" and "Writers, Intellectuals, Teachers"', in *Image, Music, Text*. London: Fontana Press.

Barthes, Roland. 1979. 'From Work to Text', in Josue Harari (ed.), *Textual Strategies: Perspectives in Post-Structuralist Criticism*. New York: Cornell University Press.

Bauman, Zygmunt. 1992. *Intimations of Postmodernity*. Routledge, London.

Benton, Ted. 1981. *Philosophical Foundations of the Three Sociologies*. London: Routledge & Kegan Paul.

Berger, Peter and Luckmann, Thamas. 1979. *The Social Construction of Reality*. Harmondsworth: Penguin.

Bernstein, Richard J. (ed.). 1985. *Habermas and Modernity*. Cambridge, MA: MIT Press.

Bhaskar. 2002. 'Women's Emancipation in NT: Interview with Mahila Comrades of Eturnagaram', *People' March*, 3(9), September.

Bhattacharjee, Ajoy. 1986. *NankarBidroh*. Dhaka: Muktadhara.

Blackburn, Robin (ed.). 1978. *Ideology in Social Science: Readings in Critical Social Theory*. Glasgow: Fontana/Collins.

Bourdieu, Pierre. 1977. *Outline of a Theory of Practice*. Cambridge: Cambridge University Press.

Bourdieu, Pierre. 1984. *Distinction: A Social Critique of the Judgement of Taste*. London: Routledge & Kegan Paul.

Bourdieu, Pierre and Wacquant, Loïc J.D. 1992. *An Invitation to Reflexive Sociology*. London: Polity Press.

Burke, Peter. 1981. 'The "Discovery" of Popular Culture', in R. Samuel ed. *People's History and Socialist Theory*. London: Routledge & Kegan Paul.

Callinicos, Alex. 1989. *Against Postmodernism: A Marxist Critique*. Cambridge: Polity Press.

Canetti, Elias. 1973. *Crowds and Power*. Carol Stewart (trans.). New York: The Continuum Publishing Corporation.

Comaroff, Jean. 1985. *Body of Power, Spirit of Resistance: The Culture and History of a South African People*. Chicago: University of Chicago Press.

Davidson, Alistair. 1984. 'Gramsci, the Peasantry and Popular Culture', *The Journal of Peasant Studies*, 11(4).

de Certeau, Michel. 1988. *The Practice of Everyday Life*. Steven Rendall (trans.). Berkeley: University of California Press.

Eagleton, Terry. 2007. *Ideology: An Introduction*. London: Verso.

Easton, Susan et al. 1988. *Disorder and Discipline: Popular Culture From 1550 to Present*. London: Temple Smith.

Epstein, Barbara. 1990. 'Rethinking Social Movement Theory', *Socialist Review*, 20(1), January–March.

Foucault, Michel. 1978. *The History of Sexuality*. Vol. I. New York: Vintage Books.

Foucault, Michel. 1980a. *Power/Knowledge: Selected Interviews and Other Writings-1972–1977*. New York: Pantheon Books.

Foucault, Michel. 1980b. *The Order of Things: An Archaeology of Human Sciences*. London: Tavistock Publications.

Foucault, Michel. 1980a. 'On Popular Justice: A Discussion with Maoists', in *Power/Knowledge: Selected Interviews and Other Writings-1972–1977*. New York: Pantheon Books.

Foucault, Michel. 1982. *Discipline and Punish: The Birth of the Prison*. Harmondsworth: Penguin Books.

Ghoshal, Upendra Nath. 1959. *A History of Indian Political Ideas; The Ancient Period and the Period of Transition to the Middle Ages*. New York: Oxford University Press.

Gluckman, Max. 1963. *Order and Rebellion in Tribal Africa*. London and New York: Routledge.

Gluckman, Max. 1968. *Politics, Law and Ritual in Tribal Africa*. New York: The Free Press.

Godelier, Maurice. 1978. 'Structure and Contradiction in Capital', in Robin Blackburn (ed.), *Ideology in Social Science: Readings in Critical Social Theory*, pp. 334–68. Glasgow: Fontana Collins.

Gramsci, Antonio. 1978. *Political Writings: 1921–1926*. New York: International Publishers.

Gramsci, Antonio. 1989. *Selections From the Prison Notebooks*. New York: International Publishers.

Greer, Germaine. 1987. *The Mad Woman's Underclothes*. London: Picador.

Gur-Ze'ev, Ilan (ed.). 2005. *Critical Theory and Critical Pedagogy Today: Toward a New Critical Language in Education*. Haifa: University of Haifa.

Gur-Ze'ev, Ilan. 2010. *The Possibility/Impossibility of a New Critical Language in Education*. Rotterdam: Sense Publishers.

Habermas, Jurgen. 1985. 'Neoconservative Cultural Criticism in the United States and West Germany: An Intellectual Movement in Two Political Cultures', in Richard J. Bernstein (ed.), *Habermas and Modernity*. Cambridge, MA: MIT Press.

Habermas, Jurgen. 1986. *Autonomy and Solidarity: Interviews*. Peter Dews (ed.). London: Verso.

Habermas, Jurgen. 1989. *Knowledge & Human Interests*. Oxford: Polity Press.
Hall, Stuart. 1981. 'Notes on Deconstructing the "Popular"', in R. Samuel (ed.), *People's History and Socialist Theory*. London: Routledge & Kegan Paul.
Hill, Christopher. 1975. *The World Turned Upside Down: Radical Ideas During the English Revolution*. Harmondsworth: Penguin.
Hoggart, Richard. 1954. *The Uses of Literacy*. London: Chatto & Windus.
Hunt, Lynn (ed.). 1989. *The New Cultural History*. London: University of California Press.
Jain, Ravindra Kumar. 1991. 'Dialogue with the Field: Ethnography Yesterday and Today', *The Book Review*, XV(4).
Kane, P.V. 1946. *History of Dharmasastra*. Vol. III. Poona: Bhandarkar Oriental Research Centre.
Laclau, Ernesto and Mouffe, Chantal. 1985. *Hegemony and Socialist Strategy: Towards Democratic Politics*. London: Verso.
Le Goff, Jacques (ed.). 1990. *The Medieval World*. London: Collins & Brown.
Lenin, Vladimir I. 1975. *On Socialist Ideology and Culture*. Moscow: Progress Publishers.
Mao, Tse-Tung. 1975 [1937]. 'On Practice', in *Selected Works of Mao Tse-Tung*. Vol. I. Peking: Foreign Language Press.
Marx, Karl and Engels, Frederich. 1970. *The German Ideology*. Moscow: Progress Publishers.
Marx, Karl. 1977. 'Preface', in *A Contribution to the Critique of Political Economy*. Moscow: Progress Publishers.
McAdam, Douglas. 1988. 'Micro-mobilisation Contexts and Recruitment to Activism', in Bert Klandermans, Hanspeter Kriesi and Sydney G. Tarrow (ed.), *From Structure to Action: Comparing Social Movement Research Across Cultures*. Vol. 1, pp. 125–54. Greenwich, CT: JAI Press.
Merquior, Jose Guilherme. 1979. *The Veil and the Mask: Essays on Culture and Ideology*. London: Routledge & Kegan Paul.
Moore, Barrington, Jr. 1968. *Social Origins of Dictatorship and Democracy: Lord and Peasant in the Making of the Modern World*. Boston: Beacon Press.
Moore, Barrington, Jr. 1978. *Injustice: The Social Bases of Obedience and Revolt*. New York: M. E. Sharp.
Morgan, W. John and Guilherme, Alexandre. 2018. 'Considering the Role of the Teacher: Buber, Freire and Gur-Ze'ev', *Educação & Realidade*, 43(3): 783–798.
Mukerji, Chandra. 1992. 'Popular Culture', in *Encyclopaedia of Sociology*. Vol. 3. New York: Macmillan Publishing Company.
O'Brien, Patricia. 1989. 'Michel Foucault's History of Culture', in Lynn Hunt (ed.), *The New Cultural History*. Berkeley, Los Angeles and London: University of California Press.

Padakusalamanava Jataka. 1957. *The Jataka*. Vol. III. E.B. Cowell (ed.). London: Luzac & Co. Ltd.

Poulantzas, Nicos. 1973. *Political Power and Social Classes*. London: New Left Books.

Poulantzas, Nicos. 1978. *State, Power, Socialism*. London: New Left Books.

Quaiser, Neshat. 1991. *Ideology, Class and Collective Action: Post '47 Peasant Movements in India, Pakistan and Bangladesh*. Unpublished Ph.D. dissertation. Jawaharlal Nehru University, New Delhi.

Quaiser, Neshat. 2016. 'Choreographic Occultation and Petrification of Meaning: Post-colonial Law and Alternative Subject', *Society and Culture in South Asia*, 2(1), January.

Rude, George. 1964. *The Crowd in French Revolution – 1730–1848*. New York: John Wiley.

Saccamkira Jataka. 1895. *The Jataka*. Vol. I. E.B. Cowell (ed.). Cambridge: Cambridge University Press.

Schwartz, Bill. 1982. '"The People" in History: The Communist Party Historian Group', in R. Johnson, et al. (eds.), *Making Histories*. London: Hutchinson.

Scott, James C. 1990a. *Domination and the Arts of Resistance: Hidden Transcripts*. New Haven: Yale University Press.

Scott, James C. 1990b. *Weapons of Weak: Everyday Forms of Peasant Resistance*. New Delhi: Oxford University Press.

Smart, Barry. 1985. *Foucault, Marxism and Critique*. London: Routledge & Kegan Paul.

Smelser, Neil J. 1962. *Theory of Collective Behaviour*. New York: Free Press.

Stedman Jones, Gareth. 1983. *Languages of Class: Studies in English Working Class History 1832-1982*. Cambridge: Cambridge University Press.

Taylor, Paul V. 1993. *The Texts of Paulo Freire*. Buckingham: Open University Press.

Therborn, Goran. 1980. *The Ideology of Power and the Power of Ideology*. London: Verso.

Thompson, E.P. 1988 [1963]. *The Making of the English Working Class*. Harmondsworth: Penguin Books.

Thompson, John B. 1984. *Studies in the Theories of Ideology*. Oxford: Polity Press.

Tilly, Charles. 1981. 'Introduction', in L.A. Tilly and Charles Tilly (eds.), *Class Conflict and Collective Action*. London: Sage Publications.

Timpanaro, Sebastiano. 1980. *On Materialism*. London: Verso.

Touraine, Alain. 1984. *The Voice and the Eye: An Analysis of Social Movement*. New York: Cambridge University Press.

Trevelyan, Sir George Otto. 1992 [1865]. *Cawnpore*. Delhi: Harper Collins Publishers.

Trimberger, Ellen Kay. 1984. 'E. P. Thompson: Understanding the Process of History', in Theda Skocpol (ed.), *Vision and Method in Historical Sociology*. Cambridge: Cambridge University Press.
Williams, Raymond. 1961. *The Long Revolution*. London: Chatto and Windus.
Wood, Ellen Meiksins. 1998. *The Retreat from Class: A New 'True' Socialism*. London and New York: Verso.

Chapter 4

The role of the research subject in Habermas' Theory of Communicative Action

Michael Dusche

Introduction

In his Theory of Communicative Action, Habermas promotes a research methodology that emphasises the role of the research subject as an interlocutor for the researcher rather than as a mere object of knowledge. The researcher cannot pretend to remain neutral vis-à-vis the value claims that arise in her interaction with the subject. Thus, researcher and subject are seen as partners in communicative action with the aim of reaching an understanding of what constitutes valid knowledge. This methodological stance goes a long way in avoiding the reproduction and reinforcement of asymmetrical relations of power between researchers and 'objects' of knowledge.

In marrying his methodological approach with Universalist ethics, however, Habermas privileges certain norms of reason as universal standards for measuring the rationality of knowledge production that can be shown to be Eurocentric (Dusche 2014). In particular, the universal norm of equality inherent in his discourse principle fails the test of universalisation before the backdrop of deeply hierarchical societies like India. This problem affects not only his discourse theory of knowledge and his discourse ethics but also his philosophy of law. Although his *Between Facts and Norms* counts among the most historically and sociologically informed works of its kind and tries to avoid the empirically uninformed 'normativism' of most political and legal theory, Habermas still shares the constitutive blindness of modern philosophies of law regarding the primacy of the state as a sole source of law (Dusche 2015b).

At least since the 1970s, a growing sociological and anthropological literature on legal pluralism has kept emphasising the ideological character of this constricted perspective on law. In reality, human behaviour, not only in the so-called developing world, but also in the so-called developed world, is not exclusively guided by state-administered law. This concerns the facticity side, but even on the side of validity, the case is not as clear-cut as modernist-statist ideology would have it. If we compare the actual working of state-administered law with the actual working of non-state legal practice and measure it by human rights standards favourable to the modernist approach, the outcome would not always support the modern statist conception of law.

Some examples of non-state legal practices presuppose what Habermas calls a 'sacred consensus', i.e., a shared belief in the efficacy of religious practice. However, those holding on to those practices are modern individuals, and their practices are intertwined in intricate ways with the legal practice of the modern Indian state. Sociology has long acknowledged its mistaken belief in the linear progression of modernity, which would entail that every developing nation would have to move along the same line of disenchantment with religion and, as a consequence, erection of a law-enforcing state as a monopolistic secular authority substituting for the sacred consensus on which society was heretofore based. We speak therefore of 'multiple modernities'. Habermas' exclusive reliance on the state as the sole legitimate authority to administer law, however, keeps promoting the Eurocentric view that legitimate law can only be state law. He thereby obfuscates the many problems associated with state-administered law, its distance from the people, its time-consuming emphasis on procedure, its authoritarian elitism, its adversarial character, etc.

In his critique of the welfare state, he mitigates against the forces leading to the colonisation of our lifeworld by the modern state, but he does not apply this to the practice of law itself. Examples of non-state legal practices show that pre-modern ways of conflict resolution can in some respects be more true to Habermas' own intention at maintaining social spaces where 'communication with the aim of reaching understanding' remains possible independently of state interference (Dusche 2016). To allow for the idea of legal pluralism within the framework of Habermas' philosophy of law would therefore be a constructive move to overcome its inherent modernist biases.[1]

The role of the research subject

In his Theory of Communicative Action, Habermas promotes a research methodology that emphasises the role of the research subject as an interlocutor for the researcher rather than as a mere object of knowledge. This methodological stance is motivated by the fact that we cannot understand the knowledge of another human being or her actions embodying that knowledge in a value-neutral fashion (Habermas 1985a: 8). In describing the knowledge or actions of our research subject, we have to take a stance as to whether it conforms to our standards of rationality, both in terms of purpose-rationality and in terms of value-rationality (Habermas 1985a: 6).

The question thereby arises as to whether the researcher may impose her variety of rationality on the research subject, thereby treating it as a mere object of knowledge, or whether understanding the research subject necessarily involves taking her serious as an interlocutor in an open-ended discussion about the very standards of rationality employed in the research methodology to which she is being subjected. In case of a mismatch between different notions of rationality, both researcher and research subject would then have to resort to a meta-theoretical discussion on the rationality standards to be employed in their mutual engagement.

It is Habermas' contention that such meta-theoretical discussions can in principle be resolved by recourse to a 'theory of rationality', or more precisely a 'theory of argumentation', that clarifies the 'formal-pragmatic presuppositions and conditions of explicitly rational behaviour' (Habermas 1985a: 2). This theory of rationality – or argumentation theory – therefore forms the centrepiece of Habermas' epistemology.

Under post-metaphysical conditions, to which Habermas subscribes, rationality cannot be conceived as a metaphysical a priori. Rationality is not to be seen as absolute but as particular to the human species.

> The critique of reason is its own work: this double meaning, first displayed by Immanuel Kant, is due to the radically anti-Platonic insight that there is neither a higher nor a deeper reality to which we could appeal – we who find ourselves already situated in our linguistically structured forms of life.
>
> (Habermas 1996: xli)

Rationality, thus, is not fixed once and for all in a Platonic heaven of ideas, but emerges in a learning process that Habermas attributes to the human species as a historical subject. Humanity as a whole is on the lookout for 'emancipated forms of life about which the participants *themselves* must first reach an understanding' (Habermas 1996: xli, emphasis in original).

This process is presented in the form of a stage theory of human development. Habermas insists that these stages neither prefigure a linear development nor should they entail any historical necessity (Habermas 1985a: 67). He thereby distances himself from any simplistic philosophy-of-history approach (Habermas 1996: xli). Instead, he leaves it open if, how and in which sequential order human societies develop to attain higher degrees of rationality. Habermas, however, does insist on a universal measure to grade degrees of rationality. The status of this Universalism, however, remains ambivalent. If seen as the vanishing-point of a learning process engaging the human species as a whole, it seems to resemble an 'internal' (Dusche 2000) and 'emergent' (Dusche 2013a) Universalism, which is thought of as contingent within the horizon of a human species, counterfactually positioned in an ideal speech situation.

However, if seen as an objective statement of a theory of rationality (or formal-pragmatic theory of argumentation), the graded notion of rationality comes with a claim to an objectivity and necessity which goes beyond any contingent understanding reachable by empirical humanity. Throughout Habermas' work, the grounding of this necessity (empirical, logical?) remains unclear. This of course impacts the asymmetries of power between so-called developing and developed societies, and it raises questions about the position of the researcher within these power relations. I would therefore like to focus on the question to what extent Habermas' methodology is able to avoid the reproduction and reinforcement of asymmetrical relations of power between researchers and their 'objects' of knowledge.

Habermas' threefold concept of rationality

Initially, Habermas distinguishes between cognitive-instrumental (a) versus communicative (b) rationality: 'From one perspective the telos inherent in rationality appears to be *instrumental mastery*, from the other *communicative understanding*' (Habermas 1985a: 11, emphases in the original). Transcendental-logically, the former is secondary to the latter or pragmatically the former is parasitic on the latter. While a greater degree of cognitive-instrumental rationality promises 'a greater independence from limitations imposed by the contingent environment on the self-assertion of subjects acting in a goal-directed manner' (Habermas 1985a: 15), a greater degree of communicative rationality promises a greater independence from limitations imposed by unquestioned background assumptions imposed by a not fully rationalised lifeworld. 'A greater degree of communicative rationality expands . . . the scope for unconstrained coordination of actions and consensual resolution of conflicts' (Habermas 1985a: 15).

Cognitive-instrumental rationality

> The close relation between knowledge and rationality suggests that the rationality of an expression depends on the reliability of the knowledge embodied in it.
>
> (Habermas 1985a: 8, emphasis in the original)

> An expression satisfies the precondition for rationality if and insofar as it embodies fallible knowledge and therewith has a relation to the objective world (that is, a relation to the facts) and is open to objective judgement. . . . [A]ssertions and goal-directed actions are the more rational the better the claim (to propositional truth or to efficiency) that is connected with them can be defended against criticism.
>
> (Habermas 1985a: 9)

Communicative rationality

> [The] concept of communicative rationality carries with it connotations based ultimately on the central experience of the unconstrained, unifying, consensus-bringing force of argumentative speech, in which different participants overcome their merely subjective views and, owing to the mutuality of rationally motivated conviction, assure themselves of both the unity of the objective world and the intersubjectivity of their lifeworld.
>
> (Habermas 1985a: 10)

> An assertion can be called rational only if the speaker satisfies the conditions necessary to achieve the illocutionary goal of

> reaching an understanding about something in the world with at least one other participant in communication.
>
> (Habermas 1985a: 11)

Ethical/expressive reliability

Communicative rationality involves criticisable validity claims in three dimensions: propositional truth, moral/legal rightness and ethical/expressive reliability (or truthfulness, authenticity, sincerity, credibility, trustworthiness etc.):

> In contexts of communicative action, we call someone rational not only if he is able to put forward an assertion and, when criticized, to provide grounds for it by pointing to appropriate evidence, but also if he is following an established norm and is able, when criticized, to justify his action by explicating the given situation in the light of legitimate expectations. We even call someone rational if he makes known a desire or an intention, expresses a feeling or a mood, shares a secret, confesses a deed, etc., and is then able to reassure critics in regard to the revealed experience by drawing practical consequences from it and behaving consistently thereafter.
>
> (Habermas 1985a: 15)

In contrast to the first two dimensions of validity claims, the third validity dimension does not refer to universal conditions (of truth or rightness) but to the general standards of a particular group of people who within their common lifeworld share the same background understanding of what counts as ethically or aesthetically commendable or appealing. Ethical/expressive validity claims therefore refer to particularistic ethical values and aesthetic tastes (Habermas 1985a: 16, 17). 'Anyone who is so privatistic in his attitudes and evaluations that they cannot be explained and rendered plausible by appeal to [shared] standards of evaluation is not behaving rationally' (Habermas 1985a: 17). Moreover, the validity of ethical or expressive claims are

> not such that [they] could be directly redeemed through argumentation as can truth or rightness claims. At most the speaker can show in the consistency of his actions whether he really meant what he said [or did]. The sincerity of expressions [or

> of deeds] cannot be grounded but only shown; insincerity can be revealed by the lack of consistency between an utterance [or deed] and the past or future actions internally connected with it.
>
> (Habermas 1985a: 41)

Rationality here is understood as particularistic. This of course raises the question of how the particular ethical and aesthetic standards of a group can be exceeded by the individual, i.e., how can an individual be innovative and achieve through her action a reform of the very standards of her reference group? Since from the perspective of ethical/expressive reliability, actions do not follow universal rules or norms, but relate to paradigmatic examples by way of analogy, actors always walk a fine line between innovation and idiosyncrasy. Here I would like to carry Habermas' analysis a bit further.

Excursus on ethopoiesis and amichanía

Habermas suggests that it cannot be predicted on the basis of general argumentative rules or moral/legal norms that an action will be deemed appropriate, embarrassing or innovative (Habermas 1985a: 16–17). Its validity can therefore only be determined post factum, but post factum also means: the background understanding of what is considered appropriate may have changed under the impact of the action itself. Thus, action A may be inappropriate with reference to some state X of the shared lifeworld, but its assessment will be carried out after the lifeworld has already changed from state X to state Y under the impact of A in such a way that A is no longer considered inappropriate. A then can be called an innovation or an 'ethopoetic'[2] act. Well-known ethopoets are: Socrates through his practice of *parrhesia*,[3] Mahavir and Jesus through their practice of non-retribution and Gandhi through his practice of *satyagraha*.[4]

The converse example would be an act B which against the backdrop of X would not be considered inappropriate, but after it has impacted the lifeworld to change into state Y would be considered inappropriate with respect to Y. B then can be called an embarrassment or an 'amichanía'. Note that an amichanía is not the same as deviant behaviour. A deviance is known to be one in advance. In other words, the shared value consensus operating unconsciously in the background understanding of the lifeworld need not change from X to Y for deviant behaviour to be considered thus.

Consequently, deviant behaviour does not give rise to embarrassment but to disapproval or scorn.

'Amichániasts' can be found among the cynics of Hellas and among the renouncers of Hindustan. Note that Diogenes, by requesting Alexander to move out of the sun, does not elicit the scorn of the emperor even though his behaviour clearly violates shared standards of etiquette. At most he will have been an embarrassment for Alexander. The wittiness of his behaviour lies in the exposure of the contingency and arbitrariness of these standards. In contrast to the ethopoet, however, the cynic or renouncer is not interested in offering alternative or better standards for society but in renouncing society and social standards altogether (Dumont 1960).

Of course, the ethopoetic way of reforming a lifeworld stands in contrast to Habermas' idea of reform through rationalisation. For him only rational argumentation can bring to the fore any freedom-impeding background assumptions inherent in the shared lifeworld. Then only can the concerned society deliberate on an eventual reform of their tacitly shared standards. For Habermas, 'a communicatively achieved agreement [on new ethical/aesthetic standards] must be based *in the end* on reasons' (Habermas 1985a: 17).

Here, Habermas' account runs into an impasse. Public deliberation would entail a rising to the level of consciousness of the implicit rules that are constitutive for the lifeworld. The lifeworld as conceptualised by Habermas, however, risks falling apart when exposed to the oxidants of public reason. What prevents this disintegration in the face of the 'ever-present risk of disagreement built into the mechanism of reaching understanding' (Habermas 1996: 21) is the support of an unconscious background understanding that is constitutive of our lifeworld. This is required, as Habermas emphasises, for society to maintain a minimum of cohesion, for as soon as these unconscious rules are brought to the level of consciousness, the ferment of public reason will dissolve their taken-for-grantedness, and we are left with the endless task of finding new common ground in communicative interaction (Dusche 2015a). There are thus limits to the degree to which a lifeworld can undergo rationalisation.

For Habermas,

> [t]here is a reflective medium not only for the cognitive-instrumental and moral-practical domains, but for evaluative and expressive manifestations as well. We call a person rational who interprets the nature of his desires and feelings . . . in the

> light of culturally established standards of value, but especially if he can adopt a reflective attitude to the very value standards through which desires and feelings are interpreted.
>
> (Habermas 1985a: 20)

In contrast, through ethopoiesis the lifeworld reforms itself without necessarily adopting a reflective attitude. With his emphasis on rationality, Habermas misses out on the possibility of ethopoetical action. For Habermas,

> [c]ultural values . . . are candidates for interpretations under which a circle of those affected can, if occasion arises, describe and normatively regulate a common interest. The circle of intersubjective recognition that forms around cultural values does not [however] in any way imply a claim that they would meet with general assent within a culture, not to mention universal assent. For this reason arguments that serve to justify standards of value do not satisfy the conditions of discourse.
>
> (Habermas 1985a: 20)

If we grant this but add the possibility of ethopoetical action to Habermas' rational discourse, then the model of interpreting cultural values may not just serve to regulate particular interests, but to set general standards in the common interest of all.

In this respect, *ethopoiesis* works through deeds just as art does through artworks. Just like an artwork 'validated through aesthetic experience can then in turn take the place of an argument and promote the acceptance of precisely those standards according to which it counts as an authentic work' (Habermas 1985a: 20), so can an exemplary deed through ethical experience function like an argument and promote the acceptance of those ethical standards according to which it counts as an authentic act of *parrhesia* or *satyagraha*. These standards, if shared by the members of a society, can then in turn take the place of moral or legal norms without even crossing the threshold of discourse. The question is whether this path of reform is any less rational than the path of discursive rationality. Habermas admits that 'in aesthetic [and ethical] criticism grounds or reasons serve to guide perception and to make the authenticity of a work [or deed] so evident that this aesthetic experience can itself become a *rational* motive for accepting the corresponding standards of value' (Habermas 1985a: 20, emphasis added). What is required again is a shift of emphasis away from an exclusive preference for discourse towards the inclusion of the non-discursive rationality expressed in the *ethopoiesis* of a transforming lifeworld.

End of excursus on ethopoiesis and amichanía

Let us return now to Habermas' theory of rationality or argumentation theory, the centrepiece of Habermas' Theory of Communicative Action. We had raised the question as to the status of the 'necessity' or 'objectivity' that for Habermas is associated with the rationality of an argument and which, according to him, explains the 'compelling' (Habermas 1996: 103), 'rationally motivating' (Habermas 1996: 182) and 'constraint-free' (Habermas 1985a: 22) force of the better argument.[5] This is important for it shall allow us to assess the nature of Habermas' universalism.

According to Habermas, '[t]he logic of argumentation does not refer to deductive connections between semantic units (sentences) as does formal logic, but to non-deductive relations between the pragmatic units (speech acts) of which arguments are composed' (Habermas 1985a: 22). These non-deductive relations are meant to be propositions of an 'informal logic' or of a 'formal pragmatics'. What does Habermas mean by these terms? Sentences of formal logics are 'necessarily' and 'a priori' true because we cannot think otherwise, i.e., they are true in all possible worlds (Lewis 2001). Habermas rejects such a strong claim for his 'universal pragmatics', but he also gives up any 'transcendental-philosophical hopes for an a prioristic reconstruction of the equipment of a non-empirical species subject' (Habermas 1985a: 2).

With his universal pragmatics, Habermas aims at the 'reconstruction of general and unavoidable presuppositions of possible processes of understanding' (Habermas 1979: 21). If we understand universal pragmatics

> in the sense of a reconstruction of general and unavoidable presuppositions of experiences that can lay claim to objectivity, then there certainly remains a difference between reconstructive and empirical-analytic analysis. But the distinction between drawing on a priori knowledge and drawing on a posteriori knowledge [as in the transcendental philosophy of Kant] becomes blurred. On the one hand, the rule consciousness of competent speakers is for them an a priori knowledge;

> on the other hand, the reconstruction of this knowledge calls for inquiries undertaken with empirical speakers – the linguist procures for himself a knowledge a posteriori.
>
> (Habermas 1979: 22)

The universal pragmatic presuppositions of human speech are 'transcendental' and 'necessary' from the perspective of the individual speaker but empirical and contingent from the perspective of the researcher or the species subject. Habermas models his universal pragmatics on Chomsky's linguistics, which he insists is an empirical science in spite of its nomological character. One can therefore say that 'if one can show that specific rules are generally and necessarily presupposed in linguistic communication or are constitutive for specifically human forms of behavior, that one can then definitely speak of a justification of these rules' (Alexy 1990: 161).

For Habermas, the laws governing human communication could be 'objective' in the same way as laws of nature are 'objective', even though they represent the enabling conditions for the creation of 'intersubjective' rules, i.e., norms that are 'objective' only from the perspective of the individual, but subjective from the perspective of the species subject. We are thus turning to the human being as an 'empirico-transcendental doublet' (Foucault 1986: 347) and to the a priori/a posteriori conditions of possibility for its collective reasoning. The question really is whether the rules enabling human communication are really objective in the naturalist sense or whether they do have the status of social facts in the sense of intersubjective rules. In the first case these rules could not be altered even if the whole of the human species agreed to it; in the latter case they would be based on tacit intersubjective agreements that could be different in different societies and subject to revision by those societies themselves or by the human species taken as a whole. As far as I can see there is little evidence for the 'laws' enabling human communication legitimately aspiring for the status of natural laws. They are man-made just as the lower-level intersubjective rules for which they form the preconditions of their coming into existence. Nothing therefore protects these 'laws' from being amended by a discourse-theoretical meta-discourse. What counts as universally rational among humans therefore is subject to communicative understanding among all humans.

As long as universally accepted rules of discourse are not readily available, it is not unreasonable to start with rules that have not been ultimately justified as yet. Alexy (1990: 163–76) provides us with a provisional 'statute book of practical reason' to begin with. He points out that the arguments of informal logic Habermas aims for, although lacking the stringency of formal logics, nevertheless are subject to certain 'objective' constraints such as consistency and non-contradiction. As he goes on to show, rational practical arguments can neither be 'objective' in a realist or intuitionist sense, nor can they be completely subjective (Alexy 1990: 151–4). Both views would run into an infinite regress of justification that needs to be broken off at some point. For this break-off point not to be arbitrary but rationally justified, Alexy invokes an empirical justification, which consists in 'demonstrating that specific rules are in fact binding, and hence are in fact observed, or that individual results producible according to particular rules correspond to our actually prevailing normative convictions' (Alexy 1990: 157). These convictions, of course, are criticisable and amendable and thus do not have the status of natural laws.

Of course, from an absolutist or Archimedean position, this strategy of justification is equivalent to committing a natural fallacy. But from an internal, being-in-the-world kind of perspective and under the presumption that the whole point of a system of norms is not to be 'true', or 'beautiful', but 'right' in the sense of being able to settle conflict in a consensual manner, an already existing consensus that *de facto* helps settling conflicts cannot be dismissed out of hand even from a *de jure* point of view. '[W]hat is at issue is a special case of inference from an is to an ought statement. This inference would . . . only be permissible if one accepted the premise' (Alexy 1990: 158). From an out-of-the-world kind of perspective of course, the existing practice or our actually prevailing convictions may not be 'absolutely' rational, if such a thing exists, but we are not living our lives from an absolutist perspective. If as real-live actors we are all agreed that our practice and our prevailing convictions are rational, then from a practical point of view there is no point of questioning this rationality. And the theoretical (absolutist, Archimedean, out-of-the-world) point of view, although theoretically possible, lacks practical motivation. Thus the question is: do we do moral theory with the attitude of a participant (which is what Habermas would advise) or from an objectifying, 'Scientistic' perspective that cancels out the being human part of the human being whose norms of sociality it investigates. Moreover, there is a limited reasonableness and a heuristic value to a consensual practice due to the fact that its existence demonstrates that it is at all possible. But of course an empirical justification is always only provisional with regard to corrections by new and more comprehensive understandings among all the concerned parties.

What can moral theory do in a situation where the comprehensive consensus among all human beings that would alone justify universally valid principles of rational discourse is necessarily a counterfactual assumption? Doesn't this lead to scepticism? I don't think so. There are possibilities of rational discourse under these circumstances of insecurity. The fact that we cannot attain an ultimate foundation does not mean that everything is equally plausible. Some possibilities are arguably more plausible than others. The reference point for such considerations is Habermas' paradigm of the 'impartial standpoint', which points to the imaginary 'assent of a universal audience' (Habermas 1985a: 35). If we imagine a counterfactual discourse taking place between two groups of people, one dominating the other, then with high plausibility (although not with logical necessity) it can be excluded that the dominated group will agree to its enslavement or annihilation. This would defeat the supposition of an agreement amongst the imaginary universal audience of which the dominated group is a constituent part. Such plausibilistic arguments, although far from carrying any logical stringency, are still valid arguments in the absence of any algorithm generating ultimately grounded laws of rational discourse. In the absence of any norm-generating algorithm, such arguments guard against radical scepticism and against normative relativism. *Ex negativo*, they can even support an argument for something like fundamental rights and liberties (Dusche 2009).

Ex positivo, there is also the option of looking at 'world culture' for the demonstration of a shared preunderstanding among participants of the 'world polity' (Meyer 2005, 2006). What Habermas notes about cultural values holds also true for world culture:

> the type of validity claim attached to cultural values does not transcend local boundaries in the same way as truth and rightness claims. Cultural values do not count as universal; they are, as the name indicates, located within the horizon of the lifeworld of a specific group or culture. And values can be made plausible only in the context of a particular form of life. Thus the critique of value standards presupposes a shared preunderstanding among participants in the argument, a preunderstanding

> that is not at their disposal but constitutes and at the same time circumscribes the domain of the thematized validity claims.
> (Habermas 1985a: 42)

One only has to extend the boundaries of the local until they become coextensive with the boundaries of the global. It is the lifetime achievement of John W. Meyer and his collaborators to have demonstrated empirically the existence of such a shared preunderstanding among participants in the world polity. This world polity, of course, is complex, layered and nested, comprising different and sometimes conflicting lifeworlds beneath the smooth surface of world culture. This pluralism of values and standards is hard to grasp from the conventional perspective of Western modernism, which can conceive of ethical, moral and legal culture only from the perspective of a state that claims a monopoly over the legitimate sources of law (Dusche 2015b).

After gaining clarity about the status of objectivity associated with Habermas' notion of rationality, we shall now turn back to our question regarding the reproduction and reinforcement of asymmetrical relations of power between researchers and research subjects. Let us review the yield of our investigation. We have discussed three types of objectivity in association with Habermas' theory of rationality: (1) transcendental objectivity, (2) natural-scientific objectivity and (3) intersubjective objectivity. Against the first, Habermas argues convincingly (1979); however, he remains ambivalent regarding (2) and (3). We have argued that only the third option is tenable. As will become apparent, however, the ambiguity encumbers Habermas' stance regarding power relations between researcher and research subject.

In his chapter on 'Some Characteristics of the Mythical and the Modern Ways of Understanding the World', Habermas (1985a: 43–74) works with a tripartite division of *mythical*, *religious-metaphysical* and *modern* worldviews. He hierarchises these paradigms on a scale of higher or lower degree of rationalisation, with the mythical representing the least rationalised and the modern representing the most rationalised lifeform. Moreover, Habermas' notion of rationality is not value-neutral, but he attaches a higher value to those forms of life that are more conducive for a rational conduct of life. Thus, for his rating of different worldviews, Habermas is interested in the 'conditions that the structures of action-orienting worldviews must satisfy if a rational conduct of life is to be possible for those who share such a worldview' (Habermas 1985a: 43–4). He grants though that modernity does not necessarily possess the highest degree of rationality. He does not suppose that 'the rationality structures specific to the modern understanding of the world are generally valid', and he is prepared instead

> to consider them in an historical perspective. . . . Mythical worldviews are far from making possible rational orientations of action in our [modern] sense. With respect to the conditions for a rational conduct of life in this sense, they present an antithesis to the modern understanding of the world. Thus the heretofore unthematized presuppositions of modern thought should become visible in the mirror of mythical thinking.
>
> (Habermas 1985a: 44)

In this historical effort to bring to light the unthematised presuppositions of the modern worldview, Habermas commits an Orientalist fallacy. By reading the infant stages of the Western mind into the minds of the so-called savages, he parallels the historical development of the Western mind with the ontogenetic development of the human child. He takes the development of the Western mind as representative of the phylogenetic development of the whole human species: '"savage thought" can be compared with ontogenetic stages of cognitive development' (Habermas 1985a: 46). This allusion to Ernst Haeckel's phrase 'ontogeny recapitulates phylogeny' – today known as the *biogenetic law*, which is largely discredited in today's biology, not to speak of human psychology – is especially problematic when comparing different cultures. The fallacy consists in not taking the 'other' serious as a fully fledged, adult human being and in taking the Western experience as the universal standard for all humanity.

Infantilising the 'other' is a well-known trope from Orientalist discourse, a problematic of which Habermas apparently is unaware. The reading of the 'savage' as childlike was used by the European powers to internally legitimise their domination over the South and the East and to make it look like a philanthropic enterprise, i.e., the 'civilising mission' of the white man. Correspondingly, there developed a homology between Western ideas of childhood and the state of being colonised (Nandy 1983: 11):

> [Ashis] Nandy stresses the 'isomorphism of oppression' taking place within the West – against women, children and men

> who did not conform to the stereotype of the aggressive and masculine adult white male . . . and between the West and the East. Naturally, the West would not spare the East where it did not spare itself. This apparent mutuality enforced, however, in a situation of dominance elucidates why the same situation could appear as if between equals (for the West) and as between master and slave (for the East). The fact of domination was less transparent for the coloniser than for the colonised. Consequently, the West could believe in the universality of its ideas of masculinity, adulthood and responsibility [since the East was not in a position to speak back].
>
> (Dusche 2010: 114)

This has changed since the establishment of post-colonial theory in Western universities. In the binary opposition *childlike* versus *adult*, the West is portrayed as having outgrown its adolescent stages, leaving no trace of the previous ones.

> The caesurae between the mythical, religious-metaphysical, and modern modes of thought [according to Habermas] are characterized by changes in the system of basic concepts. With the transition to a new stage the interpretations of the superseded stage are, no matter what their content, *categorically devalued*. It is not this or that reason, but the *kind* of reason, which is no longer convincing. A devaluation of the explanatory and justificatory potentials of entire traditions took place in the great civilizations with the dissolution of mythological-narrative figures of thought, in the modern age with the dissolution of religious, cosmological, and metaphysical figures of thought. These devaluative shifts appear to be connected with socioevolutionary transitions to new levels of learning.
>
> (Habermas 1985a: 68, emphases in the original)

Here Habermas correctly describes an experience that is typical of the whole Western experience of modernity, but it is a decidedly Western experience (Dusche 2015b). This experience is definitely not shared by differently modern post-colonial subjects around the globe. For South Asia, one can say that mythical and religious-metaphysical worldviews coexist within the modern worldview and in the same minds. The scientist or engineer who holds on to magical and metaphysical beliefs is almost a commonplace. In India,

> it seems to be the case that students study science for their exams but use different belief systems for 'everyday life'. . . . Moreover, the tendency to bifurcate the domain in which one practices science and the other in which practices contradictory to science are prevalent is not limited to students alone. In India, this is an integral part of scientific institutions.
>
> (Sarukkai 2014: 1693)

As far as India is concerned, the idea of modernity as necessarily unfolding in radically disjunctive stages turns out to be a myth. This stage-theory, however, is so much a part of the narrative that constitutes modernity that one might become suspicious whether it holds true even for the West. Since the narrative structure of modernity ideologically prescribes such radical devaluations in every step of the civilisational learning process, it is very likely that the structure of this narrative makes us blind to the remnants of magical and mythical thinking even in the modern Western mind. In fact, the very idea of progress that is inherent in the idea of modernity since the Quarrel of the Ancients and the Moderns has a magical quality to it the way it plays out as a self-fulfilling prophesy ever since the mid-seventeenth century. Religiously invoked on every occasion when something bad is hoped to change for the better – since with progress everything can only turn to the better – the unshakable belief in progress turns out to be a good example for ritual efficacy not only in modern times but as a self-mystification constitutive of the very modernity that it performatively contradicts.[6]

With Godelier, Habermas points out how 'the primitive mind' (Godelier 1977) levels 'the different domains of reality: nature and culture' (Habermas 1985a: 47). The same can be said about the modern mind. The enlightenment mystification of nature has tended to

> obscure from view a possible domain of collective . . . agency simply by declaring something as . . . natural and unchanging. . . . [Cultural rules] were represented by scholars as if they were laws of nature. Familiar terms such as 'natural law', the 'state of nature' (from where to derive the legal-ethical principles that govern society) and 'natural rights' come to mind.
>
> (Dusche 2011: 143)

'This . . . may have been a necessary myth for modern man to believe in, in order for modernity to unfold. It is a myth nevertheless'

(Dusche 2010: 67). A modern mind enlightened about its own mystifications would have to admit that in spite of its tendency to radically devalue its precursors, the rupture between the pre-modern and the modern are not as sharp as the modern mind would like to believe. It would like to believe that magical or mythical mind-sets 'do not allow action orientations that might be called rational by the implicit standards of today' (Habermas 1985a: 48). This may be true for validity claims connected with propositional truth and purposeful action. In the domain of legal, moral and ethical rationality, however, things are not so clear-cut (Dusche 2015b).

Habermas describes the processes of differentiation associated with modernisation as almost inevitable. Moreover, he is convinced not only of the material superiority associated with modern civilisation but also of its higher moral rationality. And yet he calls for the unity of reason in all three dimensions (scientific/technical, moral/legal, ethical/aesthetical) and rejects positivist and utilitarian attempts to reduce rationality only to the instrumental rationality of mastery of nature and purposive action (Habermas 1971). The opposition unity/disunity associated with primordial versus modern humanity is an old trope which dates at least from the time of the German Romantics (Dusche 2013b: 36). Like the Romanics, modern anthropology attributes this unity to mythical lifeforms. Habermas agrees that

> [m]yths do not permit a clear, basic, conceptual differentiation between things and persons, between objects that can be manipulated and agents – subjects capable of speaking and acting to whom we attribute linguistic utterances. . . . Moral failure is conceptually interwoven with physical failure, as is evil with the harmful, and good with the healthy and the advantageous.
> (Habermas 1985a: 48)

The Indian use of the term 'auspicious' almost sums it up. It means morally and physically beneficial, good, salubrious, all at the same time and without distinction. But then why does he devalue the original unity of the mythical mindset and valorise the modern emphasis on rationality?

> The magical relation between names and designated objects, the concretistic relation between the meaning of expressions and the states-of-affairs represented give evidence of systematic confusion between *internal connections of meaning* and

> *external connections of objects.* . . . Mythical interpretation of the world and magical control of the world can intermesh smoothly. . . . Thus a linguistically constituted worldview can be identified with the world order itself to such an extent that it cannot be perceived as an interpretation of the world that is subject to error and open to criticism. In this respect the confusion of nature and culture takes on the significance of a reification of worldview.
>
> (Habermas 1985a: 49, emphases in the original

As we have seen, even the modern worldview is not immune against such reifications. Just as little as mythical worldviews are 'understood by members as interpretive systems that are attached to cultural traditions' (Habermas 1985a: 52), similarly, the modern worldview is not understood by members as an interpretive system attached to a contingent cultural tradition. Its claim to universality is just as much constitutive for the modern worldview as is its contingency as a particularly European experience. Instead of admitting that modernity's rationality is fundamentally flawed in that it creates value-free spaces for morally unaccountable knowledge and action and thereby deliberately shuns the unity of reason that Habermas strives for, he holds on to both, modernity's emphasis on rationality and the lost unity of the true, the right and the beautiful. Maybe we can't have both. And who wants to live in a disenchantingly rationalised lifeworld anyway. Thus, either we give up the emphasis on rationality and take modernity as what it is, neither exclusively good nor solely bad, or we let go of the idea of unity and brace modernity's fractured lifeworld, embracing also the corresponding opportunity of morally neutral action.

Habermas guards against the 'error of simply imposing the supposedly universal rationality standards of one's own culture upon alien cultures' (Habermas 1985a: 55) by moving from a substantial to a formal concept of rationality:

> The context-dependence of the criteria by which the members of different cultures at different times judge differently the validity of expressions does not, however, mean that the ideas of truth, of normative rightness, of sincerity, and of authenticity that underlie . . . the choice of criteria [of rationality] are context-dependent in the same degree.
>
> (Habermas 1985a: 55)

As set out previously, my favoured interpretation of this formal concept of rationality points to the imaginary intersubjective understanding of a universal audience. Habermas would therefore have to take his research subject – even the person with the mythical mindset – seriously as someone who cannot be treated as if she does not matter because of her apparent irrationality. From this follows a certain principle of charity: 'We make maximum sense of the words and thoughts of others when we interpret in a way that optimises agreement' (Davidson 1984: 197), which Habermas is willing to elevate to the level of a methodological maxim: 'For the interpreter it is not a question of hermeneutic charity but a methodological precept that he proceed from the presumptive rationality of the questionable expression' (Habermas 1985a: 55). However, he also makes it clear that he is not willing to let go of the possibility of coming to the conclusion that the expression in question turns out to be irrational,[7] but irrational by what standard? Does Habermas assume a culture-independent point of view from which to judge this question? It seems so. To a certain extent he goes along with Peter Winch (1970), who understands cultures

> as linguistically articulated worldviews and correspondingly structured forms of life. Worldviews store the cultural knowledge with the help of which a language community interprets the world. Each culture establishes in its language a relation to reality. To this extent, 'real' and 'unreal,' 'true' and 'untrue' are indeed concepts that are inherent in all languages and not ones that can, say, be present in this language and absent in that. But each culture draws this categorical distinction *within* its own language system.
>
> (Habermas 1985a: 56–7, emphasis in the original)

Habermas goes along with Winch so far as to agree that worldviews taken as a whole can neither be true nor false. They make possible utterances that admit of truth.

> To this extent they have a relation, albeit indirect, to truth . . . worldviews are indeed removed from the dimension in which a judgment of them according to criteria of truth makes sense. . . . But this [for Habermas] does not mean that *the idea of truth might itself* be understood in a particularistic way. Whatever language system we choose, we always start intuitively from the presupposition that *truth is a universal validity* claim. If a

> statement is true, it merits universal assent, *no matter in which language* it is formulated.
>
> (Habermas 1985a: 58, emphases added)

By postulating the identity of propositions across languages, Habermas supposes an identity of semantic content independently of any particular (meta-) language that has been shown to be problematic (Dusche 2002). According to Quine's indeterminacy thesis,

> rival systems of [translation] can conform to all speech dispositions within each of the languages concerned and yet dictate, in countless cases, utterly disparate translations; not mere mutual paraphrases, but translations each of which would be excluded by the other system of translation. Two such translations might even be patently contrary in truth value.
>
> (Quine 1960: 66–7)

Moreover, '[w]e know from Tarski (1935) that we cannot talk about truth in the object language' (Dusche 1995: 307). Any meta-language capable of expressing the semantics of some object language must have expressive power exceeding that of the object language. Since due to Quine's indeterminacy of translation, plural but incommensurable translations from object to meta-language are possible, we cannot assume the identity of the semantic content of statements across the range of possible meta-languages. According to Tarski (1944: 248), we cannot use 'semantically closed' languages which contain their own semantic terms without running into paradoxes. 'This restriction would of course be unacceptable for those who . . . believe that there is only one "genuine" language (or, at least, that all "genuine" languages are mutually translatable)' (Tarski 1944: 249). Habermas seems to suggest just that when he speaks of truth as 'universal assent, no matter in which language' (Habermas 1985a: 58). Which meta-language we chose is however again subject to the understanding of an imaginary universal audience. It involves a decision that cannot be predicted logically due to Quine's indeterminacy but can only be motivated by arguments of plausibility.

The Archimedean footrest Habermas seems to be having in mind with his notion of truth in no matter what language therefore remains elusive, but again this does not mean that there cannot be a rational argument about the cognitive adequacy or the degree to which a worldview hinders or promotes learning processes. These would be arguments of plausibility though and not logical arguments, however informally they may be conceived. It is plausible to assume that a universal audience would agree that a lifeform is not rational when the community inhabiting this lifeform perishes because of a constitutive inability to get past its delusions. This may be true of modern lifeforms as well as pre-modern ones. If, for example, a community fails to recognise the natural causes and practical consequences of a continued draught and just keeps sacrificing more and more maidens and lads to Chaahk (the rain god of the Mayas), it is plausible to attribute a lesser learning ability to it than one that adapts its agricultural techniques to more arid climatic conditions or migrates to greener pastures. Likewise, a lifeform that keeps producing superfluous consumer products to keep an economic system running whose externalised costs include the exploitation of humans and nature and the deterioration of the planet could be called irrational because of its mythical belief in infinite progress and its inability to prevent the destruction of its own livelihood. Thus, Habermas is right that the 'dimension of "closed" *versus* "open" [to learning] seems to provide a *context-independent standard for the rationality of worldviews*' (Habermas 1985a: 62, emphases in the original), but only if we keep in mind that it is not a question of pre-modern *versus* modern rationality. Habermas, in attributing a learning curve to the human species going from primordial to modern, seems fully under the spell of the self-mystification constitutive of modernity. This mystification prevents us from thinking other than positively of modernity. In fact, however, it should be an open empirical question whether modern lifeforms constitute an improvement as compared with pre-modern ways of life. After all, with the increased potential of mastering nature and ruling human beings and thereby improving the human condition, the potential of doing harm to nature and fellow humans increases as well, and we have already seen both of these potentials being realised in stupendous ways.

Modernity taken as a discourse of self-mystification, however, is incapable of perceiving pre-modern lifeforms as prima facie equally valuable. It systematically devalues them, and so does Habermas when he follows Piaget's stage model of individual learning, transforming it into a theory of species learning.

> To the degree that the lifeworld of a social group is interpreted through a mythical worldview, the burden of interpretation is

> removed from the individual member, as well as the chance for him to bring about an agreement open to criticism.
>
> (Habermas 1985a: 71)

In pre-modern lifeforms, individuals have no less of a task than do modern individuals in interpreting their shared cultural background understanding and applying it to specific circumstances. After all, the shared background knowledge that constitutes their lifeworld is nowhere laid down in writing. It is instantiated in the individual, but it is instantiated differently in different individuals. There is no common written code to which individuals can refer when they disagree about the content of what they believe they share. It requires a large degree of creativity – and it affords a large amount of leg-space for communicative action with the aim of reaching common interpretations – for individuals in traditional lifeforms to reach an understanding about the actual content of their cultural background assumptions in the specific situation where they find themselves. This freedom is lost in modern lifeforms because erstwhile vague ideas of values have been fixed once and for all in the cold print of statute books, legal and administrative codes and best-practice manuals. It is very doubtful, therefore, whether '[t]he more the world-view that furnishes the cultural stock of knowledge is decentred, the less the need for understanding is covered *in advance* by an interpreted lifeworld immune from critique' (Habermas 1985a: 70, emphasis in the original). In a way, traditional lifeforms are more open than modern ones, and where modern ones have to be reopened by critique and through large-scale social and political processes, traditional forms of authority can more easily be bypassed and circumvented by creative acts of interpretation on the part of small groups of individuals who find themselves face to face in particular situations far removed from authority. Pre-modern lifeforms may also be far less steeped in 'dogmatism' than depicted by Habermas (1985a: 71), since their 'dogmas' are rarely cut in stone and therefore open to multifarious interpretations.

There is a strange contradiction in Habermas between his eulogy of the lifeworld and his simultaneous valorisation of the ferment of reason that threatens to divulge the inarticulate preunderstanding upon which rests the background knowledge of any lifeworld. On the one hand, he is aware of the risk involved in drawing the unconscious background understanding of the lifeworld into the light of 'risky (because rationally motivated)' (Habermas 1985a: 70) criticism, and he seeks to protect the lifeworld from the rationalising forces of modern state administrations and corporate market players. Habermas' thesis is that in the course of modernisation, the social sub-systems of market and state, by way of their steering media money and power, develop '*irresistible inner dynamics* that *bring about* . . . the colonization of the lifeworld' (1985b: 331; emphases in the original). On the other hand, he valorises the emancipatory potential of 'rational action orientation' (Habermas 1985a: 70). Already in the 1980s, Habermas was aware that in modern societies spaces become increasingly rare where groups of individuals can autonomously (i.e., outside the institutional frameworks of administration and corporate sector) establish common ways by which to live together. Meanwhile, the colonisation of the lifeworld by the forces of power and money, government and business corporations, has far advanced into the most intimate spheres of life, which leads to a complete absorption of the individual into the state and market. Increasingly, the modern individual lacks the inner distance from these forces to be able to engage in autonomous acts of seeking understanding with fellow human beings outside the purview of her state or the company she works for. The modern individual tends to be so completely identified with her state and company that she cannot view fellow human being as individuals outside their respective webs of allegiance. So much so, in fact, that the modern individual remains little more than an agent of her state and her company (in case she is unemployed in a society where belonging is regulated via work, she risks social death and is emphatically no partner with whom to autonomously reach common understandings on ways of living together). Not so in societies where traditional lifeforms have not completely been overwhelmed by the colonising forces of power and money. Here, for better or worse, traditional beliefs and group identifications stand in the way of a complete identification with the state or with the company they work for. These individuals are thus much more autonomous in their interaction and in their capacity to communicatively reach understandings regarding the shared interpretations of the values and ideas that form their lifeworld background.

In concluding this section, we may say that we can neither say that one lifeform is per se better than another nor that they are all equally valid. Lifeforms can and should be evaluated, but the standards for such evaluation are again subject to critique from the impartial standpoint which points to the imaginary assent of a universal audience. The standard embraced by the universal audience is arguable not only in rationality, but many more things against which the standard of rationality of a lifeform would need to be balanced. If we take a plausible notion of human dignity as a yardstick, then lifeforms enthralled in mythical worldviews do not necessarily rank lower than modern lifeforms. Besides, as it turned out, modern and pre-modern paradigms do not necessarily conflict with each other. The same person may be simultaneously partaking in a mythical, a religious-metaphysical and a modern worldview.

Habermas mourns 'the one-sidedly cognitive-instrumental self-understanding of modern rationality [and the illusion] that the differentiation of an objective world means totally excluding the social and the subjective worlds from the domains of rationally motivated agreement' (Habermas 1985a: 73). This comes as no surprise, however, if the driving forces of modernity are the modern state and the modern capitalist economy. As both have an interest in controlling and exploiting nature, so they have an interest in managing and controlling the intersubjective social world through the control of the subjective world that gives rise to it. The participation of the public in this process, largely absent in its initial phases (eighteenth to nineteenth centuries), has later been added on only as a smart way of co-opting oppositional forces by making them part of the more and more 'democratic' process. All along, however, this process has led to the total eclipse of an autonomous lifeworld – autonomous not in the sense of a conscious mechanism of (democratic) self-rule but in the sense of being left undisturbed by extraneous forces. This arguably is the meaning that Gandhi gave to self-rule ('svaraj', Dusche 2015a). It is a position 'neither pre-modern nor anti-modern but only non-modern' (Nandy 1983: 74). That such a position is untenable in a fully modern society of the West is evident. To believe that modernity is inevitably going to have its course in the non-West would, however, be tantamount to be taken in by modernity's own self-mystification as progress or calamity, depending on your perspective.

Notes

1 Non-State Legal Practices in India was the subject of an international conference that I organised at the Manipal Centre for Philosophy and Humanities from 5–7 December 2015. The conference volume is still forthcoming.

2 I am borrowing this term from Foucault's late work: '*Ethopoiein* means making *ēthos*, producing *ēthos*, changing, transforming *ēthos*, the *individual's* way of being' (Foucault 2005: 237; emphases in the original).
3 Another notion that I am borrowing from Foucault: 'In parrhesia, the speaker uses his freedom and chooses frankness instead of persuasion, truth instead of falsehood or silence, the risk of death instead of life and security, criticism instead of flattery, and moral duty instead of self-interest and moral apathy' (Foucault 1999). As an example, Foucault cites Socrates' refusal to comply with the unjust orders of the state of Athens in three instances. 'In the first case he contents himself with voting against the majority. In the other case, when he is ordered to arrest someone, he simply returns home. He returns home, openly and publicly, no more and no less . . . this philosophical parrēsia does not necessarily or exclusively go through logos, through the great ritual of language in which one addresses the group or even an individual. After all, parrēsia may appear in the things themselves, it may appear in ways of doing things, it may appear in ways of being' (Foucault 2010: 320). In one instance, the oligarchs ask Socrates to take part in an illegal judicial action and Socrates refuses. This is a parrhesiastic act even though Socrates has not spoken out but only acted. He has shown his commitment to the 'truth' not *logo* but *ergo*, as Foucault (2010: 319) puts it.
4 For an explanation of how Gandhi's method of *satyagraha* operates not by appealing to universal rules or norms but through the particular example, see Bilgrami (2014: 101–21) and Rudolph and Rudolph (2003).
5 'De[r] eigentümlich[e] zwanglos[e] Zwang des besseren Arguments' (Habermas 1981: 47).
6 Just to take a random example: the narrative structure of modernity in which we are caught suggests that in the US, progress has been made in racial affairs since the civil rights movement leadership of Martin Luther King Jr. Traister (2015) argues convincingly that this narrative may delude us and blind us to the fact that racism has actually never abated in the US.
7 'in order, if necessary, to assure himself step by step of its irrationality' (Habermas 1985a: 55).

References

Alexy, Robert. 1990. 'A Theory of Practical Discourse', in Seyla Benhabib and Fred Dallmayr (eds.), *The Communicative Ethics Controversy*, pp. 151–90. Cambridge, MA: MIT Press.

Bilgrami, Akeel. 2014. *Secularism, Identity and Enchantment*. New Delhi: Permanent Black.

Davidson, Donald. 1984. 'On the Very Idea of a Conceptual Scheme', in *Inquiries into Truth and Interpretation*. Oxford: Clarendon Press.

Dumont, Louis. 1960. 'World Renunciation in Indian Religions', *Contributions to Indian Sociology*, 4: 33–62.

Dusche, Michael. 1995. 'Interpreted Logical Forms as Objects of the Attitudes', *Journal of Logic, Language, and Information*, 4(4): 301–15.
Dusche, Michael. 2000. *Der Philosoph als Mediator. Anwendungsbedingungen globaler Gerechtigkeit*. Vienna: Passagen Verlag.
Dusche, Michael. 2002. 'Experts or Mediators? Philosophers in the Public Sphere', *Ethical Perspectives*, 9(1): 21–30.
Dusche, Michael. 2009. 'Nationalism, the Measles of Mankind', in Arie Kacowicz (ed.), *In the Spirit of Einstein: Germans and Israelis on Ethics and International Order*, pp. 21–30. Jerusalem: Leonard Davis Institute for International Relations.
Dusche, Michael. 2011. 'The Ethics of Ethical Expertise in Science, Medicine and Healthcare Policies', *Indian Journal of Medical Ethics*, 8(3): 142–5.
Dusche, Michael. 2013a. 'The Role of Muslim Identity in Akeel Bilgrami's Critique of Political Liberalism and an Emergentic Approach to Global Justice', *International Journal on Humanistic Ideology*, 6(1): 67–84.
Dusche, Michael. 2013b. 'Friedrich Schlegel's Writings on India: Re-Imagining Germany as Europe's True Oriental Self', in James Hodkinson et al. (eds.), *Deploying Orientalism in Culture and History: From Germany to Central and Eastern Europe*, pp. 31–54. Rochester, NY: Camden.
Dusche, Michael. 2014. 'Women's Rights in India: Hierarchical Ethics vs. Egalitarian Morality', *Südasienchronik/South Asia Chronicle*, 4: 228–53.
Dusche, Michael. 2015a. 'Whose Culture, Whose Self', Paper presented at the seminar on *Rethinking Svaraj*, 15–17 January 2015, Manipal Centre for Philosophy and Humanities, Manipal University, Karnataka, India (unpublished ms).
Dusche, Michael. 2015b. 'State Versus Non-State Law', UGC e-pathshala Syllabus *The Philosophy of Law* (http://epgp.inflibnet.ac.in/ahl.php?csrno=27#), Paper 16 (Philosophy of Law), Module 20 (State v non-state law).
Dusche, Michael. 2016. 'Būtas and Daivas as Justices in Tuḷu Nāḍu: Implications for the Philosophy of Law', *Südasien-Chronik – South Asia Chronicle*, 6: 11–36.
Foucault, Michel. 1986. *The Order of Things: An Archaeology of the Human Sciences*. London: Routledge.
Foucault, Michel. 1999. *Discourse and Truth: The Problematization of Parrhesia*. http://foucault.info/documents/parrhesia/index.html (accessed on 15 May 2015).
Foucault, Michel. 2005. *The Hermeneutics of the Subject*. New York: Palgrave Macmillan.
Foucault, Michel. 2010. *The Government of the Self and Others*. New York: Palgrave Macmillan.
Godelier, Maurice. 1977. 'Myth and History: Reflections on the Foundations of the Primitive Mind', in *Perspectives in Marxist Anthropology*, pp. 204–20. Cambridge: Cambridge University Press.
Habermas, Jürgen. 1971. *Knowledge and Human Interest*. Boston: Beacon Press.

Habermas, Jürgen. 1979. 'What Is Universal Pragmatics', in *Communication and the Evolution of Society*, pp. 1–68. Boston: Beacon Press.

Habermas, Jürgen. 1981. *Theorie des kommunikativen Handelns Band I: Handlungsrationalität und gesellschaftliche Rationalisierung*. Frankfurt am Main: Suhrkamp Verlag.

Habermas, Jürgen. 1985a. *The Theory of Communicative Action Volume I: Reason and the Rationalization of Society*. Boston: Beacon Press.

Habermas, Jürgen. 1985b. *The Theory of Communicative Action Volume II: Lifeworld and System: A Critique of Functionalist Reason*. Boston: Beacon Press.

Habermas, Jürgen. 1996. *Between Facts and Norms: Contributions to a Discourse Theory of Law and Democracy*. Cambridge, MA: MIT Press.

Lewis, David. 2001. *On the Plurality of Worlds*. Oxford: Blackwell.

Meyer, John W. 2005. *Weltkultur: Wie die westlichen Prinzipien die Welt durchdringen*. Frankfurt am Main: Suhrkamp Verlag.

Meyer, John W. 2006. 'World Polity', in *Encyclopaedia of Sociology*. London: Blackwell.

Nandy, Ashis. 1983. *The Intimate Enemy: Loss and Recovery of Self Under Colonialism*. New Delhi: Oxford University Press.

Quine, Willard van Orman. 1960. *Word and Object*. Cambridge, MA: MIT Press.

Rudolph, Susanne H. and Lloyd I. Rudolph. 2003. 'The Coffee House and the Ashram. Gandhi, Civil Society and Public Sphere', in Carolyn M. Elliott (ed.), *Civil Society and Democracy*, pp. 377–404. New Delhi: Oxford University Press.

Sarukkai, Sundar. 2014. 'Indian Experiences With Science: Considerations for History, Philosophy, and Science Education', in M.R. Matthews (ed.), *International Handbook of Research in History, Philosophy and Science Teaching*, pp. 1691–719. Berlin: Springer.

Tarski, Alfred. 1935. 'Der Wahrheitsbegriff in den formalisierten Sprachen', *Studia Philosophica Commentarii Societatis Philosophicae Polonorum*, 1: 264–405.

Tarski, Alfred. 1944. 'The Semantic Conception of Truth and the Foundations of Semantics', *Philosophy and Phenomenological Research*, 4(3): 341–76.

Traister, Rebecca. 2015. 'Our Racist History Isn't Back to Haunt Us. It Never Left Us', *New Republic*, June 18. www.newrepublic.com/article/122073 (accessed on 19 June 2015).

Winch, Peter. 1970. 'Understanding a Primitive Society', in Bryan Wilson (ed.), *Rationality*, pp. 78–111. Oxford: Blackwell.

Chapter 5

Philosophy in practice

Nataraja Guru reading Narayana Guru[1]

Sundar Sarukkai

Narayana Guru's *Darśanamāla* is one of the most important texts of the last century. It is a remarkable distillation of the philosophical visions of Indian thought and also the essence of *advaita*. The text consists of 100 verses, ten verses in ten chapters. Each of these verses has a commentary by Narayana Guru as recorded by his disciple, Vidyananda. Narayana Guru's disciple, Nataraja Guru (NG henceforth), wrote a remarkable volume on these verses called *An Integrated Science of the Absolute*.[2] This text is a journey into Western philosophy, particularly phenomenology, modern physics, particularly relativity theory and Indian philosophy. This deep and complex work constructs a dialogue between these different traditions in order to explicate the verses in *Darśanamāla*. In the true spirit of advaita and of the verses, there is a unity of disciplinary thinking that characterises NG's book.

One might be pardoned for mistaking that this book is for philosophers. However, it is important to note what NG says right in the Preface: this book 'is primarily meant for the use of disciples, and only secondarily for the general reading public' (NG 2001a: xiii). Moreover, he also goes on to add that this text by Narayana Guru will hopefully 'enhance human dignity and decrease suffering through a better understanding of life in the light of the Absolute' (ibid: xiii).

These observations must be cause for introspection. In what sense can this commentary by NG be for the use of disciples? What is the expectation on the disciples that they should be able to engage with this complex text? And most importantly, if disciples are also those on the path towards spiritual practice, how does a philosophical text as NG's commentary help? The very possibility that this text will not only benefit the disciples but also 'enhance human dignity and decrease suffering' indicates and underlines an important role for philosophical thinking, which is that philosophical reflection is integral to any practice. The suspicion towards philosophy and metaphysics (famously emphasised by Marx when he suggests that philosophy cannot change the world) is one that is based on the distinction between theory and practice or even between philosophical thought and worldly life. Such a distinction is not tenable and particularly so in Indian philosophical traditions. Interestingly, many philosophers point out that Indian philosophies do not have an idea of the a priori, as in opposition to the a posteriori. There is a related binary that is therefore missing in these traditions, namely, pure and applied. Narayana Guru's work must also be located within this idea of the unity: that theory and practice only seem disjoint but in reality are not so. NG's book continuously emphasises this unity throughout the length of the book. Right from the beginning, when he begins with the duality of a priori and a posteriori, one standing for pure reflection and the other for empirical interaction, or with the dualities of science and philosophy, he is looking for ways to meaningfully talk about these unities instead of the dichotomies. Here I want to explore how successful such an enterprise can be in the context of understanding and even practicing spirituality.

(Interestingly, this advaitic worldview can be understood alongside a dominant trait in all the Indian philosophical schools – the tendency not to give into facile binaries such as body-mind, human-god, metaphysics-ethics, self-other and so on.)

NG's *An Integrated Science of the Absolute*

The ten chapters of the *Darśanamāla* have been dealt with in detail by NG, but he has an interesting way of commentating on the verses. He begins with a Prologue, wherein he sets the stage for us to engage with the verses in ways that go beyond their immediate content. In doing so, he repeatedly points out that he is only trying to be faithful to Narayana Guru's original verses, but through his (NG's) intervention, we are able to see the larger themes in the verses. There is a Prologue and also an Epilogue for each chapter. In between are the verses, each one dealt with separately. The verses are given in Sanskrit, followed by translation into English and then the translation of the commentary by Narayana Guru.

The Prologue and Epilogue are a complex interweaving of different philosophical and scientific traditions. Right at the beginning – as exemplified in the title – we are told what NG has set out to do. He wants to develop an Integrated Science of the Absolute. The object of his focus is the Absolute, but what he wants is a science of the Absolute. In a modern paradigm, this seems to be first dissonance – the capacity to develop a science of the Absolute. NG has to thus convince us that there is indeed a science of the Absolute and that such an attempt is already part of different western scientific and philosophical traditions.

NG begins his book by remarking on an important binary, one that has also influenced the contours of this meeting. This is the distinction between metaphysics and physics. He begins by noting that his fundamental task – and the task of Narayana Guru therefore – is to unify physics and metaphysics.

Right at the beginning, he points out that when physics (which is about the physical world, is phenomenal and quantitative) and metaphysics (qualitative, noumenal) 'are treated unitively, so that the certitude contained in the one helps the certitude contained in the other, by mutual verification, we have the beginnings of a Science of the Absolute' (1). So here are the basic assumptions on which the text rests. There is a distinction between physics and metaphysics. The former is about the empirical world and consists of phenomena which are measurable. The latter is more a quality and is concerned with things-as-they-are or things-in-themselves and not as properties and phenomena. Why are these distinct first of all? NG begins with the claim that they are distinct but does not set out the reasons why these are distinct. Western thought has a long history leading to the bifurcation of these domains, and NG assumes that history.

For NG, physics and metaphysics are needed to unify the world and one's experiences – this in a sense spells out the basic assumption about the spiritual quest, namely, it is not just about subjective experiences nor is it only about the world. Here again we can see the basic assumption about the dichotomy between the subjective and the objective, or the inner and the outer. Experiences are 'internal" and subjective, whereas the world is outside and objective. For NG, the fundamental unification which is needed is between these two domains. But how then does one unify these two seemingly disparate terms?

There is a philosophical tradition which has attempted to do just this. It is also one in which NG seems to be well trained in, considering that he is Bergson's student. The Western phenomenological tradition is unique in that it attempts to overturn centuries of established belief in the opposition between the subjective and objective. From the Greeks onwards, the suspicion towards appearances (phenomena) meant that a major part of philosophy was an attempt to understand the real nature behind the appearances. Thus, phenomena were not to be taken as the final representation of reality. For the phenomenologists, only phenomena are given or available at hand. Even if there is something behind appearances, we have to discover it only through what is given to us, namely, the phenomena. Thus, beginning from 'subjective' experiences we have to discover 'objective' essences or truths corresponding to these experiences. We must note here that Indian philosophical traditions are also fundamentally phenomenological in that they are primarily about cognitive phenomena. It is from these cognitive accounts that an account of the world must be derived.

The Western phenomenological movement, particularly following Husserl, believed that phenomenology was the science of the sciences and was the highest science possible. For discovering the essences of things was more fundamental than describing how these things behave. It was also the highest science because of the certainty of its conclusions. Certitude thus becomes a mark of science as well as phenomenology. Following these paths, NG chooses science as the exemplar of certitude while at the same time attempts to find a similar domain of certitude for the spiritual. So, what is the certitude that he seeks? It is the certitude of the Absolute. Thus, it seems as if the path to the Absolute is a path of certain knowledge guaranteed by its scientific character. The unification that is at the heart of the Absolute – a unification that transcends geography, cultural and linguistic differences for NG – is a unified science 'based on the notion of the Absolute' (ibid: 3). The unified models in physics in the times in which NG lived and wrote this book seem to have been a major influence in his belief in the possibility of unification and universalism.

It is obvious that there is a vibrancy to NG's belief that is driven by the developments in science such as in quantum mechanics, field theories and so on, which he draws on. On the one hand, it might seem as if he is using science to legitimise the claims about the Absolute, but I would argue that this is a limited view of NG's engagement with science. NG is using science as an analogy and also as an illustration of different ways of talking about the Absolute. There is of course a very good reason for his use of Einstein and relativity theory – on the one hand, his advaitic project is to erase the idea of the relative and at the same time try and save the idea of the Absolute within relativity!

There is yet another reason why NG so fundamentally invokes scientific ideas in a discussion of the Absolute. To understand this, we should begin with the fundamental tension between the experiential and the theoretical. Book knowledge is very different from experiential knowledge – or at least this view has become a dominant idiom of modern times. Science is an exemplar of the bringing together of the theoretical and the experiential and thus gives us a model to understand how these two activities can be unified. As mentioned earlier, NG also grounds this distinction as one between the a priori and the a posteriori. The former constitutes metaphysics and the latter physics and the domain of experience in general. Some dominant traditions of western philosophy consider these two as being fundamentally of two different kinds. NG challenges this belief and is interested in how the unification of these two notions is possible. Again, science comes to his rescue, for he finds in modern science such possibilities.

Although NG begins with these considerations related to science, the book is primarily about the Absolute. The Absolute, according to him, is 'not a thing nor is it a mere idea' but is 'both a thing and an idea at once' (ibid: 18). Here again he reminds us of the duality of idea and thing. Things are obviously not ideas, but if we enquire closely whether it is really that obvious, then we might run into problems. In fact, this understanding of the nature of a thing or an idea is really the task of metaphysics. The idea of the Absolute challenges our most naive assumption that things are different from ideas. But then if we hold onto these dualities, there is no way by which we can understand the nature of the Absolute. Thus, NG points out that 'all dualities are to be dropped before the Absolute can be comprehended' (ibid: 19).

Here is where science again becomes important to understand the terms of the theological or the spiritual. We should remember here that NG's use of science to discuss ideas of the Absolute predates many of the more popular attempts over the last few decades. In fact, in comparison to many of the attempts to appropriate science to validate theology, I would see NG's discourse as a philosophical discourse that points out how science shares the common world of the Absolute in many important ways.

Thus, he points out the Absolute is a term that arises in science in many contexts, such as the absolute zero temperature, Euclidean absolute space, Newton's absolute space, Einstein's four-dimensional space as 'rigid and absolute' as Newton's space (quote by Einstein ibid: 21), absolute velocity of light, and (absolute) constants in physics. Space-time integration in relativity is an important model for this project since NG associates, right in the beginning, physics with space and metaphysics with time. Following an elaborate argument, he argues that Space, Time and Causality, in a manner similar to Platonic ideals, all attain the status of the Absolute (ibid: 28). We might ask here whether the notion of the absolute in science is analogous to that in theology or spirituality. NG is not making a comparative claim and leaving it at that. He sets out to analyse this claim in some detail. While I would, at this point, not comment on whether this comparison is legitimate or not, nevertheless the point is that this comparison allows NG to illustrate the complex unificatory tendencies hidden within science.

Scientific methodology can be seen as a method which is a constant attempt at unifying the theoretical and the empirical or the metaphysical and the physical. As NG points out, theories are more conceptual, 'thus tending to be more metaphysical rather than physical in nature' (ibid: 24). Moving from empirical facts to mathematics is a move towards the metaphysical. In so doing, NG is accepting an implicit assumption that metaphysics is fundamentally associated with mathematics. Through these observations, he concludes that 'dialectical methodology properly belongs to the content of the Science of the Absolute' (ibid: 42). He also draws on Schrodinger to suggest a Vedantic approach to science, namely, the belief that knowledge which we think we have and a unity of knowledge that we get through sudden experiences are already present and 'eternal' and 'unchangeable' for all (ibid: 53).

Although the primary unification is that of metaphysics and physics, there are different types of unification in NG's vision. They include the unification of *sat*, *cit* and *ananda* – a fundamental principle of advaita, as also a unification of disciplines, primarily, cosmology, psychology and theology. So the idea of unification of differences is primary and all-pervasive.

NG is much influenced by the philosopher Bergson, who was perhaps the strongest voice of the unification of physics and metaphysics. For him, both 'belong together as one and the same discipline' (ibid: 58). In an extension of this dichotomy, Bergson wanted to unify matter and intelligence (ibid: 62). This theme is another intriguing one in the context of theology and spirituality. As has been discussed in great detail, the very idea of matter has theological antecedents, particularly in the West. Both for philosophy and science, the constant attempts to define matter have led to many new disciplines and sub-disciplines. The nature of matter is also fundamental to metaphysics. At the same time, it is the starting point for classical physics. Newton begins his *Principia* by first defining mass as the quantity of matter. Major modifications to these ideas of mass and matter occur in Relativity as well as in Quantum theories.

There are many dualities inherent in our conceptualisation of matter. One interesting contrary to matter is space. Space seemingly has all characteristics that matter does not – such as extension, locality, penetrability and so on – but what adds to the complexity is the significant amount of empty space that is present 'inside' any matter. For example, the empty space that is present in a physical object, say a chair, will be more (in volume) than the amount of 'matter' that is within it. This interplay of space and matter has been a subject of interesting work in metaphysics and philosophy of space. I mention this merely to show the importance of questioning apparent dualities and also to show why certain conceptual themes in science and philosophy are fundamental to an understanding of non-duality.

The ordinary world is one defined by matter. The objects around us are filled with matter. In contrast, there is the other world comprising entities that do not possess matter: space, time, ideas, thought, mind, spirit, god, mathematical entities and so on. Even though the latter are not perceivable through the ordinary senses, many traditions around the world think of them as being real. The task of metaphysics indeed begins from here: in trying to delineate how these non-sensory entities can exist and can be called real. The status of the Absolute also belongs to this discourse. When NG quotes Bergson's attempt to unify matter and intelligence, he is pointing to the unification of a historically important duality – that of matter and mind. For the western philosophical and scientific tradition, while this duality has come to be accepted (at least in the dominant traditions), we should remember that this duality is not found in the many Indian philosophical schools which treat mind as a variety of matter. NG prefers to use Bergson since Bergson allows NG to develop a Science of the Absolute, rather than a Philosophy of the Absolute. Interestingly, NG believes that modern science can explain a difficulty in interpreting Vedantic ideas of origin of the world from pure consciousness or at least the reducibility of the physical world to pure consciousness (ibid: 156–7). Science goes beyond the material in many ways, and this is an indication of how a fundamental Vedantic idea makes eminent sense. An extrapolation of this view would lead to the claim that the world arises from mathematics itself.

Why science instead of philosophy? This question is not perhaps as meaningful as it looks since much is at stake in the definition of these two terms. After all, science was called natural philosophy until a few hundred years ago. There are at least three clear reasons for NG to use the term science instead of philosophy here. First is the notion of certitude associated with science, but whether this is outside the purview of philosophy is debatable. Second is the unification of the theoretical and the experiential that is an essential characteristic of science. NG needs this unification for any meaningful notion of the Absolute which is not in the domain of the intellect alone. For Narayana Guru, for whom these philosophical excursions are an integral part of social action, it would not have made sense to have grounded the Absolute in purely metaphysical (as NG defines it in this text) terms. Science offers the best paradigm for the distinction of the metaphysical and the experiential, and also for their eventual unification. Thirdly, and intriguingly, the use of mathematics in the sciences, which also distinguishes it from philosophy, becomes an important element for NG. Although I will not be able to discuss this point in any detail, I will make a few comments on this for it illustrates an important methodological issue in the science of the Absolute.

Like in the case of matter, there is a long history of a relationship between mathematics and religion/theology in the Greek and Western traditions. (Interestingly, one does not see such a strong association in the Indian mathematical and philosophical traditions. It is also surprising that NG does not really talk about the way the Indians understood mathematics; this was already a classic example of unifying the mathematical and the empirical.) Among other things, absolute certain knowledge is possible only in mathematics. Knowledge about God also had to have this certainty, and mathematics becomes an example of how to have knowledge that can be universal and indubitably certain. Secondly, mathematics – it was believed – arose completely out of the workings of the mind. It was a product of the intellect in every sense of the word. It was such a discourse that was the exemplar of absolutely certain knowledge. Like mathematics, theology too was fundamentally of the intellect.

Given the model of mathematics, it becomes easier to argue that the functioning of the intellect alone was enough to guarantee absolute certainty – in this case, knowledge of god.

NG in a separate section (section 25, p. 94 onwards) discusses how mathematics 'reveals the possibilities of a Science of the Absolute'. He goes on to discuss many interesting aspects of mathematics, its entities, operations, its relation to god and so on. He is also well aware and draws upon the way scientists have responded to the use of mathematics in the sciences. While recognising that there is something special to mathematics, he still does not go the full way and find the Absolute within the mathematical. He offers an interesting reason for this: mathematics does not reach the full status of the Absolute because it is seen only as 'hand-maiden to physics' (ibid: 107), and physics itself is 'committed to relativism'. Part of the problem is that Einstein, according to Bergson, does not really give time its 'legitimate place' in his theory (ibid: 106). (We need to remember here that time is the subject matter of metaphysics as Bergson and NG discuss earlier on.)

What NG is really getting at is that certain concepts (such as ensemble) in mathematics are very useful in developing a Science of the Absolute. Through his emphasis on mathematics, he is trying to reprioritise the a priori and remove the negative connotations it (and metaphysics in general) has accrued over the years. Basically, he is attempting to establish the doctrine that concepts are at the ground of everything (ibid: 111). He also clarifies that the Absolute is 'not an empty word nor a mere mathematical abstraction' but has a 'concrete universal content' (ibid: 134). That is, it has to be scientific both in the experimental as well as the intuitive sense. So the question he is asking primarily is this: how is internal experience to be scientifically certified? Here NG draws on another important philosophical movement, that of structuralism.

The question that NG is engaging with, namely, the certitude of internal experience, goes to the heart of the spiritual experience. How does one know that what we feel is indeed 'true' and refers to some transcendental term? How do we trust others who claim some truths based on their individual experiences? Extending this, how do we even read discourses that are so different from one's preferred beliefs? The difficulty of reading a text on the Absolute for those who are not so inclined is part of this problem. I also believe that the general ignorance of this book of NG by the philosophical community is also illustrative of this difficulty in crossing genres.

NG not only crosses different disciplinary boundaries and genres in this monumental book, but he also, in passing, gives us a way of approaching different texts. In section 26, he begins with an important statement: 'Each conscious person is situated inside his proper world of discourse' (ibid: 109). By this he means that we have to take 'an inside view sympathetically' (ibid: 109). 'Intuition works best' (ibid: 110) under this view. This is a methodological imperative to reach non-duality. How does one erase differences that are often apparent? One does this by first giving in to the world of the other – other discourse, other experiences and so on. NG also interprets this in another interesting manner: such an attitude towards texts (and perhaps the world itself) is a way of putting the observed and the observer together. The apparent dichotomy of the observer/observed, reader/text, etc. can be dissolved if one approaches this act of observing through sympathy.

Finally, we should note that after setting up this complex infrastructure built on philosophy and science, NG points out that in Indian thought there is already a Science of the Absolute in the *Bhagavad Gita* and *Upanishads*; it is called *brahma-vidya*. He adds that modern science can also move towards this stage if it integrates metaphysics and theology within it (ibid: 137). His primary affiliation to the Vedantic tradition is retained even through these disciplinary manoeuvrings, for he finally concludes that Vedanta has certitude like mathematics (ibid: 137).

The verses

As NG notes, Naraya Guru's *Darśanamāla* integrates all wisdom in Indian thought into one, and this is the first kind of unification. Ten 'points of view' have been 'strung together into a garland' – so as to cover all possibilities. Each of these chapters illustrates philosophical/scientific positions ranging from realism to idealism. NG titles the chapters differently from Narayana Guru in order to illustrate the theme of those chapters in the context of his comments drawing on philosophy and science. The chapter titles that he gives are: empiricism or cosmology, methodology, phenomenology, negativity, normalisation, instrumentalism (pragmatism), reason, devotion, contemplation and absorption (ibid: 145). NG also claims that *Darśanamāla* has an internal 'self-consistency' and thus the 'question of proof does not arise' since there is 'apodictic certitude at each stage' (ibid: 145).

NG also analyses the structure of the ten chapters. The first three chapters are 'directed outwards to the objective' and the phenomenological; the last three have 'axiological unity of content' and 'belong to the mystical rather than to the scientific' (ibid: 147). The other four are largely about consciousness and analysis of error. The two central chapters are the fifth and the sixth. In his own text, NG engages with the object matter of the Absolute in the first half and in the second half deals with the subject matter of the Absolute.

The first chapter is primarily about the origin of the world. The first verse begins by saying that 'in the beginning there was non-existence', and the world was created by the 'willing' or the 'dreaming' of the creator. In the commentary, Narayana Guru notes that the world of the dream is unreal in that it belongs only to that world of the dream; in the same way, the world is unreal and is of the 'same order as His will' (ibid: 176). The remaining verses describe the creator as a magician (only the magician is real and his creations are not), as an artist who manifests what he imagines in his consciousness, as a seed in which the potential of the world is already present (following the theory of effect inhering in cause), as a yogi who manifests his power through the creation of the unreal world. In this description, the world is described as 'empty of content' and thus a terrible place. All suffering arises because we do not realise that the world is unreal, and only true self-knowledge can remove us from this suffering.

How are these ideas – which are a good summary of earlier philosophical themes – related to NG's attempted synthesis of philosophy and science? In the epilogue, NG makes some very interesting connections which illustrate this synthesis. Some of it may be problematical, but I believe that it shows how to expand the vocabulary of ancient traditions in a creative yet rigorous manner. Firstly, NG points out that the first chapter is about the origin of the world. This origin is a singular point, a limit point. Phrased in this manner, one can immediately see powerful connections to scientific concepts of limits and singularities, which is precisely what NG is attempting to do. In particular these ideas in mathematics allow us a completely different hermeneutics of the origin. The explicit connection to mathematics is made by NG when he says that 'one may visualize God as an interesting mathematical entity, but not without His mysterious or mystical value natural to the mind of man' (ibid: 188). Being similar to mathematics allows God to have a truth value. Moreover, NG remarkably opens up the structure of the beginning, largely influenced by Bergson's seminal work on time and duration. Beginning has different typologies such as the beginning-beginning and middle-beginning. NG argues that the beginning in these verses is like middle-beginning and not beginning-beginning; these are 'fundamental structural features' of the Absolute – 'fully permitted and confirmed by mathematics' (ibid: 189).

Narayana Guru's commentary is about the existence of non-existence. In the beginning there was only non-existence. This statement might seem to be a classic metaphysical question, yet it is one that science has to confront in its own ways. NG goes to the extent of extending this argument to argue that facts are not as primal as mathematics (a view which will find supporters in the scientific community!). It is through this path that a priorism, as NG points out, 'enters science with full force'. Given that a priorism is associated with metaphysics, NG is showing how metaphysics gets essentially intertwined with physics. We must be aware here that although I have been using the word physics, it stands for all empirical disciplines, including the study of societies. *To extend NG's argument, one would say that the study of society as well as the possibility of social action has its origins in an a prioristic system.*

The concluding remarks by NG are also illuminating for they show how the idea of the Absolute takes on different characteristics in each of the ten chapters. NG firstly suggests that God for Narayana Guru is nothing more than a mysterious cause for the mysterious effect of the universe. In the first verse, this cause is equated with God, who is like a mathematical entity. In the second chapter, the 'same God belongs to a psychological context', biological context in the third, operational in the fourth, phenomenological in the fifth, naturalistic in the sixth, epistemological in the seventh, ethical in the eighth, creative in the ninth and causal in the tenth (ibid: 218). (NG's attempt is to bridge the gap between physics and metaphysics. In the context of social action, the real bridge to divide is the gap between social science and metaphysics. The stakes of the debate in this binary is quite different.)

Plurality and duality are first abolished by negative elimination of the unessential and the doubtful – the first five chapters do this; the last five chapters do positive reconstruction (ibid: 237). Narayana Guru reduces the world of effects to that of causes (ibid: 239). Relativity offers a way for NG to relate these notions of unification as well as causation. Here Bergson becomes very important for him since Bergson's main argument is about time, and he has five objections to time in relativity. NG relates this view of Bergsonian time to the idea of cause in Narayana Guru. For NG, Bergson's attempt to bring physics and metaphysics together is the same as the Science of the Absolute (ibid: 245).

Relativity is important for NG because it abolishes duality of space and time, but at the same time it is a problem because it accepts relative notions of space and time as against absolutist notions of these. Bergson's approach attempts to remove the duality of the first and also recapture the absolutist ideas of time. As NG notes, changing time to cause does not change anything in the methodology (ibid: 250). Duration is real time, and duration is 'essentially a continuation of what is no more into what is' – this is the lived time (ibid: 264). So essence of time has before and after but not 'absolute simultaneity' (ibid: 264). NG suggests that Bergson's method is similar to Narayana Guru's method of negative ontological reduction.

While these details of this similarity are sketchy in my summary, NG offers a sustained discussion of the same. I avoid making a judgement on whether the effort is successful or not since that is really not the point as I see it. By placing the ideas of the Absolute in a completely different framework, NG has already succeeded in opening up new ways of thinking about non-duality and the Absolute. NG also illustrates the larger structure operating behind Narayana Guru's thoughts in *Darśanamāla*. The second chapter reduces the multiplicity of the Absolute defined in the first to unity through the method of neti-neti.

The second set of verses is again philosophical and begins by describing the world as being both subtle and gross, and emphasises that the 'world is merely superimposed (adhyasta) on the Lord' (ibid: 325). It then underscores the central tenet that only causes are real and effects unreal. The confusion about the world arises primarily due to *māya* (which NG translates as relativity also). In an analogy common to Indian philosophical systems, Narayana Guru describes how a cloth is not real, and if we open up the layers of reality, we first begin with the thread but then discover that it is not real but only the cotton is and so on . . . till we reach a level of ignorance. This, according to Narayana Guru, is the origin of this reality. But even this originary ignorance can be abolished – and that is the knowledge of the Lord. Such awareness of that knowledge is self-evident and has no cause. Thus, 'it is knowledge alone that remains supreme and eternal' (ibid: 330). The world as both subtle and gross is also one that has strong resonances in science, although it is unclear how the specific notion of subtle in Indian philosophies can be equated with the idea of the 'subtle' in science. But again in these descriptions, NG discovers parallels in relativity and Bergsons' theory, and most particularly in Einstein's theory of fields. (Interestingly, for Einstein, the ultimate reality was not matter but fields.)

The third set of verses deals with non-existence in the words of Narayana Guru. NG titles this chapter under Phenomenology since phenomenology is concerned with appearances/phenomena, which in the ultimate sense are non-existent. In this set of verses, Narayana Guru emphasises the unreality of the world and the reality of the Self. Moreover, mind is ignorance, and this ignorance can only be destroyed by true knowledge of the Self. The world becomes visible only through 'willing' – drawing on the well-known example of rope/snake, Narayana Guru says that a snake seen instead of a rope is only because of willing; the snake is not of the real world nor is it an absolute truth, it only exists as a reflection. In a similar manner, the objects in the world are only 'products of the will'. Here, Narayana Guru introduces the central concept of māya as the prime cause of the world and is itself non-existent.

From phenomenology he moves to negativity – we should note that these are methodological tools in the ultimate science of the Absolute. Negativity is an important method by which one can reach the truth. In this chapter, NG engages with the various principles of negativity, ranging from Hegel and Kant to the Naiyāyikas. As far as Narayana Guru is concerned, this set of verses is on the epistemological aspect of māya. As NG points out, māya is not reality or entity in itself. The only positive thing about it is the name: 'its content denotes a negativity, empty of all reality' (ibid: 475). Narayana Guru's verse on māya sums it up very nicely: māya is that which does not exist but seems to exist. But non-existence is not absolute absence since non-existence of one thing 'always resides in the existence of another thing' (ibid: 488). So also, before the origin of the world its non-existence resides in something, the Absolute.

The other chapters elaborate many of these principles in a similar manner. While a description of all these chapters will be interesting in itself, I will not be able to do justice to the complexity of thought that characterises this analysis by NG. What I have done so far is to try and understand why NG reads *Darśanamāla* in a particular manner. What are the motivations for this elaborate dialogue between Western philosophy and science with Narayana Guru's evocative verses? Today it is too often felt that religious texts try and legitimise themselves by comparing themselves with scientific concepts. I think NG's text does not fall into the traps of such appropriations since it is an 'organic' discourse that begins by an openness to different worldviews. It also offers us a great challenge today because it is a difficult text, and it demands some amount of serious work reading and interpreting it. In so doing, NG also has a lesson for instant spiritualism, a trend which is possible only because of a manufactured suspicion towards metaphysics (theory/philosophy) and a facile acceptance of practices which are otherwise ungrounded. Narayana Guru's works shows the importance of metaphysics in all spiritual practices. His verses are not just mere poetry; they are thoughts which make us think. They make us understand the (false) presuppositions under which we live. This, ultimately, is the task of metaphysics – to let us see an alternate vision of reality, to let us not be blinded by these beliefs and suppositions. I would also argue that it is only through this process that there is a hope for meaningful social action. Here I can borrow Narayana Guru's invocation of the subtle and gross, and suggest that metaphysics and physics are like the subtle and gross elements of the same entity. It is this insight which is fundamental in Narayana Guru's own work.

Given that the spiritual is so much immersed in the metaphysical, why is there the current negative response to philosophy and metaphysics? One reason is that these disciplines have become completely textual. Ironically, in India, even as the support to philosophy has dwindled, the public consumption of philosophy through spirituality has significantly increased. In this climate of market spiritualism, metaphysics becomes a difficult commodity to sell since it needs hard work either to follow serious spiritual practices or read texts like NG's. NG himself is only making modest claims for his work. He is interested to show interdisciplinarity unity necessary for the study of the Absolute. He also suggests that Western philosophy has reached an 'impasse' and believes that Indian philosophical traditions can help them out of this. Narayana Guru's understanding of these philosophies, he believes, will help this task. His attempt to use modern science and philosophy to reflect on Indian thought is actually 'meant to enrich each other' (NG 2001b: 492). Ultimately, NG is striving for the unification of physics and metaphysics. If we remember the meanings of these terms, the unification he and Narayana Guru are emphasising is nothing more than the unity of the world of things and the world of ideas, which is the first prerequisite for a spiritual experience.

Notes

1 A draft of this chapter was presented at the conference on *Metaphysics and Politics*, Varkala, 27–30 July 2012.
2 Nataraja Guru, *An Integrated Science of the Absolute*, Vols. 1 and 2 (Delhi: D K Printworld, 2001).

References

Guru, Nataraja. 2001a. *An Integrated Science of the Absolute*. Vol. 1. New Delhi: D K Printworld.
Guru, Nataraja. 2001b. *An Integrated Science of the Absolute*. Vol. 2. New Delhi: D K Printworld.

Chapter 6

Victim(s), parasites and creative evolution

Narayana Guru and anthropology of vision[1]

K. V. Cybil

This article is written in the form of the differences in; and agreements on ideas related to the Vedanta between Narayana Guru and his disciple Nataraja Guru. The paper turns on the difference in their respective attitude towards the Bhagavad Gita as a philosophical exegesis for Monism or Advaita. Narayana Guru's reservations toward the Gita stemming from the fact that it meets with a violent conclusion (the battle of Mahabharata) which he found it difficult to endorse as a means for discursive knowledge is met with silence in the interpretations of his disciple. Notwithstanding the masterly effort to philosophize his teacher's spiritual gleanings, Nataraja Guru (1977) fails to register significance of the break with theistic Monism that Narayana Guru achieved in his negative response to the Gita as a philosophical text. In the larger picture the article tries to argue that this break also signifies his break with the Brahminical social order or the caste system and the initial steps taken towards the composition of a multitude which would take its place in a future nation.

Introduction

Narayana guru's philosophy may be summarised as an assemblage of Absolute (Brahmam) and its representations (Maya). Nataraja Guru (1977), his disciple and commentator, argues that his was a unitive (Yogic) thought that assembled unity (Ekam) and multiplicity (Anekam) into a universal, i.e., knowledge (Arivu). He called it an integrated science of the Absolute. Absolute here is the concept called Brahmam, which is nothingness achieved through the denial of everything that exists. Between nothingness and everythingness, it is reproduced in the form of the instrumentality of a soul (Jivatmavu), which is experienced in the form of life. Narayana

Guru's breakthrough of having extrapolated a concept of the self, i.e., a rational, modern, instrumental self in Vedantic philosophy of the *Upanishads* is pointed out by Muni Narayana Prasad (1997). Nataraja Guru earlier claimed that knowledge is the subject and centre of his philosophy. He also based it on Psychology and contemplated a merger with the universal plane of consciousness of the soul approximately called mystical (Turiyam), which is over and above the states of wakefulness, sleep and dream or deep sleep as the three states of consciousness given to humans. While these commentaries stress the positive nature of the self, soul, knowledge, etc., I argue that Narayana Guru introduces a notion of the self, such that a victim is presupposed in the creation of knowledge, or becoming(s) of the self. I also argue that such victimhood displays characteristics of becoming political in a parasitic mode of cultural revolt (Serres 2007).

When one reads Narayana Guru in his philosophical mood, one is led to ask what if he was an atheist? Did he believe in gods and goddesses? How is it that he built so many temples for worship of the popular deities of Hinduism when he could be an atheist? Some of the installations he has performed (for example, the mirror at Kalavamkode and Vechur Ullala and a plank of wood at Murukkumpuzha with Satyam, Dharmam, Daya and Santi – words indicating harmony written over it) can also point in the same direction.

The answer could be that he was neither a believer nor an atheist, but a mystic. Then what is that in mysticism which allows for a blend of these singular aspects of religion which cater to the imagination of people in bottomless joy. It has nothing to do with presence/existence of gods and goddesses per se but with the experience of knowing them. *Sat-chit-anandam*, from which this Vedantic phenomenon may be said to have derived, had an important role in crafting the thoughts of Narayana Guru.

French philosopher Henri Bergson, whose words 'universe is a machine for the making of gods' have been cited by Nataraja Guru (1977: 55) to describe the meaning of mysticism in the West, especially Christianity comes closest to a secular understanding of Narayana Guru. Yet, it is not possible to stop with that, because as Nataraja Guru (ibid: 159) says, Bergson identified complete mysticism with action, a feat achieved in history not even by the Greeks and only by Christianity or Christian mystics like St Paul, St Theresa of Avila, St Catherine of Siena, St Francis or Joan of Arc.

According to Bergson, calamities like famine must have stopped Hindu mystics like Ramakrishna Paramahansa or Vivekananda despite their being influenced by industrialism (Christianity and Western civilisation) from achieving such mystical harmony of thought and action (ibid: 159). The pessimism alleged on Hindu mysticism by Bergson is sought to be overcome with Narayana Guru by arguing that Christianity could not stop colonialism (which is expressed in the form of hunting and cruelty to animals) from violence by Nataraja Guru. He finally concludes with an answer to Bergson, quoting Narayana Guru's poem *Anukampa Dasakam* (Bhaskaran 1995: 490–7), that describes the virtues of affect towards a non-human universe (ibid: 215–6).

Here one may be also led to consider Narayana Guru's negativity to violence expressed in his disavowal of the *Bhagavad Gita* because it could not stop violence, which it had to finally play hand-maiden to. Narayana Guru's disavowal of violence can be the only reason behind his negative approach to the *Gita* (Devan 2002). Nonetheless, while his disciples like Nataraja Guru, Nitya Chaitanya Yati and Muni Narayana Prasad wrote commentaries on the *Gita*, it seems strange that Narayana Guru himself cared little about it. Did it have something to do with the use of the *Gita* by Nationalists in raising a right-wing discourse of Hinduism (Spivak 1999)?

Spivak's detailed exegeses on Hegel's interpretation of Gita reveal the power it wielded in establishing a colony for Brahmins in India. Her poser to colonial theory including Hegel in making the native informant into an admirer of the Gita, a text which was otherwise endlessly dispersed in several forms without a constancy of meaning or existence as a text of power is a very relevant criticism. The different interpretations of Gita, those of S Radhakrishnan and D.D. Kosambi included do not overcome this forceful impact created by the work of Hegel. The presence of this text reveals how much of a colonial power India itself might be, notwithstanding that Hegel is reasoning why India may never have one.

Separating vision and violence

Coming back to the title of this chapter or anthropology of vision, I like to point out that this vision can be understood both as vision in sense and vision as thought. This is a unique assemblage of its meanings that he derives through the concept 'karu'.

Vision as sensation may be weaned from the line where he says that all five senses are related to it (karu) as eyes:

In him who knows better than Knowledge itself
Shining forth inside and outside
Is the 'Karu'; with all five eyes folded inside
It is to be bowed to in respect again and again
(opening stanza of *Atmopadesa Satakam*,
Bhaskaran 1995: 315)

This is a prayer to the Karu beseeching its blessing for the self or Atmavu with knowledge. Vision as thought or Darsanam is constructed through an image of thought, that of Karu. So the concept of Karu has multiple uses in the works of Narayana Guru. For instance, in *Atmopadesa Satakam* he writes (stanza 41):

'This is a pot' has initially 'this' in it
Which is particular, whereas 'pot' is generic
Behind illusions of intelligence
this reason (Karu) that operates is to be seen.

Here Narayana Guru is separating this-ness (particular) and potness (universal) of the pot (Kutam). But, it is Karu that appears again as an agent, the reason causing their unity, merely an illusion. The virtual function of Karu in inducing thought through illusion is introduced here. It can also be noticed that he makes a distinction between intelligence (Mathi) which is magical and knowledge (Arivu) in these lines. But in the pursuit of knowledge of the Absolute, illusion and reality are not different from one another. Hence, Karu is at once a means and also an end in itself. As the primordial medium or instrument of knowledge, it repeats itself in the form of thoughts to the self in pursuit of knowledge. It reappears again as (stanza 45):

One religion is contemptuous for another; truth (karu)
Told in one religion is empty according to another one
That all religions share same secret in this world
Is factored into knowledge, till then, all is fantasy.

Here Karu appears as a truth generic to religions. The repetition of truth as a function in all religions is to be instrumentalised by the self in pursuit of knowledge. The plurality of religions and singularity of truth is mediated through the Karu. Not listening to the Karu or not recognising that it is the same in all deviates the self from knowledge and opens itself to fantasy. It can be also inferred that it is fantasy (Bhramam) that is opposed to knowledge and not ignorance or non-knowledge. In his poem *Jati-lakshanam* (Bhaskaran 1995: 474–80), Karu moves from the world of ideas to nature. It is written that (stanza 9):

> A blacksmith called knowledge made
> A mould (Karu) called caste once,
> Changing moulds in succession it (the Karu) will keep coming
> Repeating all that have already come into being

Here it means the species, such that it lives in all species as the means to knowledge. Here it takes the meaning related to the generic existence of life. Knowledge is described here as the creator (literally a blacksmith or Karuvan who uses a die or Karu, in which he casts tools that he makes). The die or the Karu repeats itself in different forms endlessly that nothing existing now or in future is without it, the die or Karu. Thus, both as thought and as sense, one can see the word Karu repeating itself. In its crux, it is prior to the self (Atmavu) or soul (Jivatmavu) itself. A Karu in that sense plays a virtual role, as an image of thought and also of truth in abstraction, centering the world of representation on itself and extending itself through expressions.

Creative evolution or the process by which the work of soul (Jivatmavu) may be addressed according to Nataraja Guru (1977: 169–73) has a crucial role to play in defining what is a Karu. Therefore, it involves an anthropology of vision, rather than vision of anthropology that treats evolution theory in linear and hence a different framework altogether. Advaitism has been interpreted as the process of creation through evolution of the soul by Aurobindo (Gupta 1998: 205–23). It also includes involution or a process by which the soul/spirit descends to the lowest level of itself (matter) in order to rediscover or repeat itself in the joy of creation. The concept of creative evolution that Nararaja Guru evokes to explain this mystical experience may be argued to be identical in the case of Narayana Guru and Aurobindo but for the difference that the former does not use the figure of a Godhead (addressed as Vasudeva in his *Writings on the Gita*) and instead pays obeisance to the Karu or the die/cast or the virtual moment suggestive of a victim in his philosophy taken as a whole.

One cannot but notice the miles Narayana Guru has moved away from the *Gita* through his use of such a concept as Karu. Nataraja Guru, although his steadfast disciple accepts the *Gita*, does so for a set of reasons entirely unrelated to its epic context. He sees in the *Gita* the graphic enunciation of the Vedanta at its best and even Buddhism as reflected in it (Dharma Yoga). He sees in it the axis of intuitive or yogic thought and argues that Narayana Guru positively commented on it through a chapter in Darsana Mala called Bhakti Darsanam (Nataraja Guru 1977: 324–49). What occurs as vision or darsanam to Narayana Guru is interpreted as yoga by Nataraja Guru. This is clearly demonstrated in the positivistic end to his arguments for crafting Narayana Guru's vision into a science – integrated science – of the Absolute.

I do wish to debate on the etymology of the word Darsanam, but not in this context. This chapter is not a philosophical paper. Yet, it has a philosophical context to it, undeniably that of a victim, as I have already argued before in its process of becoming political.

The *Gita* can be further examined to prove my point that Narayana Guru finds his concepts in a negative light in relation to it. The objection that Arjuna raises to Krishna that if he kills his own fraternity, it can lead to pollution of his caste as there will be no males left to perform the ancestral rites or procreate in his clan.[2] Fear of this miscegenation is what Krishna tries to remove through the *Gita* by answering that caste itself is a form of existence that is immersed in the Universal Self (i.e., himself) and not alien or external to him. Inadvertently, in refuting caste or theory that the *Gita* tries to justify caste, what Nataraja Guru does is transform purity of caste into a question immanent to the Absolute, reasons to which have therefore not to be sought outside it. He argues that it is a creation of Brahmin-Paria dialectics which can be evaded through spiritual discourse (Nataraja Guru 1995: 268–70).

Here Nataraja Guru cites a work by Narayana Guru called *Jatilakshanam* (Bhaskaran 1995: 474–80)to prove his point. *Jati* is a matter of organisation of nature, having little to do with the soul or society at large, is the view adopted by Nataraja Guru here:

> Caste (*Inam*) embodies the self
> Announcing which is its caste (Inam)
> Never is a question asked what is your caste (Inam)
> By them who have vision and eyes

Here Inam means caste or Jati in a species form, and everything is related to the work or the sense of vision. It is interesting to note that for Narayana Guru, Jati is a becoming minor, if not an animal, plant or even people in this context. But can the same be said about Nataraja Guru? I am afraid not.

Narayana Guru uses *jati* as an instrumental feature of self, conceived as the most inclusive paradigm to observe nature, but not as immanent to the soul. Though Nataraja Guru swears by his Guru's words in almost everything he says, they were both undeniably engaged in an intense debate. I think this stems from their respective interpretation of the *Gita*. Violence as a means to know the Absolute would deny the autonomy which is virtual (an attribute of the Karu) in the attainment of knowledge. In this exclusion of violence from the question of autonomy of knowledge can be detected the political overtones of Narayana Guru's thoughts.

Becoming political of Narayana Guru's Thought

That leads us to several other questions, most importantly what is the actual fate of Narayana Guru's thoughts when it becomes political?

A crucial point on which the politics of Narayana Guru's philosophy turns is that he led a movement against the caste system. He lived through a time of the colonial, ethnographic state, which had reduced all ontological questions with respect to self in India to identity. Whereas it was not so burdensome for the upper caste or Brahmins to represent Indian antiquity in a modern, ethnographic framework, the same equation posed a threat to the lower castes because it demanded ethnographically reproducing themselves as a slave caste. The critical question Narayana Guru implanted in the minds of Ezhava and other lower castes was how defy ethnographic territorialisations and repeat the acts of asceticism through which the lower castes built a procrastinated sense or feeling of community for ages – not just modernity – to come.[3] This is a significant point of departure from either Sankara, Ramanuja or Madhva, who are considered to be his predecessors as exponents of Advaita or Vedantic monism.

Nataraja Guru has synthesised his teacher's views with the major philosophers of the West and has produced a new science of knowledge. This is arguably a new platform since such attempts carry a distinctive stamp of modernity. Nonetheless, it is also true that in this effort, the Vedantic philosophy is also interpreted as a monolithic tradition of which Narayana Guru then becomes a modern face. The positive approach to the creation of a modern science of the self using the works of Narayana Guru runs into rough weather if one reckons the circumstances of his life in flesh and blood.

It has often been argued that the mendicant (Avadhutan) in Narayana Guru was at odds with the reformer in him. The escape he sought from crowds and his strong reaction to people worshipping him as a god have been anecdotally recorded by many biographers. For example, he was impressed by the composure Ramana Mahrsi maintained with his devotees seldom enquiring their whereabouts, hardly even speaking to them (Municharya Pancakam, Bhaskaran 1995: 245–50). On his part, Narayana Guru was enquiring all details about visitors, and in one instance he even asked a coconut climber, who quarrelled with his wife because he wanted to get educated in the scripture, to go back and continue in his profession and take care of his family (Balakrishnan 2006: 229). On another occasion, he was writing letters to Kuttichathan (an impish deity who provides immediate relief to devotees such that they often manipulate him for settling personal scores with enemies) to let alone one of his devotees that came to him seeking relief (ibid: 155). The haste with which a rational understanding of religion, especially Hinduism that is identified with him as I argue, has given rise to this contradiction. One of his biographers has recorded that, while living with the fishermen as a mendicant in coastal areas of Travancore, he was seeking lessons on the Yogic practices amongst Muslims and getting acquainted with the works of Dara Shikoh (son of emperor Shajahan), who translated the *Upanishads* into Persian (Kunjappa 1977: 37). If one looks at Narayana Guru exclusively in terms of his interest in philosophy, especially as a Monist or Advaitin, also the same problems tend to arise. The answer perhaps then lies in interpreting his knowledge as a desire to extension in multitudes (Tiyya, Billava, Nadar, etc.) that Ezhava as a caste of victimised identities was considering as a historic option to choose modernity.

Narayana Guru had established a break with theistic or qualified Monism (*Visishtadvaitam* of Ramanuja) that was irreparable, and he had sealed it with *Atmopadesa Satakam* (1897) or the hundred verses of self-instruction in Malayalam. It has seldom, if at all, any reference to a Hindu god or a goddess and tries to wind its way back to the denial of all forms of dualism to establish an identity of the knower and the known, subject and object, universal and particular. This is a repetition of the thought of the *Upanishads* but coded in the epistemology of a new subject called Karu. Nitya Chaitanya Yati (2005: 8–16) argues that the Karu is a symbolic form for an egg, like the Hiranyagarbham in the *Upanishads* which created the Universe upon breaking. Yati (ibid: 139) argues that Narayana Guru's vision corresponds to a modern crisis of separating the perceiver from the perceived or physiology from psychology and so on. He argues that knowledge invokes a certain mediation of the inside with a reality outside rather than a complete rupture with it. It is an answer to this crisis that has produced the idea of Karu in Narayana Guru, according to Yati. The Karu can produce multiplicities in the process of learning, but itself remains undivided (see cited lines in the following pages). This is the monistic vision of this text as interpreted by Yati (ibid: 70).

It is not difficult to follow the logic of Yati's discourse, because it attempts a synthesis of thoughts of Narayana Guru with the likes of Plato, Aristotle and Descartes while interpreting the *Atmopadesa Satakam*. This is a plot ingenious to Yati and his school, because he along with Nataraja Guru represented a global face of Narayana Guru and the legacy of Narayana Gurukulam he had started in 1923.

That brings us to another key work by him called the Vedanta sutras, which is just 24 lines in Sanskrit discovered in the late 1970s and interpreted by Muni Narayana Prasad (1997), the significance of which is yet to be assessed. Narayana Prasad claims that it is the only Sutras to be written after *Brahma Sutra* of Badarayana that precedes even Sankaracharya. A Sutra is a logical composition that aphoristically conveys the meaning of Vedanta, its comprehensive vision. Even in Sanskrit it is a long-lost tradition that Narayana Guru has discovered, before making it his own. It reflects the same philosophy of denial of dualisms and establishing the singularity of the Absolute (Brahman). In this case, he has not used the role of mediation or the concept of Karu to explain his thoughts.

The exposition of the meaning of the *Upanishads* centering on the subject or the Karu as a medium is visible only in *Atmopadesa Satakam*. That gives added reason to interpret it in the light of a crisis of modern subjectivity pointed out by Yati. But stopping at the gates of intuition in a Bergsonian sense, he hesitates to delve into the other possible meaning of the Karu than the egg. Among its dictionary meanings, the one that suggests a mould or a die used by artisans (blacksmiths in particular) I understand comes closest to the meaning he has employed in this text.

Michel Serres (1997) argues that modern subjectivity is formed of a certain kind of victimhood that is at once the instrument of punishment and also the one who suffers or merits it (ibid: 39), such that it receives all information and pain upon which the world converges (ibid: 40). It is therefore located at the centre of knowledge. Is it not what a Karu means in the context of *Atmopadesa Satakam*? Going by Serres, the victim is not the excluded outside of the system, but it's very centre. 'I rebel, therefore we are' or words of Albert Camus may be appropriate here. They were cited by Upendra Baxi in the context of human rights activism in India, suggesting the need for such activism to 'resurrect the sovereignty of the victims against the state' (Baxi 1998: 352). Extending the same logic, a victim is so much a parasite (Serres 1997: 44) of the system that once removed from its centre it will not merely lose its victimhood, but it will also cease to exist.

Once we extrapolate the meaning of a Karu to mean not merely an egg, but a mould or even a pawn used in a game of chess, we get an extension of its meaning that includes also a victim. In common parlance, Malayalam uses this word in a similar way, where being victimised is reported as being used as a Karu in a deceptive plot.

In a discursive form, such victimisation does not pertain to an exclusion from it, rather the formation of a subjectivity, a new possibility of meaning, a narrative and moreover, an intersubjectivity. This is the new dimension Karu opens in its meaning with Narayana Guru. Did the text presage the actual work of reform performed by him? This is framed as a self-defeating question that Guru's disciples find it difficult to answer. Monism or Advaita as such though have nothing to do with caste, and belong to a school that never questioned legitimacy of caste. Narayana Guru took no interest in any such discourse reflexively, and he has described caste among humans as equivalent to a species in nature.[4] It had no discursive value according to him and therefore no reason for it to be endorsed in public. The colonialist modernism often attributed to him because of his strong reaction to caste in public life leaves one stranded as to what is the crisis of modern man that Yati argues Guru is reflecting upon while writing his texts? Instead of persisting on such a separation, it may be useful to understand the meaning of these texts as creative evolution of a certain form of intersubjectivity, something along the heels of a new nationhood, including the Malayaneese, Sinhaleese, Kannadigas and Tamils the Ilava were contemplating at the moment. I would like to argue that as a prelude to such a nationalism, these works may have been written or even that this nation remains an unwritten text beneath the works of Guru interpreted as a mendicant.

Rajan and Reghu (2009) have argued that caste can be treated as intersubjectivity only when accepted into an intercommunality that exists prior to it or is precedent to it. Caste or intersubjectivity can therefore be treated only as an effect of intercommunality. This argument presumes to take forward a concept of universalism that defies meta-narratives of revolution or nation, yet espouses the cause of a subject engrossed in the act of becoming. Narayana Guru's encounter with Hinduism is thus argued to be universal in reference, especially to the different aspects of Hinduism different from the Sanskritisation of castes that seek an entry to it. While they hold that an experience of the void is crucial to the historic imagination of this encounter or the challenge to Hinduism posed by Narayana Guru's challenge to caste system and the intersubjectivity that has accrued from such an event, it fails to explain fully Narayana Guru's act of renunciation of Brahminical Hinduism itself. They have argued effectively that his renunciation of caste has to be understood as his renunciation of Brahminical Hinduism, as the latter has always existed in the form of an intercommunity of castes than in the bounded oneness of a religion. One detail that does not fall in line with this argument is their own initial characterisation of this encounter or this event within the 'becoming' of Hinduism in south India as a relation of the universal and the particular (2009: 60–2). The evolution of their logic is towards stating that Hinduism, incapable of representing universal at a particular moment, was overhauled by the reform started by Narayana Guru that produced what they termed a backwater universalism.

This remains an unstated truth about Narayana Guru in their paper because they fail to point out the fact that the reform movement embodied an impossible exchange (symbolic of death) of positions between the victim and the parasite, an intersubjectivity that implicated the oppressor and the oppressed, the master and the slave, the upper caste and the lower caste. These subjectivities that are organically linked to the system therefore retain a universality of existence proven through the parasitic body that links untouchables to the system. My argument is that Narayana Guru's thoughts to create a new theory of the self was driven by radical nihilism as a parasitic philosophical route in Indian spirituality, because he was convinced that reform as such was impossible within the caste system or Brahminical Hinduism.

It was a phenomenon of the 1920s–30s that the Ezhava imagined themselves as a community has been argued by some historians (Jayaprakash 1996). But, a strong sentiment of nation was overriding this sense of community and therefore expressed dissent with the idea of nation in a Gandhian framework (Khan 2010). To quote from Putuppalli Raghavan, renowned freedom fighter and journalist,

> if the Ilavas, the Tiya and the Chovans belong to the same group, the Sinhalas in the island of Srilanka, Lakshadweep and Malayadweep, the Eddhikas in the Kalinga, the Ekkeris in Coorg and Mysore, the Billava in Karnataka, the Shopakas in Maharashtra and the Nadars and the Cannar in Tamil Nadu all belong to the Ezhava.
>
> (Jayaprakash 1996: 12)

The emergence of Ezhava as a political subject was imagined mostly along the lines of a Sudra or a Dravidian political subjectivity, which as Pandian observed in the case of Periyar, rendered his 'nation a nation without a "moment of arrival". It was ever-fluid, remorselessly struggling for citizenship, informed by ever changing contours of rationalism and continuously violating boundaries – both in the sense of territory and otherwise'(Pandian 1993).

It was C. Kesavan who, in politically mobilising the Ezhava for a joint front with Christians and Muslims called the All Travancore Joint Political Congress in 1932, gave a holistic dimension to this subjectivity. The reason for the formation of this front was a lack of representation for Ezhavas, Christians or Muslims in the state assembly of Travancore. It had resulted in the Nivartana (abstention) movement and the boycott of the 1935 elections by the Joint Political Congress. Right when the movement was threatening to culturally upturn the traditional stronghold in politics, Sreemulam Tirunal (King of Travancore) made the Temple entry proclamation in 1936, bringing the Ezhava straight back into the Brahminical Hindu fold, from where they were drawn into the Communist movement, which completely erased the challenge raised by the Joint Political Congress (Khan 2010). The strength of a feeling of nation underpinning the community, since then, must be believed to have changed into one of a Hindu nation.

Backwater universalism (Rajan and Reghu 2009) or community overriding the Gandhian Hindu nation (Khan 2010) both espouse the peculiarity of the subject position Narayana Guru's revolt against Brahminism produced as a historical moment in Kerala. The way in which it evaded the discourse of nationalism, especially of a Hindu nation, is what makes the intervention of this moment critical. The vision of a multitude that was harbingered through this moment therefore connected cognate social groups such as the Channar, the Tiya and the Ezahava. This formed the substratum of the Nation espoused in the vision of Narayana Guru's Advaita. How different this was from parallel versions of the philosophy espoused in contemporary advocates of the same for a national renaissance in India cannot be overemphasised. Swami Vivekananda saw in it the future of a Sudra revolution affirming the victory of the labouring classes in India (Sen 2000: 75). The difference or the contrast lies in the fact that the Swami thought it was only a matter of time before the Sudra or the Pariah elevated to the level of the Brahmins and produced a Nation that comprised citizens empowered through education (Sen 2000: 78).[5] Non-Brahminism, which formed the core of the espousal of a vision of the multitude in Narayana Guru, may be argued to be the difference that needs a critical appraisal.

Knowledge, exclusion and centrality of victims

Despite its several shortcomings of having been a ploy to the creation of an elite class of Ezhava intellectuals in a modernising role for the caste and the concomitant representations of its philosophy as rooted in Hinduism, especially through the invocation of Hindu deities, the thought of Narayana Guru dwarfs its critics by erasing the distinction between ignorance and knowledge for the knowing subject. The actual significance of this view can be discerned in the use it makes of crafting an entirely innovative ethics in rules of knowledge.

Michel Serres (2007) has employed the metaphor of parasite to study a certain mode of cultural function in modernity. He has argued that culture as a field is not pre-determined by rules of knowledge or science and open to challenging subjectivities in the form of parasites (Assad 1991). The parasite is a biological entity that rules its relationship with a host but no longer exists when it stops to dominate this relationship. The pedagogy of Narayana Guru can be studied as a parasitic relation with the Hindu orthodoxy.

Certain people have found it amusing that Guru wrote letters to Kuttichathan, an impish deity of the lower castes, who was immensely powerful and believed to cause harm to enemies of his patrons. The letters requested Kuttichathan in a humorous but kind way to stop creating troubles for a follower of Guru (Balakrishnan 2006: 155). That Guru could make such loud and imaginary claims to divinity may be amusing to many, when he is identified as a spiritual modernist like Gandhi (Radhakrishnan 2013). The intellectual engagement – as in writing a letter – with lower deities of Hinduism like Kuttichathan in fact reflects a certain kind of devotion (Bhakti) and a form of transgressive sacrality that is achieved through mysticism by ascetics (Visuvalingam 1989).

It is also significant here to point out that the space of asceticism Guru was carving out for a lower caste movement through a representation of the subject was in his philosophy couched as a mould, a model, a copy, a pawn, a victim of knowledge – the Karu. After all, his humoured response to the question of which side he was on in World War I was that it was the British, because in their rule the lower castes got the freedom to choose asceticism Sanyasam (Balakrishnan 2006: 166). The tackling of orthodoxy was deftly employed by Guru in his use of teaching as a parasitic medium under colonialism. Michel Serres (1997: 4–10) uses the analogy of cross-strait or channel swimmers in oceans or big rivers to compare the ambiguities in life related to a knowing subject or soul. More or less, knowledge for Narayana Guru also represented a point in the crossing, in the life of souls, like that of a strait or channel for swimmers, of which the centre once crossed, there is only a gradual realisation for the Karu, of no turning back, with the opposite bank still equally remote.

Ramana Maharsi once remarked about Guru that he was complete in himself, although his circumstances were unfavourable to becoming so (Ramachandran 2009). The philosophy of Guru, especially his pedagogy, is about the centrality of this subjectivity, in fact an intersubjectivity of victimhood, of becoming(s) of Karu, a pawn caught in the perennial crossing of knowledge, of an alien – also the particular – with the opposite bank still remote because of the caste system, but then also of eternal returning to the universal oneness, of Vedanta. Justice, an unpremeditated category of Guru's thought, contingent and a manifestation of his anti-caste radicalism, lies here not in the fairness of things, nor in their utility, or in any original position, but from a parasitic exclusion of the subject, the victim, Karu from caste itself. Exclusion objectifies for the victim, the system, just like a parasite creates or structures its relations with a host in a biological system.

A Malayalam dictionary (Damodaran Nair 1984) describes the Karu as, among other things, a child waiting to be born, a subject in gestation. It is entirely dependent on its relation to the mother and lives a parasitic life in her womb. For the host, its mother the entire gamut of relations to this child during this period is defined by a biology, an organic system that creates the gestating subject into a real one. Once the umbilical cord is cut, the parasite is let loose into a system with no longer any organic or systemic relationships conditioning its subjectivity into a real one. The Karu has been also used to define the pawns used in the game of chess. It has been already described as a die, made of soil usually employed in the manufacture of metallic shapes. It has also been called the yellow of an egg and also a heart. It has been also identified with the platform for a building and also a drain. The one thing that brings together these different definitions is the flexibility with which it is adapted to a form it could or it is meant to assume. It defines a realm of intersubjectivity as in the shaping up of a game of chess in progress, that it is given to different possibilities, in fact infinite possibilities, but it remains stuck on the one shape which it could assume. Whether it comes to its final destination of knowledge of the absolute will always remain to itself, yet it steadfastly retains the quest for it, until such moment as it is extinct, dying in search of a justice avenging none in becoming its own fate. Herein lies the meaning of Karu as victim, when one traces it in the works of Narayana Guru.

But it is not a failed form of historic agency that is implied in this – no, not even a martyrdom. Victim is the excluded third, the witness to such a death, if it were to be. One way to understand this may be to phrase it in terms of its becoming political. The Karu must be the scattered bottom of society, its basic structure that is concealed to the outside, and therefore its base, centre and also a victim. The Karu knows no caste, even though it has its many eyes searching for it as at once being searched by many other eyes.

Ignorance, caste and the multitude

We have already seen how the concept of vision was crucial to Narayana Guru's thoughts. Narayana Guru made an installation of a mirror in one of the 60 temples he consecrated. It was a plain mirror with 'Om Santi' inscribed on it, reflecting the face of the spectator. He has elsewhere (in a poem called *Atmavilasam*, Bhaskaran 1995: 597–601) narrated the significance of the mirror as a subjective understanding of God. In the poem he explains that, when he turns his eyes inward, everything appears to him as shadows (images) in a mirror, and they exude divinity that surrounded him like a mirror, which he could see because he is now a witness to what is inside himself (Kesavan Vaidyar 1985: 90–2). The mirror represents a technology for him that ascends to the omniscience of God. It is important to note here that God sees not through his/her eyes but through a mirror. The universality of vision and the instrumentality of the mirror in achieving this remain embedded in this technology of deification. Narayana Guru is trying here to summarise the universal knowledge of the self through the metaphors of eyes and technologies of vision, i.e., mirrors.

The excessive measure of vision in dissembling the Brahminical social order can be seen in his anecdotal question to a Brahmin interlocutor about his caste that if one doesn't recognise it by eyes or sight, what is the point of asking about it? Sight is after all a significant way in which animals of similar species, of a similar caste, recognise each other (Rajeevan 2002). The implication here is that phenomenon of caste is a result not of anthropocentric vision but of the eye or sight of human beings differentiated at birth as the base of social classification/differentiation. By contrast, God, who sees without eyes, to man appears like a mirror. The importance Narayana Guru gave to eyes as also mirrors can be understood as a quest to dismantle the anthropocentrism of modern visuality to the level of identities of species and even objects. The de-centering centrality of vision with respect to faith can also be seen in the way Narayana Guru postulates the de-centering centrality of knowledge in relation to ignorance.[6]

Narayana Guru's epistemology is intricately linked to an assimilation, not of alienation, but of ignorance. He contemplates knowledge as the other of ignorance, not in a relation of dialectic or linearity, but as a passage. In fact, it rules the domain of knowledge as the only passage between the known and the unknown.[7]

The positivistic rigour of Narayana Guru's 'science' of knowledge was first articulated in the writings of his disciple Nataraja Guru. While writing on caste, he refers to a discourse centred on caste as part of the world of ignorance which has little significance for the creative evolution(s) of the self. He has treated caste at the level of species-being, i.e., all human beings are one caste. Knowledge exists beyond the realm of being, in becoming something external to species. It is a becoming in which the gestating subject or the Karu overcomes the distinctions imposed on it from the world outside and realises itself. It realises the absence of duality with the world in which it is habituated and overwhelms it to become one with it in an act of transcendence. While meditation and the bodily practice of Yoga demarcates the man of knowledge from the rest, Narayana Guru still used it – ignorance – as a door or exit from the world of lowly living into the sagely living of the ascetic.

Ignorance of caste in the discursive domain and decisiveness of caste in the natural domain did not pose a challenge to Guru's spirituality, as he consistently thought of a movement of the self in the direction of knowledge which unifies everything. Hence even ignorance is the knowledge of ignorance, which becomes one with knowledge the moment it is discovered. Knowledge or Arivu formed the basis of his thoughts and more than as a philosopher, he found poetic and political solace in playing with its different facets. He even displayed his irreverence for Sanskrit[8] at times by writing some of the most revealing of his thoughts in Malayalam or Tamil (Aiyappa Panikkar 2002).

Observed in the light of the wanderlust that marked the life of Guru, where he is reported to have stayed at no place for more than three days continuously, since he embraced asceticism this gives an insight into the welcoming multiplicity within which he contextualised knowledge. There are resonances of a troubadour (Serres 1997) searching for wisdom in the lines of Guru. He becomes the third person, the gestating subject (Karu) and transcends the duality of the world, subject (Vyashti) and Object (Samashti):

> Known is he who knows
> If it is also knowledge that he knows . . . (one who knows, knows not merely what he knows, but knows what knowledge is)
> He who knows
> In knowing it, could become six or even eight (one who knows knowledge is singular, knows it could be six or even eight)
>
> Along with the known
> Knowledge becomes seven, eight
> Knowledge becomes separate
> And becomes known in different ways if unfolded
>
> (Arivu-Bhaskaran 1995: 497–505)

Knowledge not merely represents the unity of everything, but upon knowing gives every known thing into several digits. The known exists in its permanence only insofar as it is not being touched by knowledge. There is no space for taken-for-grantedness of any known entity. All that is known is to be known, and it is then that knowledge empowers the Karu, the self or the subject to become one with itself. The challenge or the invocation to knowledge is not given by the known or the unknown, but by the Karu or the gestating subject. But the real challenge is to overcome this state of being the Karu and to become knowledge, in its undivided stage. It could possibly lead to anything from here and even multiply itself in any numbers; just as a parasite can take any shape or form conditioned by its biological circumstances, knowledge represents an escape route for the Karu to multiply itself, for the victim to destroy the system and create one of its own, different from all other systems.

Conclusion – Advaita and caste: antinomies of Hinduism?

As observed, Narayana Guru was also a Vedantin or a seeker of philosophical truth. This has often brought on him the charges that he was a traditionalist and did not fundamentally alter the society. The reforms propagated by him are thus alleged to be cosmetic. Narayana Guru's work though centrally linked to Indian antiquity (because he wrote in Sanskrit) or to South Indian antiquity (he wrote in Tamil also) is today situated within a globalised world of ideas. He is compared to a lot of Indian thinkers –both ancient and contemporary –, and a lot of Western philosophers, but which makes it difficult to distinguish most of what is Western and what is Indian philosophy from each other and the rest. It merely rises occasionally in defence of the latter as the ultimate provider of wisdom.

The paradigm for linking Narayana Guru's ideas with the systems of philosophy and the kinds of knowledge developed in the West by Nataraja Guru, nonetheless opens up an arena for the meeting of the East and the West. But does it really live up to the technological requirements of representation to articulate a form of thinking that can take care of the social injustices perpetrated in the form of knowledge or right to knowledge (i.e., the caste system) is arguable.

As pointed out by Nataraja Guru,

> For various historical reasons the critical revaluation of the subject of caste in the light of the full implications of contemplative, non-dual Self-knowledge was avoided in India. In our own times, this neglect has led to extreme forms of social inequality and discrimination, known today as caste, exclusive and segregatory, leading to the extremism of untouchability. It is Brahmin versus Pariah dialectics.
>
> (quoted in Yati 2005: 219)

Despite this potential realisation in the evaluation of the role thought or knowledge can play in determining the course of social action, there is only a general appeal to reason in deciding matters of society in Nataraja Guru, who was also a disciple of Narayana Guru. For him the attainment of self-knowledge is the ultimate aim of all social organisation, and Narayana Guru's own crusade against caste has to be seen in this perspective. He says that Narayana Guru visualised a world of a singular humanity unified in a singular caste, thus abolishing social differences ordained by humans against the rules of nature. With full realisation of these facts, Nataraja Guru is still content to leave matters of social dispute to a science of reasoning for their resolution. How a right to knowledge becomes and informs the knowledge in its realisation to the self is a ponderable area waiting to be opened in the work of Nataraja Guru.

One of the reasons why the ascetic movement begun by Narayana Guru failed to make any impact in the Malayali understanding of politics, which has continued to be dominated by upper caste notions of culture, may be this. So, in Yati (a disciple of Nataraja Guru), while discussing the course of ethical action which proceeds from the teaching of Narayana Guru, the subjectivity created is that of a condescending and exalted self, which is constructing modalities for mixing with the world outside. The complexity of caste-society is simplified in a way that makes it comprehensible to a sociologically informed self, for example, as role-playing (Yati 2005). This may not be the historic case to be precisely speaking of an Ezhava, or a lower caste subject in opening the course of ethical action in their lives.[9] Yet, there is a certain awareness or awakening to the empowerment created by Narayana Guru in the form of an urge to knowledge. It is also to Yati's credit that he distinguishes Sankara's Brahman from Narayana Guru's Arivu or knowledge. Yet they both serve like organising principles for philosophy, just like 'matter' serves a foundation for all modern physics and 'life' for modern biology (ibid).

To conclude, no lines of wisdom can conclude the postulates of knowledge (Arivu) formulated in the cast of an instrument (Karu). The requirement of a supernatural wisdom is particularly called to attention here. Therefore, my effort will be to keep this discussion as open and not given to conclusion as possible. The only escape route out of the conundrum created by thought in movement seems to be repetition of movement itself. Such is the dilemma faced by humanistic ideologies that have sought an appropriation of Narayana Guru's powerful invocations of the soul to will knowledge by becoming everything else, but knowledge itself. There is no final destination in sight as it is multiplied in nature through ever-new species. The open-endedness of creation or creative evolution has concluded the script for all beings – sociological and biological – to become more, extend themselves in multitutdes. At its zenith and also its bottom, Narayana Guru's thoughts retain this consistency. It is in this sense that they assume a coherence, a monadic spirit of nomadism, which must have informed his asceticism.

It is a speculative note on which I stop here. Philosophical excursions to Narayana Guru can provide numerous illuminations to any student of philosophy, though he had himself confessed once that he had nothing more of philosophy to offer than what has been already offered by Sankaracharya himself.[10] But then Sankaracharya may have had nothing new to offer than interpretations of the *Upanishads* or the *Gita*. Historically, the departure point he represented was thus deeper going than the cosmetic changes he achieved in creating for the Ezhava a sense of modernity as argued by many of his critics. Dalit and anti-caste movements of different shades all over India have presently accepted the fact that his vision entailed a political subjectivity of a pan-Dalit movement in the making. Needless to say, the numerous exploits of literature, arts, painting, etc. that have become popular through the rebellious mode of its engagement with culture have resonances of this subjectivity. Such modes of reading Narayana Guru may be the subject for yet another paper.

Glossary

Anekam Multiplicity
Arivu Knowledge
Atmavu Self

Avadhutan Mendicant
Bhramam Fantasy
Brahmam Absolute
Daya Kindness
Dharmam Ethics
Ekam Unity
Inam Caste as a natural metaphor
Jati Caste
Jivatmavu Soul
Karu Die, embryo, pawn, victim, etc.
Karuvan Blacksmith
Kutam Pot
Kuttichathan A popular deity with magical powers
Mathi Intelligence
Maya Representation/illusion
Samashti Object
Sat-chit-anandam Experience of mystical joy
Satyam Truth
Sutra A logical composition aphoristically conveying the meaning of the Vedanta
Turiyam Mystical
Vyashti Subject

Notes

1 I would like to thank the Sree Narayana School Reading Room and Library, Irinjalakuda, Kerala for organising a presentation and discussion of this chapter during their Reading Week (*Vaayna Vaaram*) in August 2016. Translations of Narayana Guru's poems used in this chapter are all the author's translations. I also wish to thank Dr M.M. Khan and his colleagues at the Department of History in The Government College for Women, Trivandrum for organizing a discussion on an earlier draft of this paper in December 2014.

2 At another juncture in the epic when Arjuna is escorting the Yadava women from Dwaraka after the city has fallen to the internecine rivalry of the Yadava men and their complete extinction, his caravan is attacked by robbers and the Yadava women raped, at which point Arjuna cannot rise to the occasion and protect the chastity of the Yadava women or protect the purity of the Yadava caste. Is this episode not enough reason to consider the discourse of the *Gita* as a concealed attempt to impose an ideology rather than to remove the fears of pollution of castes that may be caused due to the extinction of men belonging to that caste?, asks Devan (2002), a painter, while discussing the *Gita* in the context of the teachings of Narayana Guru.

3 See also Wakankar (2010).

4 See Rajan and Reghu (2009:33–58) for details of how Narayana Guru's thoughts never visualised itself as a challenge in thought to Brahmins or the Colonists as masters over a suppressed people.
5 'In keeping with the Yuga theory, Vivekananda looked forward to the restoration of the ideal (Satya) Yuga when each man would have turned a Brahmin and all forms of oppression and inequality would have ended' (Sen 2000:78).
6 Narayana Guru's concept of ignorance may be compared, if it should be, to that of Aurobindo. The latter conceived ignorance as the self-limitation of knowledge. It is a recognition of the limits of worldly knowledge that is implied by ignorance and hence all forms of knowledge, and those who specialise in them know their limits. The difference between the conceptions of the two may be that while Narayana Guru speaks of ignorance to mark it as separate from illusion, in Aurobindo illusion as such plays no role for worldly reality, and cosmic reality are tethered to the process of creation in the evolution of spirit. There is no such theory of the spirit in Narayana Guru such that the evolution of the spirit is not destined for a summit in the Supermind of Aurobindo, but extension in multitudes. The evolution of man is presented in transformations of the mind, which according to Aurobindo goes through a process of ascent as well as descent (evolution and involution), whereby the Supermind descends to the level of matter (or the lowest level of mind) as much as the mind ascends to the level of the Supermind or Sachidananda, the highest level of the mind. Ignorance for Aurobindo constitutes not the lowest level of mind, that is, of matter, but a stage which is delegatory to the Supermind, such that it descends to levels beneath itself in a process of transformation towards the Supermind. Ignorance is comprehensive and holds together differences, but lacks a knowledge of the absolute as a unity. He calls it the Overmind (Gupta 1998: 217).
7 It dominates this relationship in a manner, if put in Serres' words, 'as if drowned in the density of meaning, non knowledge still knew what knowledge, overflowing with information, will never know again' (1997: 65).
8 By irreverence I mean not for the language, but the Sanskritising process its use advocates by implication for example in Vivekananda, who thinks Sanskrit education can be a mode of empowerment not merely for the Brahmins but the Nation at large.
9 Pandian (2007) informs us that Pundit Iyothee Thoss of Parayar caste started the Advaidananda Sabha in 1870 Madras to 'investigate *advaidic* traditions as a way of contesting caste-based discrimination' (ibid: 104).
10 Amiya Sen writes 'Sankaracharya's abstract non-dualism had after all also been questioned by fellow-Brahmins like Madhavacharya and Ramanuja who saw more theistic possibilities in Vedanta' (2000: 15). Narayana Guru's version of Advaita in its affinity towards the version of Sankaracharya may be ascribed to the latter's adherence to abstraction over and above preference to the use of religious metaphors in expounding the philosophy of monism.

References

Aiyappa Panikkar, K. 2002. 'Arivinte Guru', in K.N. Shaji (ed.), *Narayana Guru: Jivitam, Kritikal, Darsanam*, pp. 332–9. Thrissur: Current Books.

Assad, Maria L. 1991. 'From Order to Chaos: Michel Serres's Field Models', *Substance*, 20(2): 33–43.

Balakrishnan, P.K. 2006. *Narayana Guru*. Kottayam: DC Books.

Baxi, Upendra. 1998. 'The State and Human Rights Movements in India', in Olle Tornquist, Manoranjan Mohanty and Partha Nath (eds.), *People's Rights: Social Movements and the State in the Third World*, pp. 335–52. New Delhi: Sage Publications.

Bhaskaran, T. 1995. *Sree Narayana Guruvinte Sampurna Kritikal*. Kozhikode: Mathrubhumi Books.

Damodaran Nair, P. 1984. *Lakhu Sabda Taravali*. Kottayam: National Bookstall.

Devan, Madathil Vasu. 2002. 'Guruvinu Gita Pramanamo?', in K.N. Shaji (ed.), *Narayana Guru: Jivitam, Kritikal, Darsanam*, pp. 352–65. Thrissur: Current Books.

Gupta, B. 1998. 'Sri Aurobindo', in D. Bishop (ed.), *Thinkers of the Indian Renaissance*, pp. 205–23. New Delhi: New Age International Publishers (P) Ltd.

Guru, Nataraja. 1977. *An Integrated Science of the Absolute*. Vol. 2. New Delhi: D.K. Printworld.

Guru, Nataraja. 1995. *Wisdom the Absolute Is Adorable*. New Delhi: D.K. Printworld.

Jayaprakash, M.S. 1996. *Social Protest in Travancore With Special Reference to C Kesavan*. Unpublished Ph.D thesis. University of Kerala.

Kesavan Vaidyar, C.R. 1985. *Sree Narayana Guruvum T K Madhavanum*. Irinjalakuda: Vivekodayam Press.

Khan, M. Mydeen. 2010. 'Negotiating the Hindu State and Nationalism: Travails in the Making of a Community', in K. Raviraman (ed.), *Development, Democracy and the State: Critiquing the Kerala Model of Development*, pp. 54–69. London and New York: Routledge.

Kunjappa, Murkoth. 1977. *Narayana Guru*. Alappuzha: Prakasham Publications.

Muni Narayana Prasad. 1997. *The Vedanta Sutras of Narayana Guru*. New Delhi: D.K. Printworld.

Pandian, M.S.S. 1993. '"Denationalizing" the Past: "Nation" in E V Ramasamy's Political Discourse', *Economic and Political Weekly*, 28(42), October 16: 2282–7.

Pandian, Mathias Samuel Soundra. 2007. *Brahmin and Non-Brahmin*. New Delhi: Permanent Black.

Radhakrishnan, K.S. 2013. *Gandhi-Sree Narayana Guru*. Kottayam: DC Books.

Rajan, Roby and Reghu, J. 2009. 'Backwater Universalism: An Intercommunal Tale of Being and Becoming', in Vinay Lal (ed.), *Political Hinduism:*

The Religious Imagination in Public Spheres, pp. 58–95. New Delhi and New York: Oxford University Press.

Rajeevan, B. 2002. 'Jatiyekurichulla Veendu Vicharangal', in K.N. Shaji (ed.), *Narayana Guru: Jivitam, Kritikal, Darsanam*, pp. 366–81. Thrissur: Current Books.

Ramachandran. 2009. 'Maharshiyilekoru Yatra; Guruvilekum', *Madhyamam*, 12(3), January 26: 34–45.

Sen, Amiya. 2000. *Swami Vivekananda*. New Delhi: Oxford University Press.

Serres, Michel. 1997. *The Troubadour of Knowledge*. Ann Arbor: The University of Michigan Press.

Serres, Michel. 2007. *The Parasite*. Minneapolis and London: University of Minnesota Press.

Spivak, Gayatri Chakravorty. 1999. *A Critique of Post Colonial Reason: Toward a History of the Vanishing Present*. Cambridge, MA and London: Cambridge University Press.

Visuvalingam, Sunthar. 1989. 'The Transgressive Sacrality of the Diksita: Sacrifice, Criminality and Bhakti in the Hindu Tradition', in Alf Hiltebeitel (ed.), *Criminal Gods and Demon Devotees*, pp. 427–62. New York: SUNY Press.

Wakankar, Milind. 2010. *Subalternity and Religion: The Prehistory of Dalit Empowerment in South Asia*. New Delhi: Routledge.

Yati, Nitya Chaitanya. 2005. *Narayana Guru*. New Delhi: Indian Council for Philosophical Research.

Index